# THE
# COMPANY
## OF
## THE
# FUTURE

# Frances Cairncross

Management Editor, *The Economist*

# THE
# COMPANY
# OF
# THE
# FUTURE

How the Communications
Revolution Is Changing
Management

**WITHDRAWN**

Harvard Business School Press

Boston, Massachusetts

Printed in the United States of America

06  05  04  03  02      5  4  3  2  1

Requests for permission to use or reproduce material from this book should be directed to permissions@hbsp.harvard.edu, or mailed to Permissions, Harvard Business School Publishing, 60 Harvard Way, Boston, Massachusetts 02163.

Library of Congress Cataloging-in-Publication Data

Cairncross, Frances.
    The company of the future : how the communications revolution is
changing management / Frances Cairncross.
        p. cm.
    Includes index.
    ISBN 1-57851-657-9 (alk. paper)
        1. Information technology—Management. 2. Communication
in management. 3. Industrial management. I. Title.

    HD30.2.C347 2002
    658.4'5—dc21

                                                    2001051486

# Contents

Preface and Acknowledgments    vii

Ten Rules for Survival    xi

1  Management, Information, and Technology    1

2  Knowledge, Decision Making, and Innovation    23

3  Customers and Brands    47

4  Recruiting, Retaining, and Training    69

5  Communities and Corporate Culture    91

6  Purchasing    113

7  Strategic Suppliers    133

8  Corporate Structure    151

9  Leading and Managing    175

10  The Company of the Future    193

Notes    205

Index    219

About the Author    229

# Preface and
# Acknowledgments

CORPORATE LIFE has always been full of surprises. For today's managers, that is especially true. They have to live with changes of two kinds: They must run their companies through an extraordinary technological revolution—and also survive the buffets of an economy that can alter course with breakneck speed. To live with disruptive technology and a volatile economy would be hard enough. But managers must now do both under conditions of unusual uncertainty and insecurity.

This book aims to look beyond the traumas of recession, terrorism, and war, and to chart a course further into the future. The unprecedented events of fall 2001 will long leave their marks on companies. They will think more carefully about the personal security of their staff; they will think harder about potential disruption of their supply chain; they will build in a certain amount of duplication, of data facilities, premises, and so on. Yet these considerations will, in the long run, be small by comparison with the other forces that are shaping tomorrow's company.

The basic message of the book is that Internet technologies will profoundly alter the structure of the company and of many business practices. But they will do so only if accompanied by capable management, with the support of empowered and intelligent employees. Getting corporate structure right will be just as important for making the best use of Internet technologies as acquiring the right software and hardware. No manager should be deceived by the 2000–2001 collapse of technology companies and stocks into thinking that the influence of technological change has been exaggerated. Its profitability was grossly oversold but not its significance. That will take time fully to emerge, but it may well be the single most profound force shaping the company of the future.

To catch a first glimpse of the changes ahead, look at the Ten Rules for Survival, which follow this prefatory section. They encapsulate the main themes of the book. Hurried readers can also cut corners by reading the first and final chapters, both of which give a sense of the material in the intermediate chapters. That may whet their appetites enough to persuade them to digest what lies between.

Among the themes that the book explores are those of the growing opportunities for collaboration that Internet technologies provide, of the importance of teams, and of the retreat of geographical distance as a barrier to both collaboration and teamwork. All these have also been themes in the creation of this book. It has been a truly collaborative effort. It grew initially from my "E-Management" article published in *The Economist* in November 2000. One of that article's themes, the growth of technologies enabling collaboration, was the suggestion of my colleague Matthew Symonds. Bill Emmott and John Peet, *The Economist*'s editor and business affairs editor, generously gave me time off to develop the article's ideas into this book.

At that point, the collaboration and international teamwork began. Kaija Pöysti, a successful entrepreneur, had recently sold the Finnish information technology business she had built and was in the middle of changing careers in Boston, Massachusetts. She volunteered to act as a top-of-the-range research assistant, offering the fruits not just of her wide reading of management literature but also of her corporate experience. For the several weeks of writing in early spring 2001, Kaija and I swapped thoughts electronically across the Atlantic, taking full advantage of the time difference: A passage e-mailed to her as dusk fell in Britain returned by the following morning full of helpful comments and suggestions.

A further round of collaboration began when the completed manuscript returned from Kirsten Sandberg, my energetic editor at Harvard Business School Press. As luck would have it, I was already committed to writing another long article for *The Economist* during most of the time when her comments needed review. But I was able to draw on the services of Lewis Neal, a young Treasury civil servant and a personal friend. Lewis has an impressive grasp of the interrelationship of technology and corporate structure. He went through the book, collaborating electronically with Kaija, and the pair of them produced a second round of invaluable comments. This book is dedicated to them both, with gratitude.

As with all my books, many of the most original ideas come from my husband, Hamish McRae. This book goes to press at the time of our thirtieth wedding anniversary. To live with him has been to enjoy not just friendship and amusement but constant intellectual stimulus and a sensation of jointly exploring the frontiers of practical economic ideas. I look forward happily to our next thirty years together.

Frances Cairncross
*London, September 2001*

# Ten Rules
## for Survival

NOTHING BEATS running a company for sheer complexity. New information flashes constantly on to the radar; new competitors appear from nowhere; myriad different stakeholders, from regulators to media to human-rights campaigners, clamor for attention. How should managers steer through this period of disruption, grabbing the potential of the new without sacrificing what mattered in the old? Plenty of familiar practices of good management remain, but some rules become even more important. Here are the top ten:

1. MANAGE KNOWLEDGE. A company is the sum of what its people understand and know how to do well. Value lies increasingly in creative ideas and knowledge. But ideas have value only if people share and develop them in ways that benefit the bottom line; knowledge is useful only if people can find what they need to know. Getting intelligent people to share what is in their heads is vital, and takes more than mere money or clever software. Ideas must flow sideways through a company and from the bottom up—not merely top down. And knowledge is worth storing only if senior staff set careful rules to filter and structure it. What goes into a database determines the value of what comes out. So setting central rules and standards is key to good knowledge management.

2. MAKE DECISIONS. Good judgment will remain a key skill. Managers constantly blitzed with new information require

strong nerves if they are to build in the data that matters and set aside the rest. Because production cycles are shorter, companies will often need to do things in parallel that they would once have done sequentially: This will be one of many factors speeding up the decision flow. Managers must accept that it is sometimes better to be roughly right than exactly wrong. Big-bang decisions are generally best avoided—or implemented in small incremental moves that leave room for flexibility and for altering course, if circumstances change. Accountability grows more widespread and deeper—a decision must be not just financially right, but ethically defensible too. Shareholders and other stakeholders have new ways to monitor corporate behavior and to urge change.

3. FOCUS ON CUSTOMERS. Customers matter—but some matter more than others. Acquiring new customers often costs more than making extra sales to existing ones. So companies must build loyalty and trust with reliability and good service. Given the welter of product information reaching customers, memorable brands will grow more important. Companies will not just widen their reach by finding new markets, but will also seek to deepen existing relationships. They will have more information than ever before about their customers, and must use this to offer their most profitable customers special deals and to make them feel part of an elite club. Some companies will even seek to "fire" unprofitable customers by charging them higher rates than others and restricting the services they can access.

4. MANAGE TALENT. Like its customers, some of a company's people matter more than others. That does not apply only to people at the top: Managing talent is also about capturing innovative ideas from middle managers and those further down the line. At every level, managers must identify where most value lies. In some cases, a few stars will encapsulate much of a company's value; in others, teams of employees will matter more. Some companies will want to rent the talents of "free agents"; others, to employ directly their best brains. Each case will need a different human-resources

approach; each will require new ways to measure performance and imaginative ways to reward it, not all of them
financial. Managers must strike a delicate balance between
paying enough to attract and retain talent, and offering such
lavish rewards that too little value goes to the owners of the
business and its other employees.

5. MANAGE COLLABORATION. In companies, teams will have
new opportunities to work together; companies too will
collaborate more, in alliances that allow them to outsource
production or to spread risk or to enter new markets. Both
will require lateral links, not hierarchies, and a new managerial style. Teams may be separated by time zone or by geographic distance and increasingly will work for different
employers. Effective collaboration between teams and
between companies calls for similar qualities: trust and
shared understanding, rather than the top-down, command-
and-control approach of hierarchical structures. Successful
collaboration will also require excellent communication,
and incentives that reward sharing information and working
for common goals.

6. BUILD THE RIGHT STRUCTURE. As costs of handling information in a company decline, so new opportunities open for
redefining corporate shape. In general, companies will be
less hierarchical, more modular (like Lego), with more ways
to arrange and rearrange structure. Managers must think
through from scratch which activities should be kept in-
house and which outsourced. A general rule: A company
should keep those activities it does not merely as well as, but
better than, its competitors. Such decisions now depend far
more on business logic than cost. So do decisions about what
to run from the center, what locally. True, the center can
control what happens locally more easily than ever before.
But "can" is not always "should": Business logic will vary
from one service and company to another.

7. MANAGE COMMUNICATIONS. Given the pace of change,
bosses need more than ever to be able to communicate persuasively through many channels, with their staff and the

outside world. They must also listen: The most valuable communications will frequently be bottom-up, and the folk nearest to the customer and the product now have new tools for explaining what they see. They will use these only if they feel the message gets through. More communications will also travel sideways, peer-to-peer, as teams share ideas in more depth than ever before and joint ventures cleave more closely.

8. SET STANDARDS. Ironically, Internet technologies, tools of freedom and decentralization, call for discipline, protocols, and standard processes. Only by setting standards and insisting that everyone abide by them will companies reap their potential savings. Companies need to insist on common practices in areas such as purchasing and information technology in order to harvest real productivity gains. As a result, some aspects of centralization will increase: A key task of top managers will be to provide structures and standards, and to insist that they are observed.

9. FOSTER OPENNESS. Once standards have been set, then openness and freedom should reign. Discipline and openness are two sides of the same coin: Centralization of standards makes possible decentralization of decision making. In addition, Internet technologies increase the need for a culture of openness, to foster the sharing of knowledge and effective collaboration. Companies will allow their suppliers and customers "inside the machine," as it were, by giving them extraordinary access to their databases and inner workings in order to integrate their operations and to make collaboration effective. To allow another business inside a corporation in this way requires trust, and calls for reliable ways to avoid conflicts of interest and issues of privacy.

10. DEVELOP LEADERSHIP. Without the right organizational structure, culture, and staff, a company will not fully benefit from even the most sophisticated technology. So the key to success lies much less in technical know-how than in excellent leadership to push through and build upon organizational change. At some points in a company's life, it will

need a hero-leader who can rally staff to push through the trauma of disruptive change. At other times, the right style will be the manager-as-coach, a selfless talent scout who specializes in assembling and motivating great teams. Always, the people at the top will set the tone in a firm. Their skills will determine whether it is a good company to work in and do business with. These are the main tests of successful leadership.

Armed with these ten essentials, managers in the company of the future should see the challenge ahead for what it is: the most revolutionary period this generation has ever experienced in corporate life. For many managers painfully learning to make the best use of Internet technologies, it will be frightening and exhausting, but it will also be enormously exciting. For some, who instinctively understand how to lead through difficult times, it may even be fun.

# THE
# COMPANY
# OF
# THE
# FUTURE

# Chapter 1
# Management, Information, and Technology

C AN YOU IMAGINE a job more complex than managing a business? To manage well requires extraordinary talent, good luck, and strong nerves. Not so long ago, at least it was clear what the job entailed. But no more. Almost every aspect of running a business is now in flux. The reason: the evolution of the Internet and of an accompanying cluster of new technologies for handling and transmitting information.

Back in the 1990s, managers could concentrate on running their company well: on making cars, say, or selling insurance. They had to cope with incessant change, but of a fairly predictable kind. They had to control costs, develop and launch new products, set up foreign subsidiaries, perhaps make an acquisition or negotiate a merger. Challenging as these tasks were, managers of established companies now face faster and more ubiquitous change as well as confusing new questions: Who are our competitors? Where do our core skills lie? Should we abandon our most successful, long-standing business? What are we now?

During the dot-com boom, some managers doubtless reassured themselves with the thought that when the bubble burst, such questions would disappear. It did; they didn't. Instead, what became clear was that dot-coms had failed to spot where the greatest promise of the Internet lay. Swayed sometimes by greed and sometimes by fad, they

rarely looked at the opportunities it presented—and still presents—
for real improvement and change.

In fact, on reflection the phrase "Internet company" was misleading. As Michael Dell, chief executive of Dell Computer, said in a January 2000 speech to the World Economic Forum in Davos:

> *Most successful Internet companies are really in retailing or com-*
> *puters or finance or media or some other service or manufacturing*
> *business. The Internet is just the tool they use to do business*
> *incredibly efficiently and quickly. It flows through the whole oper-*
> *ation just like electricity. A retailer doesn't say to customers,*
> *"Come into my store because I am wired up to electricity or*
> *because I keep the air conditioning on."*[1]

Instead, every company is today becoming an Internet company, just
as every company is already a telephone company.

This book is mainly about the way that change is transforming the
manager's job. But it is also about the company of the future. It looks
at how connections—within a company and between a company and
the outside world—are evolving. It reviews the nature of work: the
looser links between companies and those whom they employ, and the
difficulties companies face in extracting full value from their cleverest,
most creative employees. It looks at how the employee's life is altering, asking whether greater freedom to work as a "free agent," de-
tached from employment, is a boon or a curse. It examines the qualities that a company must have to build successful multidisciplinary
teams and corporate alliances; it discusses how companies have to
focus on customers, and especially on the needs and tastes of their
existing customers; it looks at the impacts of sharper competition and
speedier innovation. None of the changes that are taking place in a
manager's life necessarily make it simpler. More often, the task of
management grows even more complex, bewildering—and exciting.

But why should a new group of information and communications
technologies that have evolved around the Internet confound us so?
After all, the way most firms use the Internet is not particularly revolutionary. They generally allow it to perform familiar functions,
although more cheaply and flexibly than its predecessors could. The
e-mail message does not really differ from the paper memo or fax; the

electronic invoice looks much like an on-screen version of its paper form; the intranets that companies install to connect different departments resemble the enterprise resource-planning systems that many companies bought in the 1990s; even the purchasing networks that link companies with their suppliers have electronic ancestors. To the skeptic, the Internet enables companies to continue much as they have always done, though more inexpensively—and even those vaunted cost savings seem to elude them.

However, new technologies often start by mimicking what has gone before and only later change the world. And in coming to understand them, people begin by thinking of them in old terms: Consider the horseless carriage, or early television, which often seemed like radio on a screen. When factories first used electricity, they clustered machinery around the power source, just as they had with steam engines. Not until Henry Ford spotted the carcasses revolving in Chicago slaughterhouses did companies start to grasp the full benefits of electricity. Ford, seeing cows being systematically cut into pieces, realized that he could apply the same principle in reverse: start with small pieces and build them into a complete automobile. Once he had imaginatively leapt from fixed to moving production lines in 1913, others began to understand the value of taking power to the process. Only then did companies begin to develop the techniques of cheap mass production that so transformed manufacturing productivity in the twentieth century.

Many of today's Internet applications are still those of the steam age. Until we make the next leap, we will not realize their full potential. But that potential is ultimately immense. This book assumes that the Internet will, in time, be just as significant a force for transforming corporate productivity as was the switch from steam to electricity. Indeed, while people have exaggerated many of the short-term effects of the Internet (as so often happens with new technologies), they may well have underplayed its long-term impact, especially on the internal workings of the firm. That was the case with the coming of electricity. Some engineers spotted as early as the 1880s that machines fitted with electric motors no longer had to be sited near a coalfield or a stream for power, or in rows within the plant. But that was more than thirty years before Henry Ford's revolutionary development of the automated production line.[2]

The Internet may prove just as potent a force for reshaping companies in the twenty-first century as electricity and mass production did in the twentieth.

## Why Internet Technologies Matter

WHAT ASPECTS of Internet technologies make them so important? Why has their arrival already disrupted the lives of managers even more than the coming of the mainframe or the PC after it? The broad answer is that, over and over again, their uses dovetail beautifully with current trends. They provide solutions to many of the problems companies want to tackle. In particular, five aspects of these new technologies, when considered together, make them an extraordinarily powerful force for change. Of course, they should not be taken as the only effects. Others—on privacy, on managerial time, and on the complexity of decision making, for example—bring at least as many difficulties as benefits.

First, the new technologies are driving down the cost and speeding up the rate of processing, transmitting, and storing information. Remember that almost every business process involves information in some form: an instruction, a plan, an advertisement, a blueprint, a set of accounts. Businesses can handle and share all this information more cheaply than ever before. The speed at which prices have dropped outpaces that of any previous technological revolution. Over the past three decades, the cost of computer processing power has fallen by 99.999 percent, an average decline of 35 percent a year. Even electricity prices dropped by an average of only 6 percent a year in real terms between 1890 and 1920.[3]

The falling price of a new technology is one of the main forces that persuade people to adopt it. It took ninety years after the discovery of electromagnetic induction, and forty years after the building of the first power station, for electricity to account for half the power used by American manufacturers.[4] As for the Internet, in 2000 (only thirty years after its invention and seven after its commercial launch) one survey found that 57 percent of medium-sized American companies already used it for some of their sales, more than twice the number only a year earlier. Nearly all the companies surveyed were already using the Internet to buy supplies and services, recruit employees, and research markets and industry trends.[5]

Second, the astonishing fall in the cost of transferring information around the world is a powerful force for globalization. "There has never been a commercial technology like this in the history of the world," says Robert Hormats, vice chairman of Goldman Sachs International, "whereby from the minute you adopt it, it forces you to think and act globally."[6] It is not just big companies that have an incentive and a means continually to rearrange production globally in whatever mode is most efficient. Small companies can now reach a global market and "look" like big firms. One result is to allow the emergence of "sliver" companies, specializing more intensely than ever before in ultra-high-tech areas and other narrow markets. Another is to reinforce competition and therefore to drive innovation.

Third, the innumerable applications of the Internet make the changes it brings more pervasive and varied than any that have gone before. Its chameleon qualities will allow it to boost the efficiency of more or less everything a company does. The Internet is not simply a new distribution channel or a new way to communicate. It is many additional things: a marketplace, an information service, a means for manufacturing goods and services, a computing platform in its own right. It makes a difference to myriad tasks that managers do daily, from locating new suppliers to coordinating projects to collecting and managing customer data. Each of these functions of the Internet, in turn, affects corporate life in many ways.

This versatility is unique. Even electricity did not promise so many new ways of doing business. Indeed, the commercial potential of electricity, like that of steam and the railways, was mainly to transform the manufacturing and distribution of physical goods. The Internet, by contrast, mainly boosts the efficiency of services, whether provided by a corporate finance department, a travel agency, or a government department. It offers new ways to manage information, and that is the core activity of most service industries. That effect is enormously important because services account for more than half the output of the economies of the rich countries. A technology that boosts service-industry productivity makes a real difference to the prospects for economic growth.

Fourth, the Internet makes markets of all kinds work better because it increases access to information. Even the smallest businesses use the Internet for research: to check on prices, availability, potential outlets. Their employees may still pick up the telephone to complete deals, but at least they make more informed decisions than they otherwise would have done and thus drive tougher bargains. By altering the way to find information, the Internet will foster new decision-making processes and tools. It will increase the need for speedy ways to establish trust with business partners, such as suppliers and distributors.

By improving the efficiency of decision making, Internet technologies also reduce one of the main costs of doing business. As a result, individuals may no longer need companies to undertake transactions on their behalf; they may operate more efficiently alone, as "free agents."[7] The effect is to call into question the fundamental reason why firms exist: as a way to minimize the transaction costs of production.

Finally, the Internet speeds up the dissemination and adoption of new techniques. As computers grow ever more powerful, it becomes easier to design new products, whether pharmaceuticals or bank accounts. Wider competition, itself partly the effect of the Internet, increases the pressure to innovate. The Internet allows companies to connect teams of designers or engineers in different parts of the world, enabling them to hand off work to each other and use time zones to accelerate research and testing. It also allows companies to watch and to learn from what others in their industry are doing—even on the other side of the world.

This unprecedented, rich combination of qualities explains why the Internet is affecting corporate life more profoundly than any previous technology. But a glance at earlier innovations in office technology reveals that some surprisingly humble novelties have dramatically altered what goes on inside companies.

## The First Managerial Revolution

EVERY SCHOOLCHILD learns of the industrial revolution, with its spinning jenny and flying shuttle. But the second half of the nineteenth century saw a much less familiar revolution that was, in its way, just as important: the birth of modern managerial techniques, enabled by new office technologies.

Until the 1870s, nearly all businesses were small and run by their owners. Venetian merchants of two centuries earlier would have recognized the forms of information: personal correspondence, newspapers, double-entry bookkeeping. By the end of the nineteenth century, more complex corporate organization and geographical dispersion created a commercial need for method and structure.

In Europe, the demands of the army and of financial services led the way. By the 1870s, 300 clerks at the Prudential Insurance Company in London were writing more than a million life policies a year. Such clerks needed standardized policies, procedures, and structures.[8] In the United States, where large-scale data processing developed relatively late, the railways and the federal census bureau served as the entry point. Railway managers developed reporting systems to inform themselves of problems, and capital and cost accounting to improve efficiency and profitability.

As production grew more complex, argues JoAnne Yates, a historian of the period, "the demand for systematic, primarily written, information about roles, processes and outcomes" increased.[9] Coordination and control required new techniques for collecting and storing information for analysis and communication. As these techniques spread, they sparked a fashion for office rationalization and for what was dubbed "scientific management." Many of the first generation of America's salaried managers initially had trained as engineers. They devised techniques for cost accounting, processes for streamlining the flow of written orders to their staffs, and methods for communicating with their sales forces and customers.

To extend to the office the benefits that standardization was already bringing on the factory floor, they employed "systematizers," the forerunners of today's information technology consultants. These folks set about restructuring the office, introducing novelties such as typewriters and adding machines, designing standard business forms and loose-leaf filing systems, replacing old-fashioned accounting ledgers with machine billing systems, and so on.

One such novelty was the vertical filing cabinet, which, in the 1870s, began to replace bound, chronologically ordered books to enable cross-referencing of the multiplying volume of documents.

Like many novelties of its era, this deceptively simple innovation has endured. Even with the arrival of the computer, most offices still have a few filing cabinets tucked away and businesses that manage paper archives still exist. In the 1890s, not only did the proliferation of filing create a new job, that of filing clerk, it made it easier to find information and it decentralized information management, as individual departments and managers controlled local files. Then, as today, information was power, and its control was political.

Standard office procedures allowed managers a better grasp of the process, finances, and structure of their operations. They also made possible—and increased the need for—office specialists, what we would now call "knowledge workers." In 1870, the United States recorded a mere 74,200 clerical workers; by 1920, that number had leapt to 2,837,000. All sorts of new job titles sprouted up—office manager, stenographer, filing clerk, vice president of sales—just as the arrival of the Internet has brought new roles such as Web designer and chief information officer.

These new jobs emerged side by side with a boom in office innovation. The United States became the world's first country to adopt office machinery on a large scale. The typewriter, first mass-produced by the Remington factory in 1874, offered a device for rapid, inexpensive desktop production of the printed word. The first machines were intended for what proved to be the wrong market: court reporters. By the 1880s, businesses were rapidly acquiring typewriters at a rising rate, buying 150,000 machines in 1900 alone. For the first time, good typists could record information faster—more than three times faster—than by handwriting it.

Like the PC today, the typewriter was a general-purpose technology. Of course, it did not have the PC's ability to store or manipulate information directly, or to send it straight to another user; neither could it be hacked into or used for illicit games of Doom. But businesses could use it to record text or numbers. Its versatility and another strength, the common standard of the QWERTY keyboard, ensured its survival. The typewriter remained in widespread use, almost unchanged apart from eventual electrification, for more than a century and indeed is still used by court reporters. (This author wrote her first five books on manual typewriters.)

Other machines appeared to record and store more specialized information, such as the time clock to record working time and the cash register to reduce employee pilfering (and subsequently to record sales information). They too encouraged standardization. The time clock helped to standardize working hours, the cash register to standardize pricing. The preprinted fill-in-the-blanks form standardized the recording of information, making the process easier, faster, and more consistent. It also increased managers' financial accountability, although not until the Securities Act of 1933 did annual reports become a legal requirement in the United States.

Managers wanted to communicate, too: After the 1890s, stencils and rotary mimeographs allowed them to copy hundreds of documents quickly and cheaply for dissemination. The pneumatic tube carried the memorandum—two other innovations—around a plant or department store like a primitive intranet. And the telephone, even before the exchange, enabled managers to speak directly to factory foremen in a different location. Moreover, while most late-nineteenth-century office technologies encouraged managers to use the written word to transmit information formally, the telephone made it easier for people to speak informally to each other.

America's early start in office machinery was to have momentous consequences. It meant that the United States became the leading producer of information technology goods. As one perceptive commentator noted:

> *In turn, the United States has dominated the typewriter, record-keeping, and adding machine industries for most of their histories; it dominated the accounting-machine industry between the two world wars; it established the computer industry after World War II; and it dominates the personal computer industry today. There is an unbroken line of descent from the giant office-machine firms of the 1890s to the computer makers of today.*[10]

Many of the pioneering companies of the first managerial revolution survived into the computer age: Remington, which became Remington Rand in the 1920s; National Cash Register (NCR); Burroughs Adding Machine Company; and even International Business Machines, which evolved from a company that made tabulating devices to handle the data from the 1890 U.S. census. Will Microsoft, Cisco, Oracle, and Intel cast such long shadows? Only if their technologies have a comparable impact on managerial efficiency.

All of these nineteenth-century innovations allowed managers to run bigger businesses with greater speed and consistency, over a wider distance, reaching more people and more places. However, many of them—typewriters, cash machines, adding machines—also increased the productivity of individual employees and managers. They allowed managers to analyze and store data. They influenced organizational processes, but not as dramatically as did another innovation of the period: punched-card accounting machines.

These machines, which IBM was still building and selling right into the 1950s, had an enterprisewide impact. That was also true, after the Second World War, for their descendants, electronic calculators. Most people initially regarded the computer as a glorified calculator; few expected it to revolutionize management or administration. That it did is largely the work of IBM. That company sold punched-card accounting machines as part of an integrated system, so when a business bought its machinery, IBM had to reconfigure its entire information system around the new purchase. After the Second World War, IBM came to dominate business computers—in 1960, it owned 70 percent of the market—and carried this approach through to selling these new machines.[11]

Technology thus not only empowers managers but also dictates the nature of their role. How will the managerial revolution of the present century take shape?

## The Second Revolution

THE SECOND managerial revolution is still developing: We now stand at the equivalent of the 1880s, when all sorts of new devices proliferated but companies had not yet determined the best ways to adopt them, let alone realize their full impact. Many American managers began to think seriously about the Internet after the millennium passed uneventfully.

Indeed, the millennium bug may have helped to integrate the Internet into corporate networks. For two years, chief information officers, relatively new corporate creatures, had worked (often with enlarged budgets) to upgrade their control over and understanding of their existing legacy systems. But during the approach of Y2K, most companies froze spending on new applications to avoid creating new risks.

Once the new millennium safely dawned, larger companies turned to developing their Internet strategies. But they have moved more slowly than the hype of 1999–2000 would suggest. A survey released early in 2001 by the National Association of Manufacturers and Ernst & Young LLP found that only one-third of American manufacturers used the Internet to sell or procure products and services online. Just 5 percent said that they could use the Internet to track their suppliers' inventories—an innovation much touted in business schools.[12] Only when a new technology passes the stage of feverish experimentation and becomes reliable and demonstrably useful is it likely to be adopted by the great majority of companies.

However, if most American companies have been slow off the mark, then companies in almost all other countries have been slower, as a glance at comparative levels of investment in information and communications technology (ICT) suggests. In the late 1990s, ICT spending accounted for a larger share of the economy of the United States than it did in any other country except Sweden and Britain. ICT investment in Germany, easily Europe's largest economy, ac-counted for just over half the share of GDP that it took in the United States.[13]

And everywhere, large firms have been the first to seize the oppor-tunities that the Internet creates—even though, in the long run, the smaller firms may benefit more. Once companies get the message, however, they move fast. In Britain, the proportion of the smallest firms (those with fewer than ten employees) connected to the Internet shot from 15 percent to 55 percent between 1999 and 2000.[14] The survey by the National Association of Manufacturers and Ernst & Young found that more than 70 percent of respondents were planning investments to find customers or build business opportunities online, and about 30 percent planned to search for new suppliers via the

Internet.[15] In European countries that measure Internet usage systematically, such as Denmark and Finland, more than half of all enterprises with more than twenty employees placed orders using the Internet in 1999, compared with about 15 percent in 1997.[16]

Most companies initially use the Internet simply to announce their existence. They put up a Web site and maybe solicit orders from customers, who e-mail them information that must be put into the system manually. As of spring 2001, for instance, only 25 percent of Dell Computer's customers who could create orders online placed such orders electronically.[17] The rest designed orders online and then submitted them by e-mail or fax. As a result, Dell must input the information itself.

Important though a company's relations with the outside world may be, companies currently focus the most attention on running the internal organization smoothly. In the future, they will be able to satisfy more customers with fewer resources, partly because the balance between internal and external demands on a business will shift from running the company to keeping customers happy.

Many employees still move information around the business, "running errands" that good software applications can now do. In a far-sighted book published in 1995, Arno Penzias, a Nobel Prize winner and former vice president and chief scientist of Bell Labs, wrote: "Though to my knowledge no computer has yet managed to replicate the performance of a single office worker, the right combination of computing and communications can frequently replace whole departments."[18] Internet-based software applications are shrinking the amount of human time and effort needed for internal coordination.

Already, it is possible to glimpse some of the potential benefits that these uses of Internet technologies will bring. If companies are to reap them, and to minimize the drawbacks, they must make many changes. Some will seem trivial but bring profound effects; some will seem profound but turn out to be trivial. The overall effect will be transforming. Just as the new office technologies of the late nineteenth century facilitated and drove changes in the ways companies operated—and indeed in their size and scope—so today's new technologies will have equally far-reaching effects. The company of the future will look very different from the company of today.

## The Benefits

A S THE FOLLOWING chapters detail, the potential impacts of Internet technologies spread to every aspect of what companies do.

These technologies affect the way companies pool the skills and knowledge of their work forces. Thus they offer new opportunities for *knowledge management:* ways to retain and build on the learning within companies. The development of sophisticated databases and intranets enables companies to build a core of knowledge upon which they can draw globally in unprecedented ways. Managers will require better tools for making decisions because the process of decision making will grow faster and more complex.

Innovation will be speedier, bringing new products and new services to market more quickly. Already, for example, the Internet has shortened dramatically the time needed to map the humane genome. Already, inexpensive computer power has enabled such novelties as online auctions, mobile telephones, and financial derivatives. Many more new products and services will eventually appear, as the company of the future grows ever better at innovation.

Internet technologies allow companies to handle relations with *customers* in new ways: to build deeper relationships, shifting the emphasis from recruitment to retention and from the mass market to the personalized. For years, companies have talked piously about treating each customer as an individual, about retaining and realizing the lifetime value of each customer, about honing the precise product each customer wants. Now, with better tools to monitor how customers behave and to ask what they want, some companies are actually doing these things. They can discriminate much more finely among groups of customers, offering the most valuable ones the best deals.

The new technologies can also provide new kinds of choice. Up to now, companies have generally concentrated on producing more stuff more cheaply, the big benefit of mass production. But as customers grow richer, and their immediate wants are sated, they may well not want more and more, for less and less. They may want a customized product, different from anything owned by anybody else. Companies can now make a range of unique items, from bicycles to watches, for individual buyers—producing the right stuff, not just more stuff.

Even before they reach that stage, companies find that the costs of basic customer care diminish. Customers (and employees) now fill in their own forms and answer their own questions. When a customer completes an electronic order form, there is less room for error. Few customers misspell their own names and addresses, and the order-filling process itself contains internal checks that eliminate simple errors (such as omitting a vital piece of information). Accuracy is thus outsourced to the customer. Self-service, as supermarkets long ago discovered, cuts costs, and customer service and after-sales service often account for at least 10 percent of a company's operating costs.[19]

A company's most important input is what some people rather revoltingly call "wetware," the human ingenuity that puts value into hardware and software.[20] As companies change, so does the task of *recruiting, retaining, and training* talented people. Intelligence, creativity, and teamwork are the essential inputs of most businesses. Talent has grown more valuable as new communications have raised the potential return on a good idea: A piece of software or a new medicine can be produced for a unit cost that is a fraction of its market value. Yet the job market is changing too. The talented minority of the work force will be harder than ever to manage because such people are becoming scattered, mobile, restless. They know their market value and will extract as large a share as possible for their contribution.

Part of the skill of management will be to infuse a sense of *corporate community*. Here, the Internet gives companies new tools to communicate internally. As companies pass through periods of rapid change, and increasingly employ far-flung teams that spend most of their time traveling or abroad, they now have new ways for managers to explain and lead. Used thoughtfully, these tools can reinforce strategic messages and build employee commitment.

As well as changing a company's relations with its customers and with the people it employs, Internet technologies alter *purchasing and supplier relationships*. As companies move procurement online, they achieve transparency and efficiency, cutting costs and improving control. They frequently realize many of their earliest savings by pooling purchasing and negotiating centrally for items such as stationery and laptops. As of early 2001, a survey found that nearly 50 percent of a group of American companies expected to do less than 20 percent of their procurement online for at least the next two years.[21] However, the gradual pace of change will snowball as more big companies make the move. Procurement managers see little point in moving online until their existing suppliers do: As so often occurs with networks, each extra new member disproportionately increases the network's value to all the others.

In more sophisticated ways, supply chain management is putting customers in control: They click a mouse and start a production process rolling, far off along the chain. Manufacturers talk directly to their suppliers, or to their suppliers' suppliers. Companies build deeper links with fewer suppliers, replacing the traditional supply chain with something more like an "ecosystem": a network of suppliers, all connected with each other as well as with their main customer.[22] They outsource peripheral activities, keeping in-house what they do best. That allows them to invest more and respond faster to changing supplier, labor, and consumer markets.

When suppliers receive better information all along the production chain, they need not hold so much inventory. One estimate suggests that a retailer who carries an item of stock for a year incurs a cost equivalent to 25 percent of the product's retail price.[23] So cutting a mere two weeks off retail inventories saves the equivalent of 1 percent of sales—a significant sum, given that most retailers work on margins of 3 to 4 percent.

With all these changes, Internet technologies bring shifts in *corporate structure*. Companies will find more opportunities to build alliances with other firms. The Internet facilitates running partnerships, allowing one company easily to refer a customer to another or to communicate information to a supplier. So the company of the future resembles the Japanese *keiretsu*—an association of independent but interdependent businesses—or even a Hollywood studio, which assembles talent and resources for a particular movie project and then disbands them when the project is complete.[24]

In addition, the people whose skills a company draws upon will be more loosely knitted into the corporation itself. Many will be self-employed—part of the "free agent nation" described in Daniel Pink's provocative book—or will work on contract on a series of projects rather than in a particular department.[25] Managers must use new communications to create communities to which such "distributed" workers can feel allegiance.[26]

To lead such businesses calls for a different set of *leadership and managerial skills*. For example, managers increasingly need the skills required to manage alliances, and senior managers must understand how to deploy technological skills themselves in order to think strategically about how to exploit them. In addition, senior executives must spend more time communicating with their employees, their customers and investors, and the public at large. They can no longer ignore the need to explain to others what they are doing. They no longer live behind closed doors, out of sight of all but a few senior staff, but in a fishbowl. They must learn to exploit that position rather than fearing it. As Jack Welch, in his latter days at the helm of General Electric, insisted, managers must face outward as well as inward, constantly guiding the greater visibility that the Internet allows. Managers who master that skill will run companies that are more productive, open, and customer-focused than ever before.

Those trendsetting companies that have begun to put such changes in place claim to be making many gains. GE, for example, set out to cut 15 percent from its cost base of $100 billion in both 2001 and 2002. That amount is five times the typical annual growth in productivity, of 3 to 4 percent, enjoyed by even this fast-moving firm.[27] The company argues that the necessary incremental investment in hardware and software is small compared with most investments and pays off surprisingly fast. Some of those gains, however, should be discounted as hype. Oracle claims dramatic results from "eating its own dog food" partly, no doubt, in the hope of persuading other companies to buy the dog food too. Nonetheless, many of the trendsetters' productivity improvements will eventually be replicated elsewhere.

## The Difficulties

A CHIEVING ALL these savings and many more involves considerable disruption. Technological change, particularly in its early stages, always carries risk. Managers face new strains, especially on their ability to make wise decisions under pressure. Companies will find it harder to drive a good bargain, whether with suppliers, customers, or employees, merely because they have information that the other side does not. And, in spite of the trendsetters' claims, the benefits will not always accrue in terms of higher profits. Many companies will have to find ways to save money simply to remain competitive. Consumers, not investors, will gain.

The initial impact of change has often been overwhelming for managers. They have seen too many overhyped experiments pushed through too quickly by excessively young companies and often led by inexperienced people. No wonder many feel sour about the experience. Adding to their gloom is the increased difficulty of making good decisions. They confront a torrent of unprioritized information, much of which adds nothing to their output or confuses the decision-making process by demanding a quick (but irrelevant) response at a bad moment.

Internet and communications technologies potentially raise managers' productivity by allowing them to work when they would have been doing something else, such as traveling to and from the office or a meeting. Within about five years, electronic mail has become the principal tool of business communication. The average American office worker now receives an average of thirty-six e-mails a day— seven times more than voice mails.[28] As e-mail becomes accessible on mobile devices, managers use the "dead" time of a car ride or a wait in an airport lounge to continue work. The corollary: They are never out of reach. Companies expect managers to be reachable in the evenings, on weekends, on vacation, and at lunch.

There may be nothing wrong with that in itself. But in the past, the cost of communicating information was high enough to make the sender pause and ask whether the message was worth sending. That constraint has vanished. The cost of sending an additional e-mail is now a few moments of the sender's time; the cost of sending an e-mail to an additional user, even less. So questions, answers, and irrelevant copies of other people's debates pour through the wires.

In addition, many more decisions must be made out in the open. Internet technologies expose management. Employees can more easily see what managers are saying to each other and to different audiences; they can also more easily swap information with each other and find common interests. Customers, too, can quickly discover corporate information that once would have been a struggle to acquire. "You put a piece of glass into your organization and expose all your internal strife," says Pete Martinez, a senior figure in the worldwide consulting arm of IBM's global services.[29]

Constantly in reach, incessantly connected, relentlessly under the spotlight, managers must make decisions in minutes or hours rather than days or weeks. That may not necessarily produce better decisions, for the issues grow more complex.

Managers who never knew much about the technology behind their operations now must do so, in order to slot in the new technology alongside what already exists. Most companies are understandably reluctant to junk expensive computer networks for a system based only on the Internet. They call in consultants to help them to "integrate"—or cobble together—systems that try to make the best use of both what is already in place and the new opportunities that the Internet creates. The sheer complexity of such arrangements can make them unreliable and forces technically unskilled managers to make unfamiliar decisions.

Such managers frequently find that they are venturing into the unknown. Building a new production line or retail outlet is familiar: Managers understand the risks and know how to calculate the payoff. Building an online store or a corporate intranet is new territory. It may be hard to find a manager to take charge or to judge whether the project is wisely run. The risks are uncertain; the payoff, too. All these problems emphasize the importance of good decision-making processes and tools, and of understanding the reasoning that a decision implies.

Even when a manager has time to think, new dangers and uncharted debates will make the task of management harder. The flip side of connectivity is greater vulnerability to hackers and viruses. A power cut brings not just dead computers but dead customer service and lost orders. Privacy is hard to protect. New lines must be drawn on new issues, such as the obligation to protect customer data and the ownership of intellectual property.

Hardest of all, for many companies, may be the way that more fluid markets and more widely available information shift the balance of power. No longer do companies hold the best cards in their dealings with customers or their negotiations with suppliers. Even more important, no longer do they hold the best cards in dealing with their most talented staff. The brightest and best are increasingly aware of their market value and will extract it ruthlessly from an employer or move on. The more crucial individual talent becomes as a corporate input, the greater the challenge to secure some of its value for the company and its investors.

## Where Change Counts

THE GREATEST BENEFITS from the new technologies will come only to companies that change their structure to accommodate them. The revolution must also be accompanied by organizational change. What we are witnessing is not just about becoming Web-enabled but rather the start of a period of fundamental organizational change. From it will emerge a new type of company.

In many businesses, legacy structure is a greater problem than legacy systems: departments suddenly fear losing a key role to an Internet-based system. Take customer relationship management: The Internet allows companies to collect and analyze information about customer behavior much more precisely than ever before. They can see clearly which customers have bought which products and there-fore cross-sell products that other parts of the company produce. But unless salespeople have good financial incentives for doing so, they may not use the information available to them to refer one of their customers to a colleague in another department.

So, although hardware and software are essential, what really matters is the way a company is run: how it deals with complexity, speed, and uncertainty and, above all, how it trains and motivates its staff.

Teaching staff to use new technologies effectively will distinguish successful firms from failing ones. Erik Brynjolfsson, a professor at the Massachusetts Institute of Technology's Sloan School of Management, argues that software and hardware account for only about a tenth of true corporate investment in information technology.[30] A far larger amount goes into devising and introducing new business processes and training employees.

Sadly, investments in team building and training do not show up on corporate accounts. Instead, under American accounting principles (GAAP), they generally appear under expenses, such as payments to consultants. Worse, the tax man treats them like investments in old-economy physical goods to capitalize and depreciate. Yet without such spending on what Brynjolfsson calls "organizational capital," companies throw away money devoted to communications technology.

The evidence strongly suggests that winning companies must combine good people, good structure, and good software. They must change in a coordinated fashion. They cannot simply mimic others: If they do, the results will disappoint or even disrupt. However, organizational capital is much harder to reproduce than the more visible, marketable sort. Brynjolfsson and his colleagues identified such capital in a survey of 416 companies by picking those companies where employees tended to control the way they worked; where their pay was linked to their performance; where they were well educated; where the emphasis was on teams; and where most information flowed freely around the company. Judging by their market capitalization, financial markets valued these energetic, democratic, intellectually empowered companies. But the markets most valued those firms with both a high investment in information technology and lots of organizational capital.

The success of a company's Internet strategy therefore depends on how managers run the firm. A shrewd strategy obviously helps, but in addition, a company needs strength in depth of management and employee skill; intelligent, empowered employees; a culture of openness and a willingness to experiment; good internal communications; and a well-designed pay structure. It also requires absolute commitment from the top. Only determined leadership will achieve the necessary change.

## Tomorrow's Company

THE TOOLS and possibilities for a new approach exist now, but the Internet alone will not accomplish change. That is for companies to achieve, by initiating changes in organizational structure.

One result of such change will be a culture of openness. Companies must invite customers and suppliers "inside the machine," in the phrase of Peter Martin, deputy editor of the *Financial Times*. Thus customers will be able to track the progress of their orders, as FedEx already allows them to do, by reaching into a company's database, and suppliers will be able to scoop information straight from their partners' databases. Openness becomes a corporate strategy.

Another result will be a change in familiar boundaries, starting with the firm itself. Collaborating with other companies will become easier and less expensive, as will linking various operations with and between firms and buying everything from management skills and innovation to the human resources department. The boundaries for employees will be redrawn too: those between home and work, as people work from home and shop from work, and those between the individual and the company, now that the knowledge and skills of some employees may account for a large part of the value of the company they work for.

Geographical boundaries will start shifting as well. Within companies, different regional divisions will need to collaborate and share customers more than ever before to source more products globally and to foster new ideas and competition anywhere on the planet. Time zones will matter more than mile markers.

Regions will no longer be fiefdoms. Companies that once left overseas divisions to run themselves like isolated colonies of some sprawling empire will now integrate them more tightly with the rest of the business. Rick Wagoner, CEO of General Motors, holds regular teleconferences with twenty or so key executives around the world, many of whom once would hardly ever have spoken to one another. Now, new communications allow the senior figures in this giant to operate with some of the intimacy of a much smaller business.

Important though all these differences are, the company of the future, like the company of today, will require competent management and wise leadership. It will depend for its success on human inventiveness and skill. A company's skill in decision making and in knowledge management will become ever more crucial. The intellectual capital that work-force ingenuity creates will increasingly become its most valuable asset. The well-organized company will be one whose structure encourages the growth of intellectual capital; whose management recruits and retains capable people, without relinquishing the value of their output to the business's owners; and whose staff shares risk and reward.

Companies may well grow even more complex in the years ahead. Globalization, the speed of innovation, heightened demands of well-educated and articulate consumers—all will add to the demands on chief executives and their top teams. Running a business will be even tougher tomorrow than it is today, but the rewards will be greater.

# Chapter 2
# Knowledge, Decision Making, and Innovation

THE VALUE of a business increasingly lies not in factories or fleets of trucks, the sort of assets that appear on the balance sheet and are easy to value and manage. Instead, it lies in intangibles: brands, patents, franchises, software, research programs, ideas, and expertise. "Knowledge" assets such as these account for perhaps six out of every seven dollars of corporate market value.[1] Managing any of these assets is difficult, but the hardest ones to deal with are those that employees carry around in their heads.

The company of the future will concentrate on managing people more than on managing physical assets. It will focus on trying to get the best from its knowledge capital. That will require understanding what knowledge resides with its employees (and, sometimes, with its suppliers and customers) as well as its other knowledge assets. The importance of pooling the skills of the work force will grow, and new ways of building on the learning that goes on in companies will be discovered.

Happily, the communications revolution presents new opportunities for managing intangibles. It also presents new challenges. For example, Internet technologies help to spread and share ideas. But they also allow ideas to move easily beyond a company, creating the need to protect intellectual property rights. Yet too much protection of such rights can stifle innovation. So governments and companies need to be able to strike a balance between openness and protection.

The development of sophisticated databases and intranets gives companies new opportunities to build a core of knowledge that they can access globally. The enormous capacity that Internet technologies create allows for the storage of vast amounts of information (in text and increasingly in voice and video). Yet most of this information is in cumbersome and unstructured forms. Deciding what to store and how to store it will require more tools and wise judgment.

Internet technologies also provide new opportunities for companies to manage people and their intrinsic knowledge and skills, on which companies are becoming increasingly reliant for competitive advantage. One of the biggest challenges for corporate management will be to find ways to maximize the benefits and minimize the costs of the changes occurring in the workplace. Technologies provide abundant opportunities; managers must develop a corporate approach that makes the most of them.

In addition, the focus and the process of innovation are changing, turning knowledge creation into a vital competitive advantage. Research and development, once concentrated mainly in universities and defense, is now much more widespread. Services, especially financial and business services, tend to be leaders in information technology R&D.

For the first time, it becomes easier to coordinate innovation in several locations at once. The number of new patents being issued, both in the United States and Europe, has proliferated—partly because the law has changed to allow patents of new products, such as software in the United States, but partly because companies are simply innovating faster. The pressures of global competition and sophisticated business and consumer demands push companies to speed up the process of turning ideas into products.

However, although companies bandy about the terms "knowledge management" and "intangible assets," few clearly articulate what either concept means. Some interpret knowledge management as training, others as managing an online database. One useful definition is that knowledge management involves efficiently connecting those who know with those who need to know, and converting personal knowledge into organizational knowledge.

Intangible assets, to use the distinction of Karl Erik Sveiby, an authority on intellectual capital, are of three main kinds.[2] One is employee competence; a second, internal structure such as patents, concepts, models, and administrative and computer systems; a third, external structure, such as brand names, trademarks, reputation, and relationships with customers and suppliers. All three account for a vastly larger share of the value of a company than do its physical machinery or premises.

Plenty of evidence suggests that stock-market valuations correlate closely with investments in research, development, and other intangibles. For example, the biggest gap between the market and book values of U.S. companies tends to occur in those that have most rapidly boosted their spending on R&D. However, as high-tech companies constantly grumble, their balance sheets poorly reflect the value of their knowledge assets. Even within the company, good measures simply do not exist to help managers decide where to make future knowledge investments. Clark Eustace, who chaired a working group on R&D at the Brookings Institution in Washington, DC, puts the dilemma this way: "With building a factory, there are time-honored methods for calculating rates of return. But what if you are investing in R&D or software, or deciding whether to buy better people or to train more? There aren't tools for making such decisions."[3] Here, then, is a key area of decision making for which managers today lack not only adequate language and accounting principles (they still use investment terms and conventions left over from the industrial age) but also adequate tools.

The company of the future will have to develop these tools because decisions about investing in knowledge and people will matter more than decisions about investments in physical assets. After all, uniquely among assets, people can walk out of the door, taking most of their value with them. But they can also walk in the door, bringing a business new talents and stimuli. And managing people is far different from managing physical assets. Once a company has acquired a machine, it will do mainly what it was designed to do, but a human being's behavior is not so predetermined. The possibilities are infinite. So at the heart of managing knowledge and innovation will be not technology but managing human commitment and maximizing the transference from human knowledge to organizational knowledge. That requires psychology, the ultimate management skill.

## Sharing Ideas

IN A VARIETY of ways, the arrival of Internet technologies is reshaping knowledge management. Knowledge becomes accessible in new ways; it becomes easier to store and to transfer; expertise becomes easier to locate; employees can collaborate more effectively, whether they work in the same firm or time zone or in different ones. But these new opportunities will benefit companies only if they can adapt their management skills and their corporate culture to take advantage of them. New technologies must reinforce, not replace, existing human patterns of knowledge management. Technology is only half the answer; managerial ingenuity must do the rest.

For example, take one of the basic keys to effective knowledge management: converting personal knowledge into organizational knowledge. That conversion is a life-or-death matter for companies. Corporate memory is increasingly scattered in many different places: databases, filing cabinets, and people's heads. People create valuable ideas and are sometimes at their most creative when they first arrive in a company, before they become institutionalized into the corporate culture. Companies must have ways to capture these ideas while they are still fresh.

Companies also must have ways to capture the knowledge of people who move on, taking the corporate memory with them. For the moment, both the management techniques and the technology are primitive. Larry Leifer, a member of Stanford University's Learning Laboratory, describes how information accumulates in a group of people undertaking a project together.[4] Once the project is finished, most of the information and knowledge tends to disperse, and the next project has to begin almost at the beginning. People rarely write good final reports—most have already embarked on the next project by the time the first one comes to an end.

A company's best hope here may be to save the accumulated unstructured information: e-mails, reports, hasty notes of conversations. Inevitably, this is less useful than storing such memories in the human brain. Searching ragbags of data is difficult, and yet transferring information into an appropriate form is time-consuming and can be wasteful.[5] But the alternative may be that new projects start from scratch. They may thus waste precious time and repeat the mistakes a previous project made (but failed to record), while the only person who understands the quirks of a piece of customized software disappears for two months' sabbatical in Phuket or a top analyst leaves, contacts and all, for a rival firm. The challenge for companies is to find better ways to extract and share such valuable stuff.

Knowledge takes time to acquire, to absorb, and to record. But the base on which a company's institutional memory is built may be diminishing. Employees tend to retire early or to move jobs more often than they did in the past. Companies shed staff and overhaul management structures. The result may be a loss of informally held knowledge: the memory of how it felt last time there was a recession or of why the company decided to get out of some particular market. Nothing yet beats the human memory as a repository of knowledge. But as the work force alters, companies must learn to use technology in new ways to manage more effectively the human capital on which their competitive advantage depends.

Companies need their workers to share ideas more than ever before, for a variety of reasons. For instance:

- Expertise is now relatively more expensive. Given the widening premiums for skill, discussed in chapter 4, companies must pay more for top talent, so they need to find frugal ways to use it.

- The incessant innovation and refinement of new products and processes require an endless stream of fresh ideas.

- Just as workers in an old economy factory work together physically to build a machine, so workers in an office need to communicate and cooperate to build a service.

For millennia, the most durable way to pass on knowledge has been by word of mouth.[6] Information that survives for thousands of years is passed on through oral storytelling; information that lasts for hundreds, through the more modern storage technique of the book. Now, companies must find new ways for their staff to share knowledge—ways that replicate the memorable power of the fireside yarn—while overcoming the changes that make such sharing more difficult. For today, workers on the same project may be separated by long distances and time zones. They may work for different companies. The stimulating chat around the coffee machines, that time-honored source of bright ideas and quick fixes, is harder to arrange.

As tasks become fragmented among firms, so good collaboration tools also become more essential. Of course, even in geographically dispersed businesses, information long has been shared. At some companies, designers located in different time zones have passed work to each other around the clock. But until recently, they have used not the Internet but proprietary networks. Many of the most promising Internet applications aim to enhance global team building. They are designed to encourage collaboration and the emergence within companies of horizontal communities bound together by a common function or interest. These communities can now easily float ideas with each other or gossip or discuss best practice—around the clock and around the globe.

Corporate success will depend not just on using technology to store ideas but also on finding effective ways to manage the people who work where knowledge is stored. For instance, even with technology that allows teams from several firms to collaborate, the key to success will be whether the firms—or, indeed, the country where the teams are based—have a culture of sharing information outside the company. And, as with creativity, an understanding of ways to share ideas must come mainly from the bottom up. In the words of John Seely Brown and Paul Duguid, two of the wisest commentators on knowledge management, "Top-down processes designed to institutionalize new ideas can have a chilling effect on creativity. But they don't have to. Managers can learn to walk the fine line between rigidity—which smothers creativity—and chaos—where creativity runs amok and nothing ever gets to market."[7] Cultural change may have to take place before the benefits of new technology can be realized.

Managing knowledge thus entails both the management of experts and expertise and the management of collaboration. Both tasks require special skills. But the key point is that both are as much about creating the right incentives for talented individuals as about designing software or installing a grandiose chief knowledge officer. Companies must carefully balance two potentially conflicting aims: rewarding their most talented people enough to keep them on board, and at the same time developing pay structures that emphasize teamwork rather than individual effort. They must also think creatively about sharing knowledge with other companies—suppliers, perhaps, or alliance partners. Success will depend not just on maximizing the amount of knowledge shared but also on establishing the right degree of openness between them.

## Locating Expertise

W HAT DO YOU DO when you need some bit of information that somebody else in the company probably has but you do not? It might be the name of a contact or a scientific term—or perhaps something more complex, such as the background to a particular correspondence or the corporate view of a potential business partner. The answer will depend, of course, on the particular kind of information. But often, the obvious approach is to walk down the corridor, knock on someone else's door, and ask.

Finding expertise is an essential aspect of knowledge management. It involves the sharing of knowledge in a particularly precise way. Internet technologies offer new ways to structure, store, and disseminate immense quantities of important information, thus allowing a little expertise to go a great deal further. Finding what you need to know, and at the right level of expertise, is the difficulty. For companies, the question will be, What is the best way to apply technology to make that task easier? The answer will be different for different types of information, depending at least partly on whether the information is structured or unstructured.

For example, for finding certain bits of unstructured information, e-mailing a friend will always be more efficient than searching a database. Just as sharing ideas is about human networks, so is finding expertise: Since time immemorial, networks have been the way people tracked down experts. The beauty of asking a person rather than reading a book or consulting a database is that, if a person does not know the answer, he or she will be able to point you in the direction of someone else who might.

So companies must use technology to create effective versions of those networks. Here, the Internet has a great strength: It is very good at widening contacts. The Internet makes it easier and cheaper than

## The Importance of XML

A MONG THE INNOVATIONS for allowing companies to share information and knowledge with their business partners, few are more important than Extensible Markup Language, or XML. It makes it possible for a company to receive information arriving electronically from a customer or supplier and to pass it through its own system without having to print it out and manually transcribe data or change the format. XML will thus dramatically improve the interchange of online information. Its impacts on management will not be as radical as those of the Internet itself, but they will be far-reaching.

Older, proprietary systems, such as Electronic Data Interchange, or EDI, have long been able to do something similar, albeit clumsily. On the Internet, performing the trick has been harder. The code that tells a computer how to display a page of material you find on the Internet, known as Hypertext Markup Language, or HTML, specifies aspects such as header, paragraph, image, and table but does not say whether the page contains a set of medical records or instructions for installing a condenser. So search engines cannot tell from the "tags" on a Web page whether they have found a page on books *by* Charles Dickens or on books *about* Charles Dickens. As Microsoft's Bill Gates says, "if you want to learn about the fastest computer chip available, you might end up with information about potato chips delivered in fast trucks."*

That sort of problem matters most when businesses are trying to send each other complicated information about items in a catalog or stocks or invoices. HTML uses a predefined set of tags that describe, say, an invoice for truck tires as table, heading, row, and paragraph. XML, by contrast, can be used to define a set of tags that suits the needs of a particular industry. That flexibility makes it possible to use tags to label the content of the page rather than to describe what it should look like. If the invoice's tags gave price, model, quantity, and dimensions, a program could identify the document as an invoice and pass it through to the finance department to be paid promptly.

ever before to e-mail a contact on the other side of the world for an answer to a tricky question. An example: BP, the British oil giant, has developed an intranet called Virtual Team Network that links personnel on oil-drilling rigs around the world. If a drill bit develops a fault, a rig worker can log on to the network and put out a worldwide request for help to repair it.

Unlike HTML, XML does not confine the designer of a Web page to a few dozen standard words. Instead, a browser can understand that a page provides information on a book's authorship rather than the title, or that it is a purchase order, or that it is in Chinese. Because XML defines the structure of different Web languages, a page carries all the information a browser needs to understand the rules that the originator of the page has drawn up. It is as though each page were a board game that arrived with a set of rules telling you exactly how to play it. To be comprehensible, the rules must be presented in a standard way, and XML defines that standard.

The beauty of XML is that it allows different industries, research areas, and organizations to define and standardize languages that exactly meet their needs. Because XML allows the content of a Web page to be defined in terms of the type of data it contains rather than the way the data should look, it helps groups of like-minded people to share information. They simply need to agree on a language that meets their particular requirements. So a consortium of fishing fleets might agree on a standard way to describe information about fish catches: the number to be landed, the species, the average size. They could then use their own tags to store this information. A search engine would then be able to hunt for data types rather than just for words: for all the fleets that landed haddock of a certain size on a certain date, for example, rather than just any Web site containing the word "haddock."

It sounds wonderful. But individual industries and other groups need to agree on the set of tags that their particular trade will use. Otherwise, some fishing fleets will store data on catches with a tag called <size>, while others might use <weight> instead. These subsidiary standards are crucial for commercial interaction. Agreeing on them will often be a tortuous and acrimonious process. Once they are in place, however, XML will become the core of electronic commerce and a fundamental aspect of the sharing of knowledge online.

*Bill Gates with Collins Hemingway, *Business @ the Speed of Thought: Succeeding in the Digital Economy* (New York: Warner Books, 2000), 259.

The Internet thus offers an ideal way to locate unstructured information, the most difficult kind to discover. In addition, many large companies try to build databases that list each employee's area of expertise. They quickly learn that the employees themselves should not fill in the information. Some will be boastful, others modest. Better to include a question or two in the regular process of employee evaluation and have the human resources department write up the results.

Armed with material such as this, people hunting for expertise can employ increasingly sophisticated software and search engines to gauge which workers' skills are highly rated by their colleagues and which are not, or to scour directories of people with special knowledge. The Media Laboratory at the Massachusetts Institute of Technology, for example, is developing a concept called the Expert Finder: software that swaps information about various users to create a list of people it "thinks" might be able to help with a particular problem.[8] This is, in effect, an attempt to use technology to mimic the benefits of searching a colleague's Rolodex for names of people who might have a solution.

Internet technologies also provide new ways to locate information in more structured forms. For example, big consulting companies, which trade on their ability to muster knowledge rapidly and precisely, all have built electronic databases to allow their consultants anywhere in the world to tap into the company's accumulated wisdom. Accenture has its Knowledge Exchange, a vast online compendium of the company's thinking and past experience accessible anywhere in the world and at any time to all of its people. Some consultants insist that, when looking for help, the database is their first port of call.

To build such assets, the first requirement is that employees be willing to hand over their knowledge; the second, that the knowledge on the database be of high quality. The more valuable knowledge becomes, the greater the disincentive to share it—for individuals as well as for companies. Internet technologies offer a powerful tool for sharing information, yet at the same time they increase its value and so strengthen the case for protecting it. Companies must therefore coax people to help with the tasks of filtering and sharing.

Persuading employees to share their expertise, a theme to which this book frequently returns, certainly calls for incentives. These need not necessarily be financial. Some companies explicitly reward generous sharing with promotion. IBM evaluates its executives by their willingness to serve the greater good of IBM rather than their particular business unit.[9]

To ensure the value of information in a database, companies can learn from the peer-review process that filters the quality of knowledge before it appears in an academic journal. Behind the idea lies a long-established version of the fashionable concept of communities of interest. That principle has been strikingly applied by Xerox, which has built Eureka, an intranet linked to a database that allows its 23,000 service staff to share tips on repairing the company's copiers. The reward for contributing a good tip is not cash but the admiration and gratitude of one's fellow workers.[10] Whereas most databases, like most business processes, are top-down creations, the tips on Eureka are effectively peer reviewed: reps supply and vet the tips. Only after a tip has been vetted by a local expert and then checked by a centralized review process is it added to the database. This filtering is what gives the tips their value and has allowed Eureka to save the company an estimated $100 million.[11]

This emphasizes a further point: the higher the quality of information on a database, and the more tightly it is structured, the easier it will be to locate. Improving the quality of what goes in will thus raise the value that people extract. Companies find that information becomes truly useful only once it is structured. For example, General Motors uses focus groups to help it design cars that appeal to customers. It videotapes the groups to ensure that all the nuances of information are correctly recorded and conveyed to the car-design team. The trouble is, each group generates thirty hours of tape, and a dozen analysts each conduct several groups a month. Happily for GM, a software company called Virage has devised a way to digitize and analyze the content of the videos. Technicians who previously wrote out the content by hand now spend half as much time on the initial editing process, and product analysts save time finding what they need, such as all the references to a single design feature. Wholly new service industries are evolving to turn unstructured information into valuable knowledge, or at least to structure the information to make it more accessible.

No matter how well information is structured, people still have difficulty locating exactly what they want from large quantities of data. Search engines still have difficulty understanding what people really want to know and so dredge up vast amounts of irrelevant junk. That latter problem will pass. All too often, early search engines have been designed not by the people—such as corporate librarians and research departments—who know most about the disorganized and intuitive way that human beings search but by youthful techies, more interested in software than content and structure. In time, better search engines, data-mapping tools, and agents that scour the Web intelligently for information will help to solve this difficulty.

However, even the best search engine may not easily deliver the serendipity that comes from browsing through a newspaper or from hunting through the mess on one's own desk. People sometimes do not know what they are looking for until they stumble across it. One solution would be electronically generated recommendations, such as those that Amazon offers readers: "Others who bought this book have also liked the following titles." Even here, with the right management, technology has answers to offer.

## Collaborating

THE INFORMATION in one worker's head may be valuable, but that value increases if it is shared with colleagues. Collaboration is one of the most important ways that Internet technologies can help to manage the process of sharing ideas and working together.

Much of the everyday collaboration that goes on in companies is humdrum stuff. But it is immensely time-consuming to coordinate people scattered in different places, working for different employers. The Internet transforms the process. Indeed, collaborative working was the Internet's original function back in the days of ARPANET, when it enabled defense and communications specialists scattered through several companies, universities, and government departments to work together on the same project.

All sorts of new collaboration tools now allow people to share a single task. The Internet, with its open standards, makes collaboration easier than ever before. For managers faced with running a large and complicated project, that is a godsend. Online collaboration enormously reduces paperwork, limits the scope for error, and enables companies with a wide variety of skills to cooperate seamlessly. Tracking who has done what is essential, if only to identify expertise in the future and to avoid legal wrangles if things go wrong.

Take, for instance, a large building project. Meeting the need for collaboration—not just within a company but externally with dozens of businesses (architects, engineers, material suppliers) over periods of months or years—is an immense challenge. Without the Internet, each project entails thousands of transactions that must be recorded on paper. A typical $100 million building project generates 150,000 documents: technical drawings, legal contracts, purchase orders, requests for information, and schedules. Project managers build warehouses just to store them. Federal Express reputedly earned $500 million in 1999 solely from revenues generated by shipping blueprints across the United States.[12]

To reduce these costs, many companies now create a Web site to which everyone involved in a project, from the architect to the carpenters, has access in order to check blueprints and orders, change specifications, agree on delivery dates, and track progress. Moreover, everything from due dates to material specifications is permanently recorded, creating an audit trail that is a particular boon in this famously litigious industry. Swinerton & Walberg Builders, a large U.S. contractor, says that using such a Web site has reduced by two-thirds the time it needs to deal with requests for information.[13]

Using a shared Web site in this way allows anyone working on a project to post or update material. That ends the cumbersome business of sending e-mail attachments back and forth, especially irritating for people working on a laptop with a dial-up connection in a hotel bedroom. Good policy also assigns someone to act as a filter for the site, ensuring that high-quality information is easily entered and faulty information kept out. Once again, filtering is an essential part of sound knowledge management.

Mergers and takeovers generate just as much paperwork as do building projects. Davis & Co., a London law firm, now uses secure Web sites to coordinate teams of lawyers working on due diligence in large mergers or takeovers. A global takeover readily generates up to 30,000 pieces of paper and involves a variety of disciplines, from accounting to legal services. A secure Web site allows clients and specialists to monitor progress or hold an impromptu discussion of a document using an online "whiteboard" to mark up amendments. One such project coordinated fifty lawyers, fifty accountants, and fifty due-diligence specialists working in twelve cities across nine countries, from Australia to Kazakhstan.[14]

Ford uses a similar collaboration technology to handle due diligence when it acquires a company. It developed the system when

teams in Sweden, Britain, and America collaborated over the acquisition of Volvo; after that, it used the system in the purchase of Land
Rover. Staff can check points quickly by using instant messaging. The
advantage of such "e-rooms," says Bipin Patel, head of management
systems at Ford, is that they are asynchronous. So people can enter
them when it suits them. They are also always up-to-date.

Other Internet-based tools are even more sophisticated. Zaplet, a
company in California, has devised something it calls—unsurpris-
ingly—a "zaplet." It arrives in your mailbox like an ordinary e-mail,
but when opened, the zaplet becomes a window onto a server. The
information you see is whatever is now held on the server, so that you
always get the most up-to-the-minute version. The zaplet may also
allow you to use an application that sits on the server: a spreadsheet,
perhaps, or a tool for managing a customer database.

One use might be for managers to share recruitment information.
Normally, piles of applications pour daily into the human resources
department, which sorts them and forwards the best to managers, who
indicate which candidates they want to see. The department then telephones the applicants and goes back and forth trying to find a suitable
interview date. How much easier, muse Zaplet folk, if the recruiting
department could send a single zaplet to the managers who are doing
the hiring. Then they could all look at the same application and write
in comments and compare schedules to see which time slots are free
for an interview.

Groove, developed by Ray Ozzie, the man behind Lotus Notes, is
collaboration software that uses an idea similar to that behind Napster,
the hugely successful software that allowed people to share the music
files on their computers with one another using peer-to-peer links that
bypassed a central server. Groove Networks's software allows all sorts
of files—including chat, video conferencing, and instant messaging—
to be shared directly over a corporate network or over the Internet
itself. Users can simultaneously look at and edit shared files while gos-
siping with one another about the boss or the weather.

"This is based on the notion that most work is about people connecting with other people," says Ozzie with admirable simplicity.[15] It
is, according to an enthusiastic review in that high-tech bible, *Wired*
magazine, "great for small and spontaneous project collaborations
where users don't care to spend the time or money on a heavy-duty

platform."[16] Here, as so often, the mark of an innovative technology is that it makes available to everyone something that had previously been there only for the wealthy elite.

These various collaboration tools have another advantage: They will in the future allow the sort of information normally available only in corporate back offices to be readily accessible to people in the field. A salesperson, while heading for a customer's office, might be able to discover whether the customer was happy with the relationship so far, or to pull up a record of the customer's past transactions.

Eventually, the effect will be to turn a company's customers and suppliers into one large collaborative network. That will transform the relationship among companies. But it will also raise plenty of awkward issues—not least, questions of corporate privacy and trust. When your suppliers and customers have easy access to your database, you need to be sure that their security is as good as your own. And most companies will find the collaborative networking process technically harder to set up and maintain than the enthusiasts would have them believe.

## Decision Making

COMPANIES find it more important to understand how decisions are made and to build efficient decision-making processes as things happen more quickly and ever more information—good and bad—becomes available. In addition, companies must frequently deal with new and unknown players as well as with new and unknown technologies.

Internet technologies can help improve the quality of decision making in several ways:

- By increasing the amount of information available to managers, from which they can choose

- By accelerating access to information so that decisions can be based on more up-to-date data

- By allowing managers quickly—and from any place—to reach people who can offer advice and expertise

- By bringing people together to discuss a tricky point
- By searching for previous decisions made in similar circumstances

Internet technologies may also encourage group decision-making processes. People who normally hesitate to voice a view in a meeting, or who are on the road or located in another office, may now add their thoughts from their computers. Shy participants may be able to add their views anonymously through group decision software. Of course, anonymous feedback should be treated cautiously and is open to abuse. But wisely used, it may give a corporate community a greater sense of democracy. On some issues, group software enables voting over the corporate intranet.

In addition, software offers managers increasingly sophisticated tools to help understand reasoning processes, and it can do calculations based on rules, algorithms, and game theory that would be well beyond the capacity of an individual to handle. But both the Internet and the programs have an obvious limitation: They are not responsible for the final outcome. Responsibility for a decision is taken by neither the program nor its creators, who can always argue that the manager failed to appraise all possible moves or indicate all possible outcomes. Leave out some vital bit of information, and software follows the usual principle of garbage in, garbage out. As one author on game theory puts it, "The program can do no more than turn a bundle of hopelessly complex interrelationships into a more concise form that the decision-maker intuitively finds easier to handle."[17]

Ultimately, the most important aspect of decision making is "not about *what* you decide, but *how* you decide."[18] Education should therefore be more about training how to learn and analyze and make decisions, and less about teaching specific skills, which may rapidly change. Decision-making managers have always needed analytical skills, but now, in addition, they need good pattern-recognition abilities. The reason is that much of the additional information that Internet technologies offer them will be conflicting and wrong. Also, more data comes in all the time. A continuous inflow of information can bewilder a poor decision maker. Managers need to be able to spot trends, to pick out what matters from data that is constantly being updated, and to know when new material is grounds for reviewing a decision and when to remain on course.

## Innovation

C ORPORATE COMPETITIVENESS is rooted in finding new products and new ways to do things. "Innovation is now at the core of economic activity," argues the Paris-based OECD in a landmark study of the role of information technology in economic growth.[19] New ideas—such as XML or Groove or zaplets—create a double dose of value, both for the companies that design them and for the companies that use them to do old tasks more efficiently. Technologies readily leap between companies—and across national borders. Many travel in the heads of "knowledge nomads," a phrase coined by Rosabeth Moss Kanter, a Harvard Business School management guru.[20] Without bright people on board, and the ability to manage them sensitively, companies lose this key competitive strength.

Chapter 8 looks more specifically at structures for innovation and at how to manage them. But innovation also raises questions about the way companies develop and share ideas. Not surprisingly, companies spend lots of time encouraging innovation. One fashionable notion is to give entrepreneurial employees the finances and freedom to think like a startup—although the demise of so many dot-coms has made that idea less enticing. So has the realization that the dot-com business model—to grow fast and then cash out—is the wrong one for an established, conventional company to pursue. Even if it were not, when innovation is distanced from the main company something may be lost. An interest in innovation needs to infuse the whole business.

Another approach, practiced by companies such as Microsoft, Cisco Systems, and Intel and emulated in Britain by Reuters, is what Peter Job, the British media company's former chief executive, once dubbed "Buy, Don't Build." The idea is to take advantage of the more innovative, entrepreneurial climate in small companies by buying a stake in a portfolio of little businesses with good proposals and then helping them to develop and launch their products. This approach essentially turns the big company into a venture capitalist, outsourcing both innovation and some of the risk.

In general, it is easier for companies to "buy in" innovation than to "make" it all in-house (an issue that chapter 8 returns to). Sometimes, this involves creating strategic alliances between companies in different fields; sometimes, purchasing business services that incorporate new ideas. The OECD's study found that the demand for business services was growing rapidly and that services such as consultancy, training, research and development, and computing all played an important part in diffusing new ideas.[21] These service companies not only help other companies to understand how to make the best use of new communications, but they are often big users of information technology themselves.

In the excitement of launching something entirely new, however, companies must also remember how much extra value—for both company and customer—can often come from tweaking the existing range. Sometimes, this process of refinement may lead a company to realize an asset is marketable. In Europe, the ability to send short text messages to mobile telephones has been just such an innovation. Immensely profitable, it now accounts for almost a tenth of the revenues of Vodafone, the market leader. The introduction of prepaid cards for cell phones is another such refinement. It has opened a vast new market of people whose credit ratings would not allow them to take out a cell phone contract, while giving companies a stream of revenue without the expensive need to bill for calls.

Creating new business models will be as important an innovation as creating new products. This is partly because so much innovation now involves finding how to use the Internet to deliver existing services in new ways: sell books online, build cars, run an airline. For instance, Britain's easyJet budget airline, with many ideas borrowed from America's Southwest, fills its airplanes faster by doing away with numbered seats, sells onboard drinks and snacks, and gets staff to help clean the plane for quicker turnaround times. The Internet opens up all sorts of opportunities for trying out new business models and cuts the costs of experimenting.

No matter how a company sets about innovating, Internet technologies can help.

- Information and communications technologies themselves have the highest rate of innovation of any industry, when measured by number of patent applications.[22] That swiftly spreads into innovation in other industries, especially services, which are increasingly built around software, computers, communications networks, and databases. All told, about a third of the research and development carried out in the services sector is related to information technology.[23]

- Innovation feeds on shared knowledge. Because the Internet allows many specialists to work simultaneously on a new project, development is increasingly modular rather than sequential. A classic instance is the "set-based" process used at Toyota. Its people no longer design the engine and then pass it off to a second group to produce the casing, which discovers problems with the engine design just as the first team has moved on to its next project. Instead, they develop sets of solutions in parallel and gradually narrow them down as new information emerges from testing, customer trials, and so on. A gradual convergence to a final design avoids the need endlessly to redesign an earlier stage to fit in with whatever refinements subsequently emerge.[24]

- The Internet makes it easier for companies to monitor what their rivals are doing and to watch other companies around the world and in different industries. This monitoring has become an important part of the innovation process. New ideas applied by one industry in one market, such as mass customization and B2B exchanges, are quickly taken up and applied by others in other sectors.

## Ownership and Ideas

AN EFFECT of Internet technologies is to underline the value of information and knowledge. Companies claim that they are keen on the idea of sharing ideas and on cultivating openness, yet many now see intellectual property rights as a key source of income. To secure those rights, they rush to patent any novelty that seems likely to bring value in the future.

Innovation in particular confronts corporate managers with a fundamental tension between the virtues of openness and the difficulty of protecting intellectual property. One of the most interesting developments of the Internet has been the Open Source movement, which sprang up in the mid-1980s and advocates the unrestricted and free release of software, including the underlying "source" code, enabling users to make their own modifications to suit their needs.

The movement, effectively denying the need for intellectual-property rights, has had a powerful influence on innovation. It has given birth to the Linux operating system, to the Perl programming language, to the Apache server, and to Sendmail, an e-mail program. Linux is particularly remarkable. Initially created by one person, Linus Torvalds, it has been developed by thousands. Individual programmers all over the world develop the code and comment on one another's new ideas, in a giant, voluntary peer-review process. A group of "core" developers decides which of the codes is good enough to include in the core code.

The astonishing thing about open source software is that most of those who develop it give their ideas free. Thousands of programmers around the world, who have never met, work together, unpaid. Could this be a model for collaboration and innovation in the future? If so, the model requires a workable kernel (in this case, the initial 10,000 lines of code written by Linus Torvalds) to which people can easily add; a modular design, so that different people need to understand only the part they choose to work on; and a small team at the top to set broad guidelines and select the best ideas.

The most valuable development, says Alan MacCormack of Harvard Business School, who has studied the model closely, is that contributed by users. For what reward? Global recognition: "Because software code is a universal language, if I make a good patch, the world knows."[25] In addition, there is the satisfaction of seeing one's ideas discussed (often at slashdot.org, a Web site boasting "news for nerds") and then adopted.

So the process brings three key benefits: hundreds of eyeballs checking all the development for bugs, an evaluation and approval process, and a reward in terms of getting a code in the core and winning the recognition of your peers.[26]

Many of the people who come up with such collaborative ideas do so outside a corporate framework. Eric von Hippel, professor of Innovation Management at MIT, calls them "lead users" and observes: "They face general needs in a marketplace but face them months or years before the rest of the marketplace encounters them. Since existing companies can't customize solutions good enough for them, lead users go out there, patch things together and develop their own solutions."[27]

This concept of collaborative innovation is one that many companies envy and wish they could emulate. Indeed, in several ways, corporate innovation resembles Linux code writing, with its scattered teams and its modular design spread across a network of specialists. But could companies inspire the sort of altruism that has gone into developing open source software? That is harder, for two reasons. First, employees are well aware that their ideas are what bring home the bacon. Even the open source developers may not indefinitely review code for nothing, especially once an industry begins to make money from their ideas. Second, companies worry about how they can make money from the approach. There is a basic ambiguity in the concept. "Think free speech, not free beer," urges Richard Stallman, founder of the Free Software Foundation.[28] But most free software is also distributed free of charge.

To foster innovation, an effective reward structure includes a pat on the back and a sense of recognition: Everybody likes to feel appreciated by their colleagues. A review by McKinsey & Company of practice at thirty companies—fifteen judged successful at innovating and applying their new ideas, and fifteen not—found that the successful companies used all sorts of devices to coax more brainwaves out of their staff.[29] They used technology constructively, building and regularly updating procurement databases that could be read by product developers, for instance.

Many did more gimmicky things. They ran ideas contests and offered opportunities to work on projects not directly linked to their employees' usual work. One global machinery company assigned product developers to the shop floor to supervise the production of the articles they had designed. A big electronics company even developed a "virtual Hollywood" and got employees to present "scripts," or improvement ideas, to "investors," or general managers. This device apparently resulted in submissions from 200 teams in the first year—although the study does not record how many were turkeys rather than box-office hits.

So money is not everything. But it certainly helps. The McKinsey study found that more than two-thirds of the successful companies linked individual incentives to product development targets; only a quarter of the unsuccessful ones did so. Indeed, one high-tech U.S. company gave employees cash incentives to file patent applications. The aim is "to bring ideas into the open and discourage the hoarding of knowledge"—and, no doubt, make some money if the idea took off.[30]

From a company's standpoint, the value of new ideas has grown, thanks to a vast expansion in patenting, principally in the United States, where every innovation, whether for computer software or even for business methods, now seems to be legally locked up. For some companies, "intellectual capital" has come to mean not the brainpower of their employees but the commercial value embedded in patents for products, business processes, and dreams of processes yet untested. Among the ideas to which America's patent office has given monopoly protection are such simple ones as group buying, the matching of professionals with other people seeking their advice, and one-click shopping.[31] "Software and algorithms used to be unpatentable," complained James Gleick in a *New York Times* article. "Recent court decisions and patent-office rule-making has made software the fastest growing category, and companies are rushing to patent the most basic methods of doing business."[32] No wonder that every self-respecting e-commerce company now has its own favorite patent lawyer.

An example of the spread of patenting is that of Dell Computer, which in the mid-1990s lodged several applications to patent not its PCs but its new way of doing business, by building machines in response to orders. By 2000, it had seventy-seven patents protecting different parts of the complex building and testing process involved in its build-to-order system. Henry Garana, vice president of intellectual property at Dell, confesses that, at the time, many people regarded these patents as a waste of effort. Now, he says, "They make people go away. In this business, that's what matters."[33]

Companies initially saw such patents as Garana did, as a way of defending a good idea—or even a business. Both Texas Instruments and National Semiconductor avoided bankruptcy in the early 1990s by the aggressive use of patents, which brought in a stream of useful licensing revenue.[34] Gradually, companies have realized the commercial value of patents as a form of property and have become more systematic in their patenting policies. IBM, for example, claims to get ten patents every working day and to have generated $30 billion in revenue from licensing the use of its patented technologies.[35] Financial services firms and accountants are starting to patent their techniques (a classic instance is the patented Merrill Lynch Cash Management Account), which in the past never would have occurred to them. Companies even patent ideas requiring technologies that do not yet exist. If a company can plausibly describe how something might be done, then it can patent it.

The authors of a famous study of the strategic use of patents call them the "smart bombs" of the business war and add, "Companies that treat their patent portfolios as a strategic asset and a new core competence will enjoy a big advantage over those that don't."[36] Again, the Internet will help them. Automated systems can help companies to organize and analyze their "Rembrandts in the attic" and to describe their innovations more precisely and speedily.

This proliferation of patenting is surely bad for competition. In the long run, too, the fragmentation of knowledge will harm research. The excessive protection of proprietary knowledge will distort the cultures of openness that companies must foster to make the best use of Internet technologies in other ways.

Moreover, it will ultimately boomerang. Each time a company's successful innovation, patented and exploited, makes money for its shareholders, the people who made that innovation possible will wonder whether they were right to give away so much of their own intellectual capital. The greatest challenge for innovative companies will be more fundamental than developing an innovations strategy or a patents database. It will be getting incentives right.

# The Future of
# Knowledge Management

INTERNET TECHNOLOGIES have the power to transform the collection and accessibility of knowledge and information. Companies must find ways to ensure that knowledge and ideas bubble up from the bottom, as the clearest symptoms that a company has a healthily creative culture. They constantly need to be aware that the most vibrant and useful ways in which people share knowledge online will often be electronic versions of the ways human beings have always contacted each other and picked each other's brains.

The decreasing cost of communicating information does not mean that everything should be put online or should be stored in a random and unstructured way. Knowledge in a database is like food in a freezer: Nothing ever came out in better shape than it went in. If knowledge is to be truly useful, it must be collected and stored with great attention to how it will be used in the future. That may be hard to predict, but it may be worse to store for too many contingencies than for too few.

Knowledge therefore must be filtered at the point of collection. However, that in turn requires making difficult decisions about what to store and what to leave out. The task of setting guidelines for filtering the input of knowledge in this way is not one that wise managers will delegate to junior staff, any more than they would delegate the task of deciding what make of computer to buy. Corporate knowledge is an asset whose value will be determined at least partly by how skillfully it is harvested and structured.

In looking for ways to capture and use good ideas, companies face a trade-off. They must balance the need to provide wide access and freedom to contribute with the need to filter and structure. Many areas of corporate activity will have to confront this consequence of Internet technologies: Real benefits will flow only when the center first provides order and structure and then devolves access throughout the organization.

Companies must also think about how to reward those who produce ideas. The ownership of ideas is at the heart of many commercial ventures. Ideas, however, spring not from companies but from individuals. The more companies seek to profit from ideas, the more they will have to split the takings with those who first produce them. People are not like machines: They can easily discover what their intellectual output is worth and take their creativity elsewhere if they feel insufficiently rewarded.

# Chapter 3
# Customers and Brands

FROM TIME TO TIME, most companies tell themselves that their customers are their lifeblood. Many, however, do not behave as though they believed it. Most thought that Internet technologies would offer new ways to reach the customer—but then seized the opportunity to hide behind a Web site and to automate customer contact. However, Internet technologies have a brighter potential. They dramatically cut the cost not only of delivering some products and services to customers but of other key tasks: identifying and keeping the small minority of customers who account for most of their profits; developing new ways to sell their wares on the basis of service, not merely of price; and persuading the customer to come back, again and again and again. Taking advantage of these opportunities and building durable customer loyalty will make the difference between success and failure.

The cost savings from persuading customers (who in this chapter are mainly individuals, not businesses) to shift transactions to the Internet can be considerable, but they can also be elusive. Most companies already have elaborate physical distribution networks that they are rightly reluctant to discard.

In one sense, Internet technologies make the task of dealing with customers much more difficult—by making the customer's life easier. Customers can search for and compare products and prices more readily than ever before. Many, though, still choose not to do so.

A study of consumer click-through behavior found that most online buyers actually shop around very little: 89 percent of online book buyers purchase from the first site that they visit, 81 percent of music buyers, and 76 percent of electronic goods buyers. Fewer than 10 percent of Internet users, in a separate study of North American consumers, turned out to be aggressive bargain hunters.[1] However, the Internet increases the risks of competing on price alone. To do so is to risk being commoditized—whether the product is books, PCs, or a loan. That spells misery: Most industries have room only for a tiny number of large-scale, low-cost producers. Everyone else needs to find ways of preserving margins, differentiating the product through differentiating the relationship with the customers.

Internet technologies provide new tools for doing just that. Their greatest value is the scope they offer for understanding the customer and for developing customer loyalty, either to a brand or to a company. They can help managers to identify valuable customers and offer them more targeted products. Managers may estimate that 10 or 20 percent of customers account for about 80 or 90 percent of profits— but up to now, they have found it hard to tell which customers mattered and why. The Internet makes it possible to segment customers into different groups as well as to bundle together packages of products, so that companies can offer the most valuable customers the best treatment—without offending the rest.[2]

Better still, Internet technologies help managers to crack a problem that they have long perceived but been unable to tackle effectively: the need for customer retention. It is far less expensive to keep an existing customer than to recruit a new one. Managers know that two of the simplest ways to make money are to turn a one-time customer into a repeat buyer and to sell an additional product to an existing customer.[3] Here, Internet technologies offer advantages similar to those that (as later chapters argue) they provide in employment and in supply chain management: They facilitate better analysis and deeper relationships. Some ways that managers use Internet technologies to recruit and retain online customers will also be helpful in recruiting and retaining employees. It is the power of these technologies to reinforce a relationship—even more than their power to reach out to new markets—that will be their great strength.

This chapter looks first at the changing ways in which companies attract customers, using self-service to cut costs and brands to build loyalty. Then it examines what companies do with their customers once they recruit them: how they learn about them and spot and retain the profitable ones. It discusses the ways in which Internet technologies allow companies to offer customers mass customization and treat each individual as a market. Finally, it looks at the longer-term managerial implications of change: the dangers of channel conflict and the need to improve customer focus.

## The Savings of Self-Service

CARING FOR CUSTOMERS costs time and money. How much better, many companies think, if customers could look after themselves. In grocery stores, after all, customers select and transport their own purchases; in self-service restaurants, they carry their own food and clear the table (more or less) when they finish. Technology companies, which pioneered so many Internet applications, found that customer services was one of the first opportunities for change the Internet offered. For other companies selling a product that can travel over a wire, the Internet has the same potential.

Training customers to place orders online can bring enormous savings. For example, Ryanair, an Irish no-frills airline, sold 92 percent of its tickets online in 2000, cutting its sales, marketing, and distribution costs by a staggering 62 percent in the second half of the year.[4] General Electric calculates that accepting a simple order on the telephone takes about four minutes and costs around $5. If the order comes in online, it costs 20 cents.[5]

When customers have problems, companies can also make big savings by persuading them to find the answers online. John Chambers, president and chief executive of Cisco Systems, claims to have saved nearly $400 million a year and raised output per head by 200 percent by moving customer support online.[6] And, says Ward Hanson of the Stanford Graduate School of Business, huge gains are to be made from applying the usual 80/20 rule: If the staff answers only the truly complicated 20 percent of questions, its work is more interesting and productive.

But what about the customers? Do they mind? Not in cases when support staff is so scarce that the alternative is ten minutes on hold. Online service eliminates those infuriating waits on the telephone, listening to "Your call is very important to us. Please stay on the line." In addition, it guarantees customers access, twenty-four hours a day and seven days a week, to services that were once available only for limited times, such as banking and airline bookings. This may turn out to be a mixed blessing from the company's viewpoint: Round-the-clock, round-the-week online access raises customers' expectations of the speed and immediacy of service online and off.

Some people, of course, prefer to deal with a human being: For that reason, State Street, a Massachusetts bank that uses lots of voice response to answer calls, makes extensive use of call center operatives as well as seeking to improve the provision of help online. John Fiore, the bank's chief information officer, explains: "Some customers simply want to talk to someone."[7] But in other circumstances, people may prefer the apparent anonymity of a Web site. Of course, neither the telephone nor the Internet allows true privacy: With both, companies learn something about the customer. But customers may sometimes prefer to conduct their business themselves: How many amateur investors would not prefer to liquidate their dud buys quietly online rather than having to give a telephone instruction to a broker and imagine his smirk?

That point emphasizes the importance of studying and responding to customer preferences. Most current automated online solutions are still at an early stage. In time, though, they will grow more sophisticated. Already, at one Finnish company, for example, the computer "listens" to the pitch of a caller's voice to determine if it is an older person, in which case it forwards the call to a human being. Companies now must refine ways to deliver help online rather than over the telephone, and they must learn to identify both customers who need to talk to a human being and those who are happier online. At present, the customer who suddenly needs human help with a truly complex issue often has to scour the company's Web site for clues. ("The gray area," says Ward Hanson, "is trying to hide the help desk telephone number from the remaining 80 percent. I usually go to 'investor relations.'")[8] Companies must recognize that there will always be a point when it is easier for customers to talk to someone rather than do it for themselves.

# Brands

FOR MORE THAN a century, the clearest link between a company and its customers has been through the medium of its brands. That connection will remain at the heart of customer relationships in the Internet age, for brands bring trust. They emerged in the first age of distance shopping, when nineteenth-century families left the country and moved into the town. In the country, the customer knew exactly what the butcher put in the meat pies because the butcher lived just across the road. Once the customer moved to the city and bought pies made by distant, unknown hands, a brand became a substitute for personal knowledge and trust. Brands provide the customer with vital evidence of the origin of a product. The foundation of their value is the returning customer: A brand is trustworthy mainly because trust is what secures loyalty.

In addition, consumer brands have come to stand for more than the reliability and quality of a product. They have become the best defense against margin-wrecking competition based on price alone. Most products now meet an adequate standard, and if one product is as good as another, buyers will often settle for the cheaper. They may, however, pay more for a brand—not merely because they trust it but because it seems to represent a way of life or a set of ideas. Increasingly, the importance of the brand is shifting from the product to the image or very essence of the company. Companies now must target people's emotional needs as well as their desires to consume.

Hence Nike's "just-do-it" attempt to convince runners that Nike sells personal achievement and Coca-Cola's relentless effort to associate its fizzy drink with carefree fun. The aim is to convince the consumer that using a brand of soap powder marks him as being a certain kind of person or belonging to a particular social group, just as much as his haircut or his home does. In brands, the anatomy of fashion is to belong—even when a brand purports to stand for bold individualism.

In the future, a product's competitive edge may come not from technology or design but from its story. As one author puts it, "The company with the best story wins; consumers will pay for the story that sparks how we want others to see us. What are the most important raw materials of the twenty-first century? Stories that will translate information for consumers into accessible emotional terms."[9] Some companies deliberately build a story around their service or product, turning a run-of-the-mill purchase into something more rewarding—and thus desirable. An example: When a policyholder with Progressive, an insurance company in Ohio, has an accident, a claims officer goes straight to the scene, gives the unfortunate victim a cell phone, pulls out a laptop, and, in 95 percent of cases, hands over a claim check on the spot. No wonder some customers say, "I wasn't a member until I was hit by one." The service, not the price, sells the product.[10]

What if a company sells a physical product? How then to create what Joe Pine, coauthor (with James Gilmore) of *The Experience Economy,* calls a "wow" experience? An example might be to offer people buying a two-seater Smart car several weeks' rental of a larger car each year. In that way, a manufacturer and dealer together can turn a physical product into a continuing service, retaining a link with buyers long after they have driven away.

Some retailing is increasingly becoming a "wow" experience, as companies compete to make shopping more pleasurable by, for example, putting cafés in bookstores and books in cafés. The Internet is accentuating this trend—after all, no online bookstore can offer the shopper a cappuccino. A growing number of markets may thus split in two, with the cheap and functional on the one hand and the entertaining and pricey on the other.[11]

Overall, the Internet increases the importance of brands. Faced with more choice than ever before, consumers will head for names they recognize. A winner-take-all outcome may result:[12] Global brands, such as Microsoft and Sony, will have a special power to inspire trust in far-flung consumers. Brands will thus to some extent revert to their original role, as a device to win confidence. Will that launch a proliferation of global or regional, rather than national, brands? Probably not. Consumer products are already closely tailored to the tastes of different markets: Coke tastes different in different countries, and

McDonald's offers different types of food in different countries. Rather than homogenize corporate images, communications technology allows companies both to unify and to diversify their service.

When it comes to building a brand, the Internet makes the task easier in some ways, harder in others. Online brands evolved in the 1990s with amazing speed. Coca-Cola took fifty years to become a global brand; Yahoo! did the same in five years. But this may have been a transient phenomenon. Certainly, the Internet has breathed new life into some branding techniques, such as viral marketing. Just as a shopper at Harrods carries an advertisement for the department store around London, emblazoned on the distinctive green carrier bags, so anyone with a Hotmail account sends an advertisement for free e-mail tacked on to the bottom of every missive to every correspondent. Indeed, the Internet seems ideally suited for passing on tips about the coming trend, emulating word of mouth. One of the most striking examples was the success of *The Blair Witch Project*, a (very) low-budget horror movie that grossed $140 million at the box office. But such triumphs are rare and fleeting: The sequel to *Blair Witch* was a flop that took in only about $30 million and cost far more to make. *The Blair Witch Project* was a discovery—but nobody could possibly claim to have discovered *Blair Witch 2*.

For now, brand building remains overwhelmingly easier to achieve through traditional media: Indeed, at the height of the dot-com boom, advertising by dot-coms desperate to make a "landgrab" poured revenue into television networks and newspapers. Without the dot-com premium to pay for billboards, companies seeking to create an online name from scratch will struggle to pay the entry fee. That is no accident. Only reliable, enduring firms can generally afford to advertise widely in traditional media. Customers therefore trust their staying power—even if they are skeptical about the message.

While the Internet makes brand building a bit easier, it does wonders for brand smashing. Critics can all too readily use chat rooms or a Web site to smear a product or a company—and the company may find it hard to fight back convincingly. One such site is www.sucks500.com (formerly www.americasucks.com), which features a long list of corporations and angry comments about them. Another example is that of a disgruntled Nike customer who wanted to have the word *sweatshop* stitched on the back of his customized trainers. Nike refused, citing various elaborate reasons. The customer's tortuous e-mail exchange circulated widely on the Internet. The Web, argues L. Jean Camp, an associate professor at Harvard University's Kennedy School of Government, "will increasingly become the mechanism of angry customers and employees in the future."[13]

A bigger problem for brands will be the way the Internet aggravates the fragmentation of markets. Most brands represent a big, simple idea. But the impact of Internet technologies is to segment customers and tailor products for individuals. Besides, if customers are growing more individualistic, they may not want to project a Nike image, just like everyone else. Instead, they may want to be part of a small, elite group—or of no group at all. It may be impossible to attract customers to the idea that they are part of a "mass elite" or are "the same but different." So in hunting for ways to make each customer feel like an individual, companies may unwittingly undermine the value of brands.

## Learning about the Customer

NO INVENTION has ever been more effective at accumulating customer data than the Internet: As shoppers meander around electronic networks in general and the Internet in particular, they drip data wherever they go. Companies have never before known so much about their customers. But knowing what to do with all that knowledge can be a burden. Most of the information that companies hold is strewn among many different databases, each attached to a particular product line or sales channel.

As later chapters describe, Internet technologies offer elegant ways to collect all sorts of data about the preferences and purchasing record of corporate customers. In dealings with individual customers, though, these marvelous tools must be used with care. Their potential is great. "The Web allows companies to draw a graph of a customer's lifetime value," says Ward Hanson. "You can learn how customers end up in your fold, which are the best and the worst ones, and why some abandon their electronic shopping trolley before they make the final transaction."[14]

However, to know so much about individual customers involves trespassing on their privacy. In a bricks-and-mortar store, that happens less. Shopping is a relatively anonymous activity. You may browse the shelves under the watchful eye of a security camera, but your hesitations and ultimate purchases are recorded in a far less structured way than they are on the Internet, where tracking what was bought and where is much easier. Pay cash in a store, and nobody has any record of who you are and what you purchased.

In the future, companies will increasingly have a record not merely of who bought what but of exactly where a customer was at the crucial moment. As wireless applications evolve, companies will learn to use them to target users geographically. That will allow users to give companies feedback at the precise moment when they are making use of a product or service. But it also has difficult implications for privacy: Do you want your whereabouts constantly monitored?

Companies will benefit from the accumulation of data on customers only if they—and all their competitors and suppliers—earn the customers' trust. When online customers see their personal data traded like any other commodity, they worry intensely about privacy. Rightly, for some companies have betrayed their trust. ToySmart collected a great deal of information about children, promising not to pass it on to third parties. Yet when the company closed its operations, the list went up for sale.

Establishing trust is harder online than through personal contact (although that may change as younger people grow accustomed to buying online). For the moment, people resent intrusive questioning while they are trying to reach the service they want. They will be more likely to hand over personal data if they are confident that it will be used to provide them with better deals than the run-of-the-mill customer can enjoy.

To offer such deals, companies must often skillfully integrate the data they collect on a single customer from several transactions. That way, they hope to present their customer with one, coherent face. The customer who telephones his bank of ten years to ask for a credit card *and* is rejected because the credit card department did not know what was on the personal savings department's database will be justifiably enraged. Instead, databases should be sufficiently interconnected to reveal that the customer's regular savings habits earn him the approval for a credit card *and* a special deal on life insurance. Bingo! A happy customer and the extra sale that makes the difference between modest profit and celebration. In fact, such simple coherence may be easy for young companies. For most older companies, making multiple databases compatible with one another involves huge payments to consultants and endless frustration.

In addition, information is more likely to be truly useful if it is filtered at the point of collection and carefully structured. Often, the part of the company that collects information when the customer buys is not the part that uses the information for selling. As always, the care taken when data is initially collected and stored will determine its eventual value. Enormous quantities of information about individual customers may be rendered useless if the marketing department cannot extract from them ways to spot which customers are profitable and why.

Information will also be more useful if the departments that collect it do not insist on "owning" the customer. If each individual department squirrels away information on transactions by product rather than by customer, a company will never succeed in presenting the customer with a single point of access. As long as the credit card department and the personal savings department think of themselves as separate empires, the company will find its fancy systems integration is worthless. To be truly beneficial, new technology requires skillful management and an appropriate corporate culture.

## Spotting the Profitable Customer

WHEN COMPANIES accumulate customer information efficiently, they learn more about which customers generate the most profit. Then they must segment customers, cosseting the most valuable ones and shaking off the unprofitable. A wide range of studies has pointed out, over the years, that a small minority of customers frequently produces almost all the profits companies make. A PricewaterhouseCoopers survey for the British retail industry, for example, found that 4 percent of customers accounted for 20 percent of sales and 29 percent of profits, and another 26 percent of customers accounted for 50 percent of sales and 55 percent of profits. In other words, more than two-thirds of customers accounted for a scanty 16 percent of profits.[15]

For some companies, the pattern is different: The profitable vast majority of customers spends tiny sums. BOC, Britain's biggest industrial gases company, for example, takes in most of its money from the huge number of customers making small yearly purchases that do not qualify for discounts. Because these accounts are small and all very different, competitors would find it more expensive to chase after them than to target larger accounts.[16]

Spotting customers who are definitely unprofitable is also important, especially for companies faced with the high acquisition costs that characterized the frenzied dot-com days, when many start-ups sold products at a loss just to attract enough customers to underpin their share price. For instance, Scandinavian teenagers, those great wireless chatterers, quickly learned that switching cell phone service providers was a great way to amass free minutes at the companies' expense. There may be little point in spending good money to acquire such footloose customers.

As information grows more detailed, companies increasingly segment their customers, trying to concentrate on those from whom they gain the most. Charging all customers the same means, in effect, getting the profitable to subsidize the unprofitable—and thus making them easy prey for competitors. The greater the spread of profitability, the greater the danger. Pinpointing that top 20 percent is one of the best ways for a nippy new entrant, unencumbered with "legacy" customers, to overcome the disadvantage of size.

Segmentation calls for delicacy. It may make sound commercial sense to charge valuable customers less than unprofitable ones, and it is easier to do on the Internet than in a bricks-and-mortar store. Some kinds of price discrimination do not appear to erode customers' trust. In banking, for example, the top 20 percent of customers can account for more than 100 percent of profits; the bottom 20 percent actually lose money. So banks often pay better interest rates and charge no fees on accounts with higher balances. Most people seem to accept such price discrimination. In other situations, discrimination leads to a fuss. Lots of bad publicity hit Amazon.com in 2000 when it quoted different prices to would-be buyers of the same book. If companies are going to price-discriminate, they then need to do it unobtrusively or in a way that customers accept.

This realization leads companies to pursue two main segmentation strategies, both of which combine price discrimination with linking purchases to offers of other products or services. One strategy is to create customer clubs, discussed in the following section. Customers accept that the holder of a platinum card gets a better deal than the holder of a bronze one, even though they dislike the idea that Joe Bloggs pays less for his airline flight than Mary Doe. The other strategy is to bundle products together—setting up a bank account that includes free travel insurance, say, or selling a cell phone contract that gives free text messaging. Such devices make it harder for customers to compare prices while allowing them to feel they are getting something extra on the cheap.

The line between the extremely profitable and the extremely unprofitable customer may be a narrow one: A credit card company loves the customer who accumulates vast outstanding borrowings but hates the one who defaults. However, when customers are clearly unprofitable and likely to remain so, companies must learn to fire them. The notion of firing customers—by, for instance, deliberately raising the charges they pay—makes many companies squirm. In these customer-conscious days, it seems heresy to suggest that some people might cost a company more than it will ever make from them. But banks gingerly have begun to grasp this particular thistle: Back in 1995, the First Chicago Bank imposed a surcharge on customers who chose to use a bank counter for certain transactions that they could do—far more cheaply—through an automatic teller. When the inevitable fuss subsided, the bank found that the use of ATMs had risen sharply and operating costs per customer had declined.

Price discrimination in markets, as thoughtful commentators such as L. Jean Camp have pointed out, is not inherently bad.[17] Bricks-and-mortar stores discourage unwanted customers, as anyone who has ever walked into a designer clothing store in cheap jeans knows. However, differential pricing on the Internet cannot easily be based on gender or race. In used car lots, women often pay more than men for cars. Online, in the words of the famous New Yorker cartoon, nobody knows you're a dog . . . or a woman.

## Recruitment and Retention

M OST COMPANIES offer higher levels of service to profitable customers, for they know that recruiting customers costs far more
than retaining them. Indeed, many businesses need a certain level of
retention to make any money at all. Subscribe to a magazine, and you
will be a loss-making reader in your first year, profitable if you renew
for one year, and extremely profitable if you renew for a second. The
same arithmetic applies to many businesses, from cell phone service
agreements to home loans.

This basic business truth dawned on companies more than a
decade ago, but it gained force as dot-coms poured their investors'
money into buying online customers. Because they lacked both established brands and physical stores, the dot-coms spent far more than
other retailers on customer acquisition. Amazon.com, the online
bookstore, was fairly frugal compared with most of its breed, reput-
edly spending 29 cents per dollar of sales on customer acquisition ver-
sus retailers' 4 cents average.[18] Other dot-coms spent more—indeed,
sometimes much more—than a dollar per dollar of sales. Foolishly: A
study by the consultancy Bain & Company estimated that it would
take more than a year and a half for online grocery stores to make sufficient profits on a customer to exceed the acquisition cost, and more
than four years in the case of online buyers of consumer electronics.[19]
As it happened, many purely online retailers never lived long enough
to test such calculations.

The growing emphasis on the benefits of building a continuing
relationship with individual customers is one sign of the high cost of
acquiring them. In the past, such relationship building has been easier
for companies selling services than for manufacturers. But the Internet provides new opportunities. Its interactivity allows companies to
establish what they fondly call a "conversation" with the customer.
And online activity generates all that useful information, which can be
used to give customers the impression that a company has remem-
bered their particular tastes and whims. Theoretically, the customer,
having once divulged all sorts of personal details to a company, will be
less likely to move to another provider and have to start the whole
process again.

In an article with the encouraging title "Do You Want to Keep Your Customers Forever?" one team of management gurus spells out how such relationships ideally work. "Customers," they point out, "do not want more choices. They want exactly what they want—when, where, and how they want it." The authors go on to depict the greeting-card company of the future: "It would be able to remember the important occasions in your life and remind you to buy a card. It . . . would display past selections, either to ensure you don't commit the faux pas of sending the same card to the same person twice or to give you the option of sending the same funny card to another person."[20] Some customers, of course, would find such ersatz coziness infuriating. Others might dislike the intrusion into their privacy and worry about other ways in which the information might be used. In time, no doubt, better data analysis will filter out such curmudgeons.

Meanwhile, an alternative approach to retention is to convert the cadre of top customers into a club. This is a familiar concept: Airlines have had loyalty clubs for a generation. But other companies have been slower to see the club as a way to convince their top shoppers that they are not just purchasers of services but members of an elite. Internet technologies slash the costs of reaching members with special offers and even of fulfilling those orders. They also greatly extend the range of options. The concept of the club can be widened to include people who join without application, such as loyal shoppers in grocery stores, or it can be narrowed to become highly exclusive. As so often with the Internet, both widening and deepening are possible.

The sort of club that enlists supermarket spenders or frequent fliers may be a long way from the traditional concept of the club as a group of like-minded people with a common interest. All that those frequent fliers have in common is jobs that require them to spend many hours sitting beside each other in the sky. But members of such ersatz clubs seem much more willing to part with useful information than regular customers—and that makes it easier to cross-sell.

Involving the customer in refining the product is another way to create a relationship. Computer companies have done this for some time. More than 650,000 customers tested a beta version of Microsoft's Windows 2000—some even paying a fee to do so.[21] Other companies are trying to emulate this concept of "co-opting customer competence," as it has been dubbed. Procter & Gamble invites visitors to its

Web site to say what they dislike about existing products—and to ask for new products that do not yet exist. Eli Lilly, the maker of Prozac, e-mails those users who have asked for a reminder to tell them to take their pills (although in July 2001 it temporarily suspended the service after an embarrassing glitch allowed recipients to see each other's addresses). This is not altruism but shrewd business practice: Of all the prescriptions written for Prozac, only 79 percent are filled, and seven months after receiving an initial prescription (the average prescribed length of treatment), only 21 percent of patients are still taking their medicine. That represents a huge loss of potential revenue.[22]

Some of the techniques that companies apply to recruit and retain online customers will also help them to recruit and retain employees. The principle here is similar: Teaching new workers the ropes is expensive, and only after several years does an employee understand a company well enough to make a truly valuable contribution. In addition, as Fred Reichheld argues, companies that are good at building customer loyalty often do so on the base of loyal staff.[23] Loyalty, in other words, is a hallmark of a successful corporate culture rather than merely a marketing tool.

## Mass Customization and Content for One

As COMPANIES LEARN to fit the Internet into their relationship with their customers, they quickly notice that easy interactivity and information collection allow them to give the appearance of a personal touch. They will try to treat each customer as an individual and to hone the precise product each wants. That will bring a shift from the mass market to the personalized—or rather, to "mass customization," a familiar idea that can now, thanks to Internet technologies, be extended and developed.[24] Companies hope to use it to combine the low costs of mass production with the premium pricing and desirability of a distinctive, tailor-made purchase, thereby jacking up margins and turning a one-off purchase into a continuing relationship.

Services that can be delivered electronically are easiest to personalize in this way. Banking, stockbroking, communications, online information—all pop up on your PC with your name attached. Anything that can be digitized can easily be customized. However, many companies now customize physical products as well. The aim is to move beyond the mass market, which brought low prices at the cost of a lack of variety, to offer the unique appeal of a tailor-made producer at off-the-rack prices.

So, for instance, IDtown.com, a company based in Hong Kong, offers an almost infinite variety of watch designs. Customers click their way through a series of choices to create a product made of standard parts but unlike any other, for which they pay little more than they would for a mass-market watch. Reflect.com, created by Procter & Gamble to sell beauty-care products online, is combining Internet technologies with what is, in effect, catalog shopping for customized products. The company transforms information from customers into cosmetics, shampoos, and other products that match the customers' coloring and complexion. Reflect.com has developed an ingenious way to deal with a problem that plagues online retailers: the abandoned shopping cart. Between 75 percent and 90 percent of online shoppers abandon their carts before they have to pay for them. Reflect.com sends messages to these shoppers, offering them a free customized lipstick if they complete their purchases or buy at least one extra product. A gratifyingly large number return to do so.[25]

Levi Strauss, whose famous blue jeans now compete with cheaper copies, can body scan customers in its flagship Union Square store in San Francisco. Half-an-hour later, a Levi Strauss factory has downloaded their vital statistics off the Internet and cut the jeans of their choice. This process has two advantages. One benefit is that returns, which usually run at up to 40 percent of mail-order sales, decline to single digits. The other is that store employees learn about coming fashion trends from their customers who buy this way, presumably because the process appeals to the most fashion-conscious. The salespeople noticed, for example, that customers who designed their own jeans wanted them slung low on the hips months before the average customer stopped buying "high-rise" jeans.

This example shows how a manufacturer and a retailer can collaborate to give customers more personalized products. In another instance, two makers of high-margin sports bicycles, VooDoo Cycles and Cannondale, work with retailers to add an extra dimension of tailoring to their products. They increasingly take customers' orders directly and only then start to build the bicycles. But a costly bike requires much last-minute tweaking to make it roadworthy. That job is done by retailers, which reduces the danger of expensive returns by dissatisfied customers. Besides, the customer who drops in to a shop to pick up a new bike may also want a new helmet or some Lycra shorts. The retailer can thus benefit from and reinforce a continuing relationship between the customer and the manufacturer.

## Delivery and Channel Conflict

HOW TO REACH the customer—and especially that elusive creature, the individual profitable customer? When, in the second half of the 1990s, new online companies sprang up selling everything from toys to tickets, older companies worried about the future of their bricks-and-mortar distribution channels, which appeared to cost so much more to run. In some cases—stockbrokerages, travel agencies, and music companies, say—such worries were understandable: Their products or services could be delivered electronically, and customers were happy to buy that way. But the dot-coms often quickly realized that fulfilling online sales could be done only by physical distribution—which was both complex and costly to arrange.

For established businesses selling products that can be easily distributed online, the coming of the Internet has been an earthquake. Banks, travel agencies, and stockbrokerages all have had to redefine the role of their physical distribution chains. Music and video stores may eventually follow. The cost savings that online distribution allows may well wipe out the slender margins that some businesses—such as travel agencies—typically trade on.

The pressure has been the greater because high-income customers are typically the first to go online. But once things start to settle down, physical branches will clearly have some advantages. For example, Charles Schwab, the pioneer online broker, finds that 70 percent of new account openings occur in its branches.[26] Wells Fargo, a bank in San Francisco that has offered online services longer than almost any other company, finds that attrition is lower and balances are higher among customers who bank online. But, notes Avid Motjitbai of the bank's Internet services group, the company still sees a significant role for branches, where closing a sale is easier than in the more anonymous territory of cyberspace.[27] Perhaps customers are better persuaded to sign on the line when the sales staff can see the whites of their eyes.

Getting a physical product to a customer runs up against at least five problems that make it difficult and expensive—whether the customer orders online or not.

1. Order processing and warehousing need to be done on a large scale to be profitable.

2. So does delivery. A study by McKinsey & Company estimated that a company must penetrate between 10 and 15 percent of a neighborhood before it can afford delivery capacity of its own.[28] But without its own capacity, its product is just one more package on the truck.

3. Shipping is time-consuming. That impulse buy may take just a few clicks, but it then may require a day to pack and a couple more days to ship.

4. There shippers hit what they call the problem of the "dark house." Each missed delivery adds an extra day to fulfillment, so spanning the last mile to the home may take as long as all the rest of the process.

5. Finally, there is the problem of returns, an issue that conventional retailers such as Nordstrom and L.L. Bean handle gracefully and efficiently, but that can easily cost both customer and company much time, money, and frustration. "Consumers will remember the lost Saturday morning spent at the post office far longer than the 20 minutes spent making an online purchase," comments one study.[29]

A physical store offers answers to these problems. The customer carries the cost of selecting the product and bringing it home, and returns are lower because it is easier to get selection right first time. So while the first wave of online commerce focused on using technology to acquire customers, the next may well focus on using technology to improve delivery.

Meanwhile, the traditional relationship between manufacturers, wholesalers, and retailers is changing. The challenge for managers will be to create a form of distribution that realizes the potential of the Internet. They must define the role of each delivery channel relative to the customer segments that prefer it. Physical delivery channels must complement electronic ones.

For example, Office Depot uses its physical stores to promote its Web site and its Web site to tell customers what products are in stock where. Customers can choose to buy online for delivery or to visit a nearby store and pick up the product themselves. The company has similarly integrated its catalog and online operations: A catalog buyer telephones an agent who uses a Web interface to call up that customer's details and to check stock. When the staff of corporate contract customers log on to buy online—and companies get a discount for ordering electronically rather than over the telephone—they see exactly how much they are authorized to spend and what they can buy.[30] This mix of integration, segmentation, identification, and authentication will grow more common in the future.

One result is that companies are moving away from one-size-fits-all physical branches; another, that companies are deciding when they should own their distribution chain (as banks have traditionally owned their branch networks) and when they can piggyback on somebody else's. Indeed, a rejuvenation of physical branches may occur as companies find new ways to use them. There may, for example, be a move back to smaller stores, linked together in a local network. A pioneer in this strategy has been Dollar General, which competes with Wal-Mart's prices but through thousands of conveniently located 6,000 square-foot stores rather than Wal-Mart's typical 92,000 square-foot monsters.

Such stores benefit from the realization that people do not particularly want to be offered ninety different brands of almost identical dog biscuits. Instead, they want a big choice of individual products— dog biscuits, cat food, fish flakes, and so forth—and they are more likely to live or work near a branch of a smaller store than a huge one. And electronic networks make it easier to organize distribution routes inexpensively as well as to manage peaks and troughs in staffing and inventory among stores in a single town.[31]

Sometimes, the retailer will become part of the manufacturing process. This, of course, already happens in some industries that people think of as services, such as the fast-food business, as a visit to McDonald's shows. Every branch is filled with workers flipping identical rounds of raw meat on a hot grill and packing french fries into cardboard cartons. Are these people working in a service industry or in the distributed manufacture of cooked-meat products? As one observer puts it, "The hectic repetition of different tasks, the loading and unloading of the cooking machines, recall nothing so much as a car assembly line. If Charlie Chaplin were alive today, then he would film 'Modern Times' in a fast-food joint."[32]

As the old line between manufacturing and service blurs, more and more products will be created on the customer's doorstep, as it were, tailored to his personal tastes. Companies will aim for McDonald's ubiquitous consistency and quality of service, and they will add the variety and distinction of an upscale restaurant.

The balance of power between manufacturer and retailer is shifting in ways that vary from one business to another. In some situations—such as the issuing of airline tickets—it will be easier for producers to sell directly to customers, bypassing traditional distributors. In many others, retailers will still be extremely important, although their role will change. They will become the customer's assistant and guide, more actively managing the customer relationship. They will offer the serendipity that only a physical experience of shopping can so far provide. They will be crucial to customer recruitment and retention. And increasingly, they will become part of the production process itself, as they measure shoppers for customized clothes or perhaps download and bind electronic books or package customized CDs. Bricks, not just clicks, will have a future.

## Organizing for Customer Focus

As companies grow more sophisticated at managing customer relationships, they move from mass marketing to targeting. Neither requires much organizational change. But then some companies realize that different groups of customers behave differently and have different needs, so they start to reorganize their sales activities around customer segments. At that stage, the manager in charge of each customer group must reach its members through any or all of the company's delivery channels: the telephone, the Internet, a shop, direct mail, its suppliers, other customers, and other products and services. Tailoring products, services, pricing, and communications for the appropriate group will be essential.

Increasingly, companies will want to measure more precisely the long-term profitability of customer segments—just as they increasingly try to measure the long-term profit contribution of individual employees. Companies frequently track such sales metrics as levels of and increases in purchases. But some now want to go much further and measure even the rate of return that the individual customer brings a company on its investment. For this, a business must balance the costs that may arise if an apparently valuable customer pays bills late or plagues the help desk with calls or needs special service. These costs and benefits will be harder to capture if they are scattered throughout an organization still designed around functions or distribution channels. On the other hand, the deployment of Internet technologies should make them easier to track.

In 1998, the Economist Intelligence Unit surveyed almost 200 large companies around the world and found that only 18 percent were organized around customer segments.[33] But almost half expected to move that way in the following five years. That movement may be going more slowly than companies then expected, but structures based around product lines, services, or geography are on the way out. Taking advantage of information technology will call for organizational change.

Reorganization, however, may be immensely difficult. For, as with so many of the changes that Internet technologies call forth, it involves an element of centralization, giving a single manager a clear view of the products on offer to the customer and of the way they are distributed. "The relationship manager—the sales organisation—is essentially a quarterback," says John Ruane, senior director of sales at American Express Bank. "It calls the play and positions all the players. A central leader is needed; otherwise the left hand will not know what the right hand is doing."[34]

Such a role runs slap into a new version of an ancient problem: how to motivate one salesperson in a company to hand over a customer to another. Without incentives to share customers and adequate talent to grasp the opportunities that arise, the most elegantly reconciled data and segmentation plan will make no difference. Breaking down the tyranny of the distribution channel requires immense willpower and perseverance on the part of senior management at the highest level. "In large companies," observes George Colony, chief executive of Forrester Research, "tremendous political power has built up around these channels. It takes the CEO to force the breakdown of the walls."[35]

In shaping companies' relationships with their customers, Internet technologies offer not merely a way to cut costs and to collect customer data. They will, in time, boost the importance of brands and of the "story" attached to a product or service, redefine the relationship between manufacturers and retailers, encourage companies to segment markets more finely and to discriminate more vigorously among different customers, and shift markets from mass production toward personalization. In the emphasis that companies will increasingly give to retaining existing customers rather than recruiting new ones, there will be striking parallels with the job market, to which we now turn.

# Chapter 4
# Recruiting, Retaining, and Training

N OTHING MATTERS more to a company than to find the best people for a job and then to keep their skills right up to date. For every business, acquiring and grooming talent is the single most important challenge. The job market for some skills has collapsed since 1999–2000, when people talked incessantly of the "war for talent" and companies went to dire lengths to poach one another's best personnel. But the hunt for good people may actually intensify, particularly for young workers: Demographic trends indicate that there will simply be fewer of them. The impacts of higher education and training on increasing the supply of young people with appropriate skills will appear only after several years' delay. Every company, therefore, will need a well-honed recruitment and retention strategy.

As with customers, as described in the previous chapter, so with employees: There are the best, and then there are the rest. The difference is that, in the case of employees, the best generally know their value. Many companies will find they get along with plenty of staff in the "adequate-to-okay" category as long as they have a few first-raters who can provide the product ideas, the strategy, the inspiration, and the drive. One really capable person is worth a half-dozen mediocrities. But the "adequate-to-okay" lot will need excellent training to keep their skills at the top end of their potential. And the first-raters will know to the nearest cent what they could command elsewhere. The best workers will set their own terms. They, not companies, will call the shots in the job market, even in bad times. Indeed, the power may shift more to the best staff when things are tough because that is when the best will be in the greatest demand.

So managing people will remain a demanding, time-consuming business. Already, good managers spend hours finding the right people—about a third of their time, say some. Important today, talent will become even more critical in the future. Internet technologies have changed the job market fundamentally, in ways that put a premium on finding and keeping highly skilled staff.

When Rosabeth Moss Kanter asked 785 companies around the world about barriers to making successful use of the Internet, the number one barrier was "the unit does not have staff with adequate technical or web-specific skills."[1] That was in boom times, but those skills matter, although they will matter less in the future as the number of people with Web skills rises and new software allows people without specific programming skills to design Web sites. Other skills, often harder to measure or define, will become ever more essential. At the top of the list will always be an ability to exercise judgment: That, says Bruce Tulgan, an authority on staffing, "is the 'killer app' of the human brain, and it is the new standard for human talent in the workplace."[2]

Thanks to its amazing ability to search, the Internet will help with the task of locating talent. But acquiring and training good people will continue to be difficult and expensive. So companies will need a clear strategy for identifying the people they most want to keep and for tackling the controllable causes of high staff turnover. Just as the Internet helps companies to keep tabs on customers that are most likely to leave and to measure how much it matters if they do, so it will make corporate retention strategies more sophisticated.

Companies will find that, while money plays a part in the decision to leave or stay, other factors seem to matter more. These include opportunities for career development, responsibility, and professional satisfaction. Good people like to work for companies with reputations for honor and competence. They also like companies that give their employees control over their working lives, opportunities to make decisions, and rewards for performance. Not surprisingly, these are the very qualities that Erik Brynjolfsson's work, described in chapter 1, find determine a company's ability to make the most of new communications technology. Only a company that can match its investment in technology with the necessary organizational change will make the most of its initial investment.

The main evidence for the increasing value of top talent lies in the widening of wage differentials between skilled and unskilled workers, which has been happening in many countries. In the United States between 1979 and 1999, according to the Department of Labor, average weekly earnings of college graduates grew by more than 60 percent compared with those of high school dropouts. Even more striking, earnings of the brightest have risen relative to those of the fairly bright: Earnings of college graduates have risen by more than 30 percent compared with those of high school graduates, bringing the gap to its widest in at least sixty years. As for those right at the top, their rewards have soared. In 1980, an average chief executive earned 42 times as much as a typical factory worker. By 2000, that had soared to 475 times.[3]

What has been going on? One persuasive view is that different technologies seem to favor different skills. In the nineteenth century, the relative demand for unskilled workers increased as factories sprang up and highly skilled craftsmen, such as weavers and blacksmiths, were replaced by machines and unskilled labor. By contrast, computers, and now Internet technologies, seem to favor the best-educated workers. One explanation may be that skilled workers are typically the ones with the most ability constantly to learn new tasks. Some companies build this notion into their production pattern: General Electric's continuous improvement program requires that factory workers learn at least one task "before and after" their task in the process, in order to ensure that people can fill in for each other and thus to increase staffing flexibility.

Moreover, while the proportion of people entering higher education in most rich countries has risen steadily, some of the skills companies need most are scarce. Time will partly resolve this problem: Today's most necessary skills were almost unknown a decade ago. In addition, the Internet boom came after a period when students had turned away from technical subjects. In Germany, for instance, the number of students majoring in them dropped 50 percent in the decade from 1990 to 2000.[4] In the United States, the number of degrees awarded in engineering, mathematics, and computer sciences fell between the mid-1980s and the mid-1990s.[5]

Other factors, such as globalization, may also play a role in widening the pay premium: The workers who have most felt competition from cheap imports have been the relatively unskilled. With technical tasks too, the least-skilled work (such as document processing) is likely to shift to low-wage countries, as are the more routine aspects of computer programming, while the tasks that call for the greatest creativity and judgment will remain mainly in the rich-world companies.

At the top end of the job market, where companies fight hardest for talent, the rewards may go to the best through a winner-take-all effect. Back in 1981, Sherwin Rosen, an economist at the University of Chicago, drew attention to the way a few top film and sports stars are paid massive sums, when others who seem only a whisker less brilliant earn many whiskers less.[6] Electronic technologies with increasingly global reach vastly magnify the effect in the world of entertainment, giving talented individuals the power to reach a world, rather than a national or local, market.

And the effect has spread beyond Hollywood. In all sorts of professions, the best earn vastly more than the second-best—much more than the gap in skills would appear to justify. When it comes to attracting customers, the top bond dealer is far more valuable than a nearly-as-good rival; and what company would hire the second-best chief executive in the industry if the head-hunter could deliver the best? Sometimes, the effect touches a whole team. In investment banking and advertising, a single charismatic figure may win business but also will have loyal support staff, who will follow (for higher salaries all around) when the star moves to another company. Even in less star-struck businesses, a company that hires a top chief executive or vice president will usually find that he or she brings along a ready-made top team that supplants most of the company's existing cadre.

However, as Robert Reich, secretary of labor under Bill Clinton, points out, the winner-take-all effect may be less powerful in businesses where the emphasis is on team, rather than individual, work.[7] Those businesses must motivate a range of people involved in the production process. Splitting pay between the best and the rest will be one of corporate management's toughest tasks.

## Recruiting Insiders

THE BEST have become more valuable, and Internet technologies magnify the rewards to top talent. No wonder companies seek new approaches to recruiting, retaining, and training.

Before recruiting talent from outside the business, however, shrewd managers identify the talent they already have within. Recruiting outside, especially at senior levels, is often risky and disruptive: Companies rarely think through the impact on middle-ranking staff of acquiring a new manager who may import an existing entourage. Recruiting insiders has several advantages. It costs less. It creates career paths and raises expectations among existing staff. And it is, of course, a safer option: A company already knows the person it is promoting and so faces less risk than with a new hire. As with customers, retention generally makes better economic sense than acquisition. As Fred Reichheld points out, employees may cost a company money in their first year and earn significant profits only after a couple of years in the job.[8] Good staff who stay with a business acquire a deep understanding of its culture, its customers, and its limitations.

Internal recruiting also becomes increasingly important the more companies use mutating teams of employees to run particular projects. Each time a project is set up, a miniature recruiting exercise has to take place. Happily, Internet technologies can help to make the process speedier and more efficient by building on the social networks that people typically use to locate talent.

To find talent—and, indeed, to weed out the duds—the best tool is bound to be personal contacts. On a corporate shuttle bus, Eric Schmidt, chairman and chief strategist of Novell, asked two engineers for a list of the company's best engineers.[9] He then went to meet all the people on the list and asked them the same question. After a while he found the number of new names trailed off. That simple exercise identified some of the best people in his organization. Internet technologies extend such networking, by connecting the more distant work force. As a result, the internal labor market widens. It becomes easier for someone in the Bangkok office to be aware of the opportunities in the London office. They are all on the intranet, accessible to everyone across the world.

In addition, a company can store the details of an employee's work experience in a database. That also builds a more efficient internal market for talent. Using a password, a manager can call up and examine a potential recruit's work experience, past assignments, and willingness to relocate. The manager can also look at a candidate's latest job review. Armed with such information, managers can search the database for a particular set of skills—language, specialist computer knowledge, or whatever—a task that once would have required help from the human resources department. So, much of the work of recruiting can shift from the HR department to the line manager, who may well know more precisely what abilities to look for. At the same time, a company's internal job market will widen, sometimes to an astonishing degree.

There are, of course, some snags in using internal databases for recruiting. Employees may not much like the idea that managers in other departments can sneak a look at their latest job review without their consent. That concern for privacy may change in time, especially in companies where employees trust their managers, in which case the companies that gain most will be the ones that are most open about sharing information. For the moment, if a company posts employees' photographs, it may find itself dealing with a discrimination case if a nonwhite face is screened out of a suitable job online (the technology will reveal whose records were considered).

Most important, though, a database may not answer a recruiter's biggest question: Just how good is this person? At SAP, for instance, Thomas Neumann, director of human resources, admits that his vast database of 22,000 people in fifty countries works "better for skills than for competencies."[10] But the managers who use it still claim it saves them time. It may be a coarse sieve, but it will become finer, and for the harassed manager it is a better starting point than to ask in a fairly random way who is good.

The HR staff may still play an important role here, as "human capital knowledge managers." A database of employees is useless if nobody assesses the quality of candidates on relatively objective criteria. As with knowledge management in general, the quality of a database depends on filtering the information added to it and setting clear standards that its content must meet. The task of the HR department, then, becomes to ensure that the data is collected and structured in a way that gives it true value.

## Recruiting Outsiders

H ERE IS what it sometimes feels like:

*You have a job opening in marketing and you need to fill it pronto. The person suddenly gave two weeks notice and was out the door before your over-worked HR people had time to speak with the department VP about recruiting. So now you put ads in a few newspapers and on a few web sites and send out that e-mail you always send out to all staff asking if they know anyone (they never do).*

*You get 674 resumes and have two people and about two days to go through them, so you do the usual qualifications check: You arbitrarily decide you'll eliminate anyone with less than three years of experience in a marketing department in your industry. . . . You then eliminate anyone without a marketing degree, then randomly discard a few whose resume fonts . . . are ugly. . . . You're down to 8, and you call them in for interviews.*

*. . . Of the eight, you love one, like another an awful lot, and think three more would be OK.*

*You offer the job to the one you love, and she turns you down. You offer it to your second choice, and he says . . . he's waiting on one other offer (which he had told you about before). . . . You decide he's arrogant and you can't wait. . . . You finally offer the job to Contestant Number Four.*

*He accepts, and you close your eyes and wait for the disaster, which about 30 percent of your new hires turn out to be.*[11]

That despairing sketch comes from the peak of the 2000 job market. But recruiting is always a laborious process. The company of the future will hunt for ways to make it easier.

Good recruiting brings many competitive advantages. In making a good hire, a company gets much more than another pair of hands. Newcomers bring new ideas, new expertise, new contacts. People who spend their lives with the same company naturally think that its procedures are the normal way of doing things, a mind-set that can become a barrier to strategic change. Staff recruited from outside bring with them the experience built up by rivals. So well-planned recruitment can help a company periodically to rethink how it does things and where it is going. Each new hire ought, in theory, to raise the average quality of a company's employees. (The effect, in other words, should be the exact opposite of that of the Scottish migration to England, a phenomenon well known among my fellow Scots simultaneously to raise the average IQ of both countries.)

For employees, too, changing jobs every so often is desirable. No longer is the ideal employee the "Organization Man" who spends a lifetime with a single employer. Judicious job switching provides a way to acquire that blend of experience and skills called human capital. Good companies work hard to increase their employees' human capital (one of the nonfinancial benefits that an individual company can offer and one reason why large firms can still compete with smaller ones). Some companies, such as management consultancies, can offer a sufficiently wide range of experience to go on building that capital for a long time. But most companies, by their very nature, offer fewer opportunities. So the wise worker moves around companies, picking up experience and skills. The richer that blend, the bigger the paycheck.

Some companies, embarking on new ventures, deliberately pick people with different expertise to augment their own. As Peter Cappelli, author of *The New Deal at Work,* has observed, an airline that wants to improve its customer service hires executives from Marriott, a hotel group; a power company preparing for deregulation scours the telephone industry for people who have already been through that experience.[12] Other companies use "strategic poaching" to get into new industries. When AT&T wanted to break into computer-systems integration, it decided not to buy a company already in the business. Instead, it asked headhunters to locate the top fifty systems integrators in the country, snapped them up, and opened its own business.[13]

In time, Internet technologies will simplify recruiting. Companies advertise a growing number of job openings online. Some post them on online billboards such as Monster.com, some on the "come and work for us" page on their own Web sites. Many companies insist that applicants file résumés online to disseminate them more widely. Two of the groups most in demand, information technology specialists and university graduates, are also more likely to use the Internet to hunt for jobs.

Some companies put great thought into their recruitment sites. Safeway, a British supermarket chain, allows potential graduate recruits to read about the experiences in different departments of young people who have recently joined. Others, such as Siemens AG, a big German high-tech firm, use online games to test for the skills it most needs, such as an ability to work in a team. These games attract the attention of young engineers, who are in desperately short supply in Germany. The company invites those with the highest scores in for interviews.

Of course, one consequence of advertising online may be a flood of the wrong sort of applicants. When Taylor Woodrow Construction, a British building company, began advertising online, it received lots of unsolicited résumés from Russia and the Middle East, where it would never normally recruit. But sometimes, the Internet offers a way to trawl unusual markets deliberately. When two British supermarket groups, Somerfield and Kwik Save, merged in 1998, they needed extra information technology staff and so created a "microsite" to attract workers from Australia and New Zealand.[14]

Online job markets, like any other market, will benefit from a network effect: Their value will rise disproportionately as more people use them both to advertise and to search for jobs. Once a critical mass of people posts résumés online, the Internet becomes a much more efficient job market than rival forms of recruiting. At that point, online recruiting will become a way to save time. Already, a survey of fifty large American companies found that the average company had cut about six days off its hiring cycle of forty-three days by posting jobs online instead of in newspapers, and another four days by taking online applications instead of paper ones and more than a week by screening and processing applications electronically.[15]

However, companies need additional ways to locate and lure the cream of the crop. They should apply three principles to hiring in the communication revolution.

1. Hiring is a useful exercise in its own right. The job interview itself can teach much to an acute employer. It tests a company's reputation in the wider marketplace, and it helps a company to learn about new trends. How else do most

executives have a chance to talk to middle-rank talent at
rival businesses? In addition, one potential hire may locate
another. At Dell Computer, interviewers always ask, "Which
manager has had the greatest influence on you?" They pop
the names into an electronic mailbox set up specially to
locate executive talent.[16]

2. Finding good people requires teamwork. Just occasionally, a
   manager has such a good nose for talent that one person can
   take charge. Usually, though, hiring should not be a solitary
   activity. Companies will increasingly create teams to brainstorm for good candidates and to interview: After all, a new
   person who does not fit in with the rest of the team is not
   usually the one to recruit. Bonuses for recommendations that
   lead to good hires are worth paying. Why spend money on
   outside searching if the staff come up with a better name?
   Good employees will know who else in the job market is
   good—in the external market as well as the internal—and
   what it will take to hook them. Employees already know the
   company and what kind of people are needed. The key will
   be to strike a balance between like-minded and different
   employees, combining experience with new thinking. This
   balance will be different for every company—and a good HR
   department will be aware of the balance and work to maintain it.

3. Constantly be on the lookout for talent. It is always worth-
   while to stockpile contacts, polish networks, and follow up
   on good résumés. When an employee decides to leave, there
   is rarely time to fill the post without an awkward gap.
   Recruiting in a hurry is a recipe for bad decisions.

In following these principles, managers will continue to find that
what really counts in recruiting is contacts. Hiring good people comes
down to knowing who the good people are. And the best way to know
who the best people are is through word of mouth—either in the
office corridor or in an e-mail. The Internet can extend word of
mouth around the globe. For all its transparency, its main impact here
is to magnify the importance of social connections.

## Retention

W HEN EMPLOYEES LEAVE, companies are sometimes delighted. They want to get the headcount down; they want to end that particular project anyway; they have an awkward bunch in the purchasing department who think they are worth much more money than they really are. Fine. Fine, too, if a company employs a succession of bright young things with good ideas—"knowledge nomads," in Rosabeth Moss Kanter's nice phrase. When they pitch their tents for a few months, they bring with them the latest in new ideas from other companies they have passed through. They provide (to switch metaphors) a handy way to cross-pollinate industries with new ways of doing things and thinking about problems.

The nomadic life attracts more admiration in some cultures than others: In the United States a willingness to move on is impressive, while in Japan it smacks of social unease. In America, some of these nomads are the "free agents" described by Daniel Pink.[17] They will undoubtedly become an increasingly significant force in the job market. As they do, the challenge for managers is to embrace this trend: to focus not on retaining employees in the traditional sense but on keeping their skills, outsourcing their talents in the ways described later in this chapter.

While employees may move to being contractors, retaining their loyalty will be key. In general, though, retention matters. Just as it costs much more to acquire a new customer than to keep an existing one, so it costs much more to recruit new talent than to retain existing capability. Besides, in fast-moving businesses, people hold much of the institutional memory in their heads—and institutional memory is one of the few things that can save a company from making the same mistake twice. However hard companies try to persuade their staff to share ideas (the subject of chapter 2), most of what a company knows will always have two legs and a maddening tendency to leave for a better job offer.

People have long had some idea of the salary game: just apply for a job in other companies, get an offer, and then lobby the boss to match it. But the Internet may make retention harder.[18] Employees can check their salaries against those offered elsewhere more easily online, using surveys such as that by Robert Half International posted on Monster.com. And rivals can locate good employees, even if they are not job hunting, and woo them with tempting offers.

Companies will therefore work harder to identify the people they most want to keep. They may sometimes use Internet technologies here, for instance to discover how coworkers rate each other's performance, using the powerful tool of 360-degree anonymous appraisal. Overall, though, human resources policy must move beyond merely trying to reduce employee turnover across the board. Part of the HR task in the future will have much more in common with customer-relationship management: It will be to segment employees according to their value to the company and to design appropriate strategies for each group. The correct goal is to influence who leaves and when. As author Peter Cappelli puts it, "If managing employee retention in the past was akin to tending a dam that keeps a reservoir in place, today it is more like managing a river. The object is not to prevent water from flowing out but to control its direction and its speed."[19]

That means assessing how long the company ideally wants various employees to stay. It may want to keep a few people indefinitely: a creative product designer, say, or an inspiring business leader or a gifted engineer. Another group will be people worth keeping for shorter, well-defined periods of time: employees with specific skills in short supply or members of a team working on a particular project. A final group will be people in easy-to-fill jobs or with skills that are not much in demand; no need to invest in retaining them.

Each group requires a different approach. Just as companies increasingly use technology to tailor the services they offer each customer, so they must look for similar ways to meet the needs of each employee. The people whom a company wants to keep only for a limited time period may, in fact, prefer to be told that rather than to drift along, uncertain about when their jobs will fold. The people a company really wants to keep need red-carpet treatment.

Cappelli describes two companies that have developed this approach. Prudential Insurance, the American financial services giant, has developed a sophisticated planning model that projects talent requirements and attrition rates. The aim is to allow managers of business units to target retention programs on people with particular talents and to create cost-effective contingency plans for filling potential skills shortages.

United Parcel Service redesigned a key job to retain some of its most knowledgeable and valuable workers: its delivery drivers. Replacing a driver costs time and money: A new hire may spend months learning a particular route. When UPS studied why drivers left, it found that they hated the tedious task of loading packages at the beginning of a run. So the company gave that job to a new group of workers. Driver turnover fell sharply. Turnover in the new loading jobs was "an eye-popping 400 percent per year," says Cappelli, but the jobs are simpler to learn and easier to fill with part-timers and students.[20]

So to keep your most valuable people, it is not just a matter of paying them more. However, explaining pay differentials within companies has grown harder as the job market has become more transparent and as patterns of employment shift. Old patterns, built around hierarchy and length of service, survive in some companies. Egon Zehnder International, the executive-search consultancy, for example, still pays a premium for length of service, having decided that the people it most wants to keep are those who want to be with the company for the long haul.[21] Other companies depend partly on recruiting knowledge nomads and twenty-two-year-old Web designers. But the basic reasoning behind the new patterns—"that is what we are willing to pay to keep you"—may seem harsh to many people.

That is why companies will increasingly use not only pay but benefits, flexibility, training, and atmosphere as retention tools. They must strike a balance—and make sure that their staff understand it. They must also discover which aspects of the job valued employees most love or hate. That calls for guile. One study interviewed 4,500 key workers and managers in technology-intensive businesses in North America, Europe, Asia, and Israel. It found significant differences between what people claimed they liked about their jobs and what actually influenced their behavior. For example, men claimed to value a good work/life balance and job security. But when researchers looked at how men in their twenties, thirties, and forties behaved in the market, they discovered that career advancement and pay were the main things that kept these people in their jobs.[22] Employees are a hypocritical lot.

The other—unsurprising—conclusion of this study: Different people value different aspects of a job. Human resource departments, which so often see the Internet as a way to reduce costs and automate benefits, must also use it to build richer relationships with individual employees. They must mine employee data just as carefully as marketing departments mine customer data and offer staff better service in exchange. They must look at which managers have departments with the highest turnover rates and which succeed in developing new talent within the firm. They need to look at ways to tailor jobs and career paths to the needs of individuals rather than assuming that one size fits all.

Companies clearly need a variety of ways to ensure that they keep their best staff and ensure commitment. True, they need competitive pay. But, as Rosabeth Moss Kanter observes, "The hard part for many companies is not giving people financial incentives. It is giving people opportunity, power, and meaning."[23] Only well-run, self-confident companies will know how to give people trust and respect. Those two qualities may not be enough to buy talent—but without them, talent surely won't stay.

The relationship between employer and employee is undergoing a fundamental transformation. Jobs have become more modular; fewer people expect to spend a lifetime working for the same employer; more work on contract or freelance. As a result, the skills that managers need to retain the best staff are more complex and sophisticated than they used to be. The trick will be to pick and keep the best, and accept that it may often make sense to outsource the skills of the rest.

## Outsourcing Talent

GIVEN how hard finding and keeping bright people is, companies sometimes need other options. One is to outsource. Sometimes, the best way to deal with an intractable skill shortage is to let someone else deal with it.

Bruce Tulgan's advice to companies is to "staff the work, not the jobs."[24] During times of rapid technical change, staffing needs are unpredictable; when the economy is shifting gears, lots of work takes the form of projects that start and boom and then come to an end, leaving surplus people on the payroll. Tulgan recounts how Ogilvy & Mather, the international advertising firm, found that many of its creative people—artists, writers, directors—were leaving to start their own small firms. So the advertising giant simply became its former employees' best client. The work once done internally is now done externally—and only as needed.[25]

Another approach is to cooperate with other companies. Most companies see the quest for talent as a zero-sum game: I poach, you lose. Sometimes, though, companies can share employees. Peter Cappelli reports on several such instances. In one particularly interesting case, Cascade Engineering, a manufacturer of plastic parts in Grand Rapids, Michigan, teamed up with a local Burger King to coordinate recruitment. Applicants who did not have the skills that Cascade needed, but who appeared likely to be good workers, were offered jobs at Burger King. Successful employees at Burger King who wanted more challenging work might be taken on at Cascade. "The career development that individuals in the past would have experienced within a single company now takes place across two companies," comments Cappelli.[26]

Cooperation of this kind may be rare. However, it might usefully be extended as a way to link the various parts of a company's supply chain more closely together. After all, a key to success will be that businesses in such partnerships do not compete in the same markets. But there would be considerable benefits for, say, a small company in Dell Computer's supply chain from letting a manager move to Dell.

One thing is sure: Employees' career paths will become more complex and less uniform in the world of tomorrow. People will work for a succession of shifting, forming, and re-forming projects and teams. They may work one year for a large company and then, a few months later, do the same job for a small company to which their previous employer has outsourced the work. Experiments will flourish. And with each new job, employees will hope to acquire more knowledge and skills.

Outsourcing will not suit every company: It is, for instance, much easier to maintain quality and discipline among employees than with freelancers. Nor will every worker willingly choose to become a free agent: Many people, particularly those without star talents, would prefer the relative security, the benefits (such as health care), and the social life of a job. To some extent, the recent interest in outsourcing reflects the peak of a boom and will pass with prosperity. However, the broad direction of change is likely to be away from permanence in the job market and toward more instability and fluidity. Even if change occurs only at the margins, the outlook of companies will alter.

## Training

ONCE GOOD PEOPLE come on board, the next challenges are to keep their knowledge fresh and to expand it. Training is the main way in which companies invest in their people and create value for shareholders. Given that new employees rarely earn back their employment costs for several months—or even years—after they begin their jobs, a company has a huge financial incentive to train them as quickly as possible—and the more value a company hopes eventually to extract from them, the more important that training becomes.

Companies need to earn a return on their training, just as on any other investment. Nobody wants to train an employee for a year and then see these expensively delivered skills walk off to earn money for another company. When a company invests in a new factory or a piece of fancy machinery, it can choose whether to keep it or to sell it. Employees are a different sort of investment. They can leave at a moment's notice, taking their precious capital value with them. And there is nothing much an employer can do to stop them—apart from rewarding them adequately.

Businesses therefore have to think carefully about training in the most cost-effective way possible, and then capturing the benefits institutionally. Ultimately, the best way to make training cost effective is to persuade employees to see it as a partnership: Their employer invests in them, and they match that investment in terms of their time, if not of their money. The employee contributes to the cost of training—not necessarily by paying for it but by accepting that it comes as part of the total compensation package. That is only fair.

Training is no longer an optional extra but a necessity to keep up with the pack. Done properly, it can deliver both short-term adaptability to innovation and real long-term advantage. However, the speed at which companies now introduce new products and processes gives employees less and less time to master more and more information. Besides, because so many employees are on the road or are working alone, they are less likely to have a colleague nearby who can explain unfamiliar material to them. "Working beside Charlie," the traditional way in which new staff absorbed corporate wisdom, is less likely to happen. Charlie is probably several miles away, on a different sales call.

Internet technologies create radical new opportunities for training programs. With traditional corporate training, people often assemble from different locations, stay in a hotel, and spend time away from their desks, which is great for bonding and team building but expensive and time-consuming. Delivering on-the-job training to staff constantly on the road is difficult. And providing training of all kinds in exactly the quantity and at the level that employees need is also hard to do. Most people end up dozing through much of any training course—either it tells them what they already know, or it tries to convey something complicated in too little time.

To solve all these problems, companies are turning to the computer and the Internet. E-learning has become every corporate training program's hope of salvation. But is hope triumphing over experience? After all, companies have dabbled for years in replacing teachers with screens. The results have generally been dire. And attempts to deliver formal education electronically have so far met with decidedly mixed results. Even the University of California, Los Angeles, a campus at the forefront of using information technology to advance education, has found only modest success with delivering online learning. Regardless of whether professors put all the course material on the Web, the students still come to lectures. For many people, learning and the creation of new ideas are social processes, hard to replicate electronically.

Corporate training, on the other hand, seems better suited to online delivery. Students do not necessarily need to be taught to analyze and argue in every work situation, two constants of university education. Moreover, workers often have much more compelling incentives to acquire information than university students may have: Their pay and promotion, or simply keeping their jobs, may depend upon absorbing some particular piece of coursework.

Many companies, in practice, use a combination of traditional teaching and online delivery. As John Coné, head of learning at Dell Computer, puts it, online learning is like the microwave oven: It is not a complete replacement for the traditional model, but it does some things better.[27] To minimize loss of working time, well-organized companies provide a mix of classroom learning with computer-based courses, supervised help from fellow employees at the workplace, and solo study in a worker's own time.

Electronically delivered training has several benefits:

- It delivers training in new forms.
- It delivers the information when it is needed.
- It allows employees to study material where they want and at their own pace.
- It allows easy access to experts: One good instructor can teach everyone.
- It is fast and inexpensive to update.
- It allows the progress employees make and the courses they take to be readily monitored.
- Courses can be tailored to an employee's individual skills and requirements.

Some companies use live, interactive, two-way video conferencing to allow their staff to take courses in scattered locations. A far-flung group of employees can assemble for a class, watch a lecture or demonstration, ask questions online, and then debate the material locally. Merrill Lynch is using this technique to help employees in several cities to earn college credit from a university without leaving the office. One effect is to save time; another, to give employees an intellectual perk that may help to keep their loyalty.

More common, though, is the use of asynchronous, on-demand training that employees can participate in as their workload allows. Using the Internet to deliver training to employees' PCs is particularly appropriate for the two groups that often pioneer online training in companies: sales personnel and information technology staff.

With more sophisticated tools, companies can take advantage of inexpensive and extraordinarily realistic simulation techniques. For instance, Pratt & Whitney, the giant manufacturer of aircraft engines, has developed a simulation of a running Boeing 777 engine. Students who fly through it, using virtual reality, learn ten times better than they do from an instructor using audiovisual equipment.[28]

One potential strength of online delivery is that it can be provided to workers at any time and in any place. Exploiting that requires careful thought. Internet technologies do not reduce production costs, but distribution costs fall sharply. So the economics of electronic training will depend largely on the relative costs of production and distribution. To fly a high-quality trainer to classes around the world is expensive, but to bring a few key people to hear the trainer speak is not.

At Germany's SAP, for instance, Rainer Zinow, head of knowledge management, says that his Web training program is the most expensive one he designs, requiring between 100 and 200 hours of production time to create a single hour of material. The important thing, he says, is to realize that "my classroom is a room in a medium-sized hotel in Connecticut," with a dial-up computer and a consultant who will pay attention for at most an hour between 6 P.M. and 7 P.M.[29] The need for accessibility is important when training employees who may have to cut nonelectronic classes because they are traveling to visit customers or working on urgent projects.

Designing an online training program to cope with irregular sessions is also essential for success. At clearly marked points along the road, employees need regular checkpoints—tests to measure what they have absorbed. Training may also have to be sliced into small bits. Conscious that mobile learning may eventually come to mean learning from a cell phone or a personal digital assistant, researchers at Stanford University's Learning Lab have studied the possibility of teaching people something useful in sessions as short as a few minutes at a time. Among the first-cut answers are that it is easier to practice the already familiar than to learn something new, and that the learning must be delivered in extremely simple, intuitively obvious ways.

A further benefit of online delivery is the speed with which it can be updated. "When we start teaching a five-week course," says Rob Koehler, associate director of interactive technology at SBC/Ameritech, a telephone giant, "we find that 75 percent of the material needs to be revisited by the time the course is finished."[30] Not all businesses change so rapidly, but clearly material available online can be updated much faster and more cheaply than can paper manuals or CD-ROMs. People must also have information on hand: technical data, say, or knowledge of formal constraints, such as regulations.

Ultimately, one of the biggest potential benefits of electronically delivered training is that it can be tailored precisely to the needs of the individual. Like those markets of one that companies offer their retail customers, companies now can provide online training for one. Dell Computer has found that produces savings. The company used to pack new employees off to boot camp for three weeks to be taught about systems and processors, rules and regulations on selling, and the finer points of Dell's product lines. This was wasteful: Some recruits knew most of it already, others knew nothing. Now the company first tests what people know and then offers part of their training online. This personalized approach has allowed Dell to cut a week off initial training—and two weeks off "initial ramp time," the time it takes a newly hired salesperson to achieve a full sales quota. New salespeople thus cost less to train and are job-ready more quickly than they previously would have been. The company argues that online learning works better than the old-fashioned sort.

In time, electronic delivery may change the thinking behind many concepts of training. Given the availability of online help, "dedicating time to make people retain things is sometimes a waste of time," as Rob Koehler of SBC/Ameritech puts it.[31] It may be speedier to teach people how to use online help.

One important possibility will be to use the "anywhere, any time" nature of online training to provide what might be called "just-in-time learning." Because the information is online, it is quick to update and easy to search. At Pratt & Whitney, Richard Wellman designs teaching programs for the company's airline customers. In the past, the aviation industry has pioneered many training devices, such as simulators. Now, his team is designing a wireless-based, voice-activated device through which a mechanic will be able to swipe the bar code on a new part when fitting it to an aircraft. That way, the computer will be able to track the part's history and dictate instructions for installing or repairing it into the mechanic's earpiece. The effect, Wellman points out, is more precise than a training course because it teaches people "what they need to know, when they need to know it."[32]

Instant training of this sort would free training departments to concentrate on teaching employees more subtle skills: how to learn and analyze and make decisions. That in turn may call for classroom, not electronic, teaching. Coné believes passionately in the power of online training. But he admits, "The only thing we can't do asynchronously online is to have an individual attempt to display a learned behavior, and get immediate feedback based on judgment."[33]

Some of the most important training that employees receive will always be delivered not electronically but by their coworkers. Managers must take that into account. They must consider such strategies as moving key staff to cross-pollinate knowledge. They must also consider lending staff to a partner firm, partly to undertake a specific task that will build up their skills but also to deepen relationships with other companies with which the firm has close links. As people have more modular careers, training will become a part of job choice and of compensation, a part of company building and culture creating, not just the dry acquisition of technical knowledge and skills.

# The Future of Human Resource Management

GIVEN HOW MUCH companies claim to value their staff, they have devoted remarkably little effort to making the management of human resources more efficient or the goals more integrated with corporate strategy. That is changing, for two reasons. First, Internet technologies impose new demands on human resources departments. Second, the job market itself is changing in fundamental ways.

Indeed, some imagine that the company of the future will be a mere talent broker, employing few people directly but outsourcing most activities to free agents—freelancers or "e-lancers" who work for themselves. They argue that the market for talent will come to resemble more closely the market for other desirable and scarce commodities. Some signs point that way. At the height of the dot-com boom in 1999–2000, thousands of individuals auctioned their services on the Monster Talent Market at Monster.com and at Bid4geeks. At eBay an entire virtual project team put itself up for sale. In *Digital Capital,* Don Tapscott, David Ticoll, and Alex Lowy imagine companies trading human capital as they might trade company stock. They illustrate the notion with this imaginary conversation:

> BOB: *"Let's try to get Greg Munro to work on this project. I just checked Monster.com, and he'll be available in a month."*
>
> JOANNE: *"Are you kidding? Have you seen what he's trading at?"*[34]

The people who will determine whether the company runs well or runs superbly will be the Greg Munros. Identifying them, watching them, making sure they are properly rewarded and planning their replacement when—inevitably—they walk out: That will be one of the main human resources tasks in tomorrow's company. Recruiting them will sometimes make HR directors feel like casting agents, luring a star for a tempting role. Indeed, the question will often be: Do we buy or do we rent? Do we try to recruit a key person for the (fairly) long haul, or buy him or her by the month? Some tasks (turning round a wobbling business) will call for the former, some (launching a new product) may suit the latter.

While there may be more Greg Munros in the future, there will be many more ordinary Joes who continue to work for an employer. A solid core of workers will still value the "three Ss": security, stability, status. Remember, too, that at the end of the 1990s, more than fifty American public companies employed more than 100,000 workers. In the mid 1980s, only eighteen did so.[35] And those talent auctions were notably unsuccessful. The eBay team withdrew, unsold.

# Chapter 5
# Communities and Corporate Culture

T HE COMPANY is changing—and so is working life. Many people no longer work where their employers can watch them. They no longer have jobs with easily measurable output. They no longer work next to their closest colleagues; instead, their colleagues may be half a continent away. Few employees now work in the same company office, week in, week out, for years at a time. Instead they travel constantly; they work on projects, in teams that coalesce and then disband; they work on contract. And their working and domestic lives increasingly interweave. They finish a project at home; they book a vacation at work. Employment thus becomes a more fluid concept than it used to be.

As the institutions on which corporate loyalty once rested fade away, the company needs new ways to bind its work force together. Creating a strong sense of belonging will be vital for several reasons. It offers some answer to that conundrum of the information age: how to persuade somebody with a bright idea to let the corporation exploit it for the benefit of shareholders. It allows a company to build up a body of expertise in a field—constructing aircraft, say, or designing Web sites—that justifies its brand. It helps to ensure that customers get a uniform quality of service. It makes it easier to retain high-quality staff, a company's single most important asset.

Inevitably, commitment is partly at the mercy of the job market: Staff will be more loyal when firms are firing than they were in the heady days of the boom, when everyone was hiring. But in good times and bad, companies need some sort of corporate glue to bind their staff together. In a small firm, it might be personal loyalty to the owner. In a new business, it might be the shared excitement of innovation. In a large firm in a company town—Dow Chemical in Midland, Michigan, say, or DuPont in Wilmington, Delaware—it might be the hours that workers spend together, either in the office or at social gatherings after work. For many companies, an effective corporate culture is an intangible—but invaluable—commodity.

A strong culture benefits a company in many ways. Its employees understand instinctively the defining qualities of the business and the way they should react to any issue that confronts them. New staff quickly absorb a sense of appropriate ethics, of what is "done" and what is "not done." That provides a useful element of self-policing. It helps with recruitment if a company is self-confident and has a clear sense of its mission. It also helps with branding: Customers know what to expect.

In a stable, slow-growing, and well-established company, diffusing a common culture is fairly straightforward. You send each year's new recruits off to boot camp for a fortnight and teach them the company history and the meaning of the mission statement. The task was easier when the work force was relatively stable, working in the same buildings and sharing common memories and experiences.

Now, instability and speed make culture creation harder. Dot-coms tried to create instant cultures and often found they turned sour when under pressure. Maintaining a culture is undoubtedly more difficult when workers are scattered. And mergers and acquisitions force one bunch of employees to abandon their corporate creed for another. That is destructive but vital. Mergers fail when two cultures prove hard or impossible to integrate, as is dismally clear from Compaq's difficulty in absorbing Digital or from Daimler's struggle with Chrysler.

Employees who deal directly with customers especially need to buy into a company's culture: They are, after all, the people who define the firm to the customer. Frequently, the voice in the call center sounds entirely uninterested in the company whose products it is supposed to sell. That is the peril of outsourcing. Free agents may have their own values and goals that do not square with the corporate identities of the half-dozen firms they occasionally work for.

Creating an appropriate corporate culture is difficult even at the best of times, let alone in times of change and uncertainty. Managers must be on guard for signs of sickness: closed doors or people muttering into cell phones outside their cubicled offices, apathy at company meetings, no contribution to internal Web site discussions. Now their task is made even harder by the fact that they can no longer impose a corporate culture from the top. In the past, culture—of a sort—flowed down from on high. Lowly clerks had little influence on the concept, and the ones who disagreed were out quickly. Men were their companies: Thomas Watson, Sr., with his "Think" photograph, defined the culture of IBM.

One of the key aspects of Internet technologies is that they allow bottom-up and peer-to-peer flow of information. Another is that they require centralization in order to avoid anarchy. The Internet may thus allow companies to turn on its head the old pattern of culture creation. The role of the center, as so often, becomes that of setting standards and of establishing a framework for the culture; maximizing the benefit of the Internet, the periphery is then left free to express itself. Establishing a culture, then, becomes partly a question of expressing an idea and persuading others to join, and partly a matter of establishing ways for employees to express opinions, and for managers to react to them quickly. The model becomes more like that of Linux, with its multitude of loosely coordinated programmers scattered far and wide but striving for the same goal, rather than that of the disciplined ranks at Microsoft.

Like those Linux programmers, the company of the future will increasingly comprise a collection of online communities. Some will be purely internal, and some will reach beyond the corporate boundary, bringing together teams working on a particular project, perhaps, or salespeople and their key customers or suppliers and buyers. Some of these communities will grow organically from the bottom up. To manage them, executives need a light touch. They must recognize that communities often form around shared jokes, resentments, and gossip. If well managed, these communities can help to diffuse a company's culture.

The Internet will help both to spread corporate culture and to link communities together. Through corporate intranets and e-mail, the scattered workers of the future will keep in touch, share gossip, and learn at a distance. Even so, managers will need new skills for the job: skills that emphasize communicating, not command or control.

## The Shifting Work Force

COMMUNICATING in old-fashioned ways with a new kind of work force, in which more key people are based away from the head office, in markets abroad, a day's air travel away from the main office, or just constantly on the move, will be harder. In many companies, the salesforce and the maintenance people rarely come into the office. At the same time, the divide between work and home has eroded. Companies now expect their people to work from home more than ever in the past, because technology makes it easier for them to do so.

By some counts, 37 million American workers (of a work force of 141 million) spend at least one day a week on the road, traveling to meetings, customers' premises and so on.[1] At some companies the proportion of staff on the road is higher: 25 percent of IBM's work force, for instance, is now mobile. These IBMers spend at least 80 percent of their time off-site, usually working from home or on the road. At GE, the number of sales offices fell by half in four years at the end of the 1990s, as more and more sales staff began to work on the road, from home, or from their customers' premises.

These itinerant workers will be rarely out of the employer's reach. Some estimate that 65 percent of calls made from cell phones are from cars, which have become mobile workstations.[2] In 2001, IBM equipped each of 6,500 of its staff with a BlackBerry, a mobile device that allows them to read their office e-mail while traveling. So employees find that they can use the "dead" time of a car ride or a wait in an airport lounge to continue to work. Given delays in road and air traffic, that creates lots of time to do business—and may offset just a little of the estimated $78 billion of output that Americans appear annually to lose in traffic jams.[3]

This invasion of work into leisure was once the burden only of those at the top of the tree. In the 1850s, James de Rothschild, a scion of the famous banking family, complained about the telegraph. It meant that "even when he went to take the waters from his summer holiday, there was no respite from the business: 'One has too much to think about when bathing, which is not good.'"[4] The Internet, the laptop computer, and the cell phone have all helped to democratize that intrusiveness.

The office will increasingly be more than just a place to sit and work. Of course, there will still be many "factory-offices," such as call centers and data-processing plants, where white-collar workers will sit in rows performing routine tasks, just as Henry Ford's production-line workers once did. But some "offices" will be hotels and airports. Some will be entirely portable: "My office is on my hip." Other offices will mutate into clubs. Employees will use them as a place to network and to brainstorm, to meet for a coffee, or to catch up on gossip. Accenture (once Andersen Consulting) has shown the way here, with offices run by former hotel staff, the profession most skilled at dealing with short visits from big egos. Accenture's offices have desks that can be reserved by the hour, "huddle rooms" with cozy chairs for intense discussions, brainstorming rooms with springy chairs for bright ideas, cubes, enclaves, and pods. The aim is to encourage not comfort (although employees will surreptitiously find ways to recreate some personal territory, however small) but creativity, collegiality, and contact.

More and more companies operate "virtual teams": workers whose main contact with their colleagues and their company is by e-mail, the cell phone, and the intranet. For them, life is not about the journey to work but the journey as work. Their life may be the delightful calm of logging on every morning from an office at the foot of the garden. Or it may look more like the world depicted in a British study called "Meet You at Junction 17," which paints a hellish picture of sales reps riffling through papers while stuck in traffic jams, or parked on side streets, frantically plugging laptops into the cigarette lighter to hunt for clients' details.[5]

Managers must imbue sales- and maintenance people with a sense of corporate loyalty. They are the people, rather than the workers in the back office, whom most customers associate with the company. They are its ambassadors. But as long as they are on the road, they cannot participate in the water-cooler conversations that generally help to instill a sense of corporate belonging. In addition, they constantly meet potentially more attractive cultures and prospective employers.

Some people who need to acquire a strong sense of a company's mission are not employed directly at all but work for subcontractors. As companies outsource more and more activities—their call centers, their servicing, their repairs and maintenance facilities—so they place their reputations in the hands of strangers. They need ways to teach these strangers to share their values.

Pulling these threads together, the company of the future needs the following:

- Strong communities that reinforce the corporate culture, both within the company and—a new problem—across companies as outsourcing and supply chain integration become more important
- Techniques for managing mobile workers
- An imaginative approach to managing e-mail and the intranet, its main tools for talking to its staff and allowing them to talk to each other

## Spreading the Message

MORE THAN any previous technology, the Internet allows companies to ensure that every employee has access to the corporate news, views, and vision. But its sheer availability can mislead managers into believing that communicating effectively is easier than is the case.

Certainly, the Internet offers new ways to disseminate the vision of the company's mission to staff. Some companies use the Internet to explain their ethical code—and to communicate it to their suppliers and customers as well. A good example is Boeing, whose Web site offers an online "ethics challenge."[6] Employees can test their moral instincts for such delicate issues as "acceptance of business courtesies" (what do you do if a client offers you a set of golf clubs to swing a contract his way?) and "proper use of company, customer and supplier resources" (should you circulate an appeal for a charity on the Boeing intranet?). Boeing uses the test to give its employees "ethics refresher training" each year.

Managers can also tell staff electronically where they want the business to go. For example Jacques Nasser, chief executive of Ford, sends the company's staff a weekly "Let's chat" note (a curiously matey idea for such a notoriously tough boss). The company runs a purpose-built newsroom; employs a team of professional journalists who update several times a day a Web site that is available to Ford's employees around the world and to staff in its recent acquisitions, such as Volvo; and runs what it claims is the world's largest corporate intranet. The aim is to use company news to help to create a sense of belonging.

Ford thus handles its internal communications with as much care and professionalism as most companies apply to their external public relations. That is surely sound policy. Most companies spend much more time and money on talking to their customers than to their staff. Yet, if a company cannot communicate its values to its employees, how can it expect to sell them to its customers? In addition, in the past (and indeed still today), trade unions have often dominated the connection between a company and its staff. Internet technologies give managers a chance to bridge the divide directly.

Not only does the Internet allow managers to talk to their staff: It allows them to discover whether their staff are at least pretending to listen. William Nuti, a senior executive for Cisco Systems, produces a monthly video to send to his staff, explaining where the business is going. What happens if employees choose not to watch? Happily, the Internet allows you to track who opens an e-mail and when. "I know everyone who clicks on it and those who throw it away, and I make phone calls to people, saying 'it's important you watch this.'"[7] Not surprisingly, Nuti's monthly videos enjoy high viewing figures.

However, only a foolish boss would imagine that staff who read the "chat" note or watched the video would also buy the spiel. For starters, in a multinational company, the same message may go to people in different countries—and be heard with differing degrees of cynicism or enthusiasm. Moreover, the Internet is not a one-way channel.

It allows staff to communicate directly, for the first time, with senior executives whom they have never met in person. At Siemens, a large German company, Chittur Ramakrishnan, the chief information officer, has noticed a "very significant number of e-mails to top management. The idea of going through a secretary to get an appointment has changed. People can send e-mails to anyone and expect a response. It's very democratizing."[8] That assumes, of course, that the top brass do not delegate to a minion the task of replying. The technology, as always, is no guarantee of cultural change. But it creates the opportunity for managers to see what really worries their employees. That opportunity can be amplified if corporate pages feature real questions from employees rather than ones invented at the top, demonstrating that their questions are genuinely being heard and answered.

The erosion of hierarchy, such a primary aspect of the company of the future, is not always welcome. Questions may arise over who should address whom. Once, information trickled down a company, layer by layer, conveying authority to each subset of managers who delivered the word from on high. Now that is no longer necessary. When SAP, a German business-software giant, created an elaborate Internet-based communications system, it found that middle managers objected to the chairman's e-mailing all employees. The middle managers' authority had rested partly on their role as a source of information, and without it, they felt exposed. As so often with Internet-driven changes, the implications of what initially appeared to be a simple, time-saving measure turned out to be more complex and politically sensitive.

Finally, if the chief executive is to be the chief communicator, the job requires a whole new set of skills. It needs that rare quality, an ability to write clearly and persuasively. Managers will frequently need to carry an audience with whom their main link may be the written word. Good writing, as Peanuts' Snoopy has observed, is hard work. Communication also requires an ability to use video effectively. A chief executive may be a brilliant strategist, but some of that brilliance must emerge on camera if it is to inspire confidence in employees, customers, and investors. The leaders of big companies thus need to be rather more like effective politicians than they have been in the past, able to inspire and lead from a distance.

If messages travel only from the top down, they will have modest impact—and sometimes may do more harm than good. True employee commitment will depend upon creating a sense of belonging to a community or a team. In order to be secure, productive, and creative, most people need to feel they belong to a group.

How, then, to create a new sense of belonging? And can the Internet help? One part of the answer is to create smaller units to which people can feel they belong. *The Wisdom of Teams,* by McKinsey consultants Jon Katzenbach and Douglas Smith, points out that "large groups of people . . . have trouble interacting constructively as a group" and suggests an ideal scale of the units in which people operate effectively: "Virtually all the teams we have met, read, heard about or been members of have ranged between two and 25 people."[9]

Some large companies deliberately encourage small units. At Carlton Communications, a British media giant, Michael Green, the chairman, decided not to consolidate staff scattered in offices across London into a single unit, arguing that smaller groups feel more entrepreneurial. At St. Luke's advertising agency, also in London, the rule is that when a work group has more than 35 people, it splits. Bill Gross, founder of Idealab!, an American venture capital company, argues that people cannot tolerate working in a group of more than about 100, because a group of that size becomes too impersonal.[10] Few people can remember the names of more than 100 colleagues.

People are more committed to other individuals than to an amorphous corporation. Team members work harder because they do not want to let down the other members. If pay is tied to team performance, peer pressure will encourage members to work for the good of the team. Not only do smaller groups enjoy a greater sense of belonging, but they are more effective. Whenever a company—or indeed a government—wants to achieve a goal, it creates a task force, a hit squad, a committee, or a team. As workers become more dispersed and disconnected, they increasingly need to participate in teams.

The Internet not only allows teams to talk to each other around the world. It also makes it easier for several teams or small groups to behave as though they were a single large one, collaborating where they gain benefits from size. The Internet fosters lateral connections within a company—or even between people in different companies.

People feel commitment to a team; linking that to the culture of the corporation will be the challenge for management. A company's success may lie increasingly in its ability to work across business units, joining teams and communities with the glue of common culture.[11] Defining the proper links between individual communities will be difficult, but those links will hold the company of the future together.

## Managing Mobility

I F PEOPLE work from home or from their cars, then their relationship with the company is inevitably more tenuous. They can no longer easily go out for a drink after work with their colleagues. They quickly lose esprit de corps. They lose institutional learning too—the almost imperceptible sharing of ideas and information that occurs when people work physically side by side.

Yet these people may be the employees that a company's customers meet most frequently. Some companies recognize that fact. GE Medical, for instance, gives its maintenance people special training because they often spend more time in a customer's office than anyone else. Mark Lurie, chief executive of @hand, a company making software for mobile devices, argues that companies must "empower the field force" because the people who deliver see the customer more than either the back or the front office at a company.[12] Yet companies tend to leave those people until last when they are investing in new computer systems. Even the people who deliver Dell computers, he points out, offer the customer a clipboard with a piece of paper and a carbon copy and ask for a signature.

The task of managing mobility involves recognizing the importance of the internal intranet as a way of keeping such workers up-to-date, and using it to fend off the inevitable sense of isolation. Companies put boundless imagination into designing the online face they show to their customers—ensuring that it is easy to understand, current, and fun. Few devote nearly as much energy to the face they show on their intranets.

However, companies must design their intranets with far-flung workers in mind. Most important of all is reliability: If the system crashes, then people in the head office can just walk next door and ask each other the time of the meeting; the people out on the road are sunk. An online calendar is a wonderful means of coordinating work flow—until it goes down.

Almost as maddening is the experience of sitting in a distant hotel room, puzzling over in-jokes and allusions in an e-mail that mean something only to the people who were physically at the meeting. An intranet's design must acknowledge this. It must acknowledge, too, that many traveling workers will not enjoy a capacious T1 connection, cable modem, or ADSL line. Many telecommuters log on using dial-up connections on ordinary telephone lines and curse the elaborate graphics and fancy features that take ages to download.

E-mail can help to keep people in touch, but voice calls are better and physical meetings better still. Some companies hold regular weekly conference telephone calls, having first e-mailed an agenda to all participants to ensure that time is used efficiently. Most find a way to bring scattered staff together at regular intervals, even if only for a cup of coffee in a highway service station at Junction 17. Physical meetings undoubtedly have qualities that even the fanciest broadband connection lacks. John Seely Brown and Paul Duguid make this point repeatedly in *The Social Life of Information,* in which they describe how the repair people at Xerox, fed up with instruction manuals that were hard to follow and to apply, began solving problems by getting together for regular breakfasts to share repair war stories. Sometimes, there is no substitute for the give-and-take of a chin-wag over a real, not virtual, drink.

From the manager's point of view, virtual teams bring other problems. One may be conflict. Francois Gossieaux, head of eRoom Technology, a company that makes software for dispersed employees, argues that conflict is rarer in virtual than in physical teams. When it does arise, though, it is much harder to resolve. Individuals who have never or seldom met in a physical work space have fewer social restraints than those who know they must sit at adjacent desks the next day and the next.[13]

The toughest problem is creating trust. Companies increasingly must judge and reward their staff by output rather than hours spent at the desk. That is a revolution in itself: The clock, after all, is one of the most entrenched standards of the industrial age. For years, workers have clocked in, done their eight hours, and clocked out.

So changing this aspect of corporate culture will be especially tough. With salespeople, the original road warriors, measuring and rewarding is easy. With other telecommuters, it is harder. But if managers cannot see their staff, they have little choice. The team will take over some of the role of the manager in ensuring that employees deliver. For nobody knows who is slacking better than the coworker who picks up the slack.

The tools managers must devise to cope with dispersed workers will, in time, benefit their relationship with their in-house staff. The Internet raises all sorts of new issues of workplace trust—and, fortunately, suggests some answers too.

## Using Corporate Intranets

THE DIFFUSION of corporate culture and the inclusion of mobile workers unite on the corporate intranet. Wall off a bit of the Internet, and a company has a virtual space where all sorts of services can be offered. They include not just news and information, from the company history to a constantly updated telephone directory and service guide, but the many personal services that companies provide staff with in order to motivate and retain them. Not surprisingly, business-to-employee communications are one of the fastest-growing areas of Internet applications.

How do employees differ from customers? They don't, in this respect: The company's external and internal message must be the same. With the Internet, discrepancies will be noticed (and made public) faster than before. "Managing in a fishbowl" is the phrase that Novell's Eric Schmidt likes to use: Nothing a manager says or does within a company is likely to remain confined there.[14] Managers must assume that they are on public view almost all the time.

With a corporate intranet, the manager's role is once again that of filtering and structuring information. As with knowledge management, the task of deciding what appears on the intranet is vital, but once there, the information should be available to everyone. To get across a common goal and message, companies must quickly move to pull together all internal communication that they want to post.

The first step is to ensure that everyone has access and a common point of entry. Intranets draw on one of the Internet's great strengths over previous, proprietary, systems: Managers can use them to provide services to everyone in a company. But not everyone has a PC, which is still people's main entrée to the Internet. So some companies, such as Ford and American Airlines, are giving their employees computers to use at home; Ford had issued about 166,000 to its staff in the United States by mid-2001.[15] In the case of Ford, two-thirds of its employees are hourly workers who cannot use their computers to do company work from home. But that is not the point. Ford is creating a way to teach its entire staff to think online as well as to reach every employee with a single global message.

The other essential of online internal communications is consistency. Initially, every department may set up its own Web site, perhaps protected from the rest of the company by a password, and often designed to boost the department's self-esteem. Companies quickly move to end such anarchy; if communications are to be effective, they need a single organizing principle.

Once intranets have woven the staff together as part of a single network, companies can move a step further. They can create a corporate "portal," a centralized home page with links to various services, items of information, and tidbits designed to entice employees to keep checking in. Sophisticated portals offer links not just to internal services but sometimes to the wider Internet. The home page can be personalized, just like MyYahoo!, so that an employee in a production department does not have to look at links designed for the sales force and people in the marketing department do not get a deluge of news clippings on camshaft design, reducing the nasty feeling common among people in large companies that they are tiny cogs in a vast machine.

Some of the information available through the portal may be extremely work-a-day: Click for a map of each floor of an office, say; click again for a photo and a few personal details about who sits where. Elsewhere there may be links to the day's news and pages that allow workers to fill in expense reports, order office supplies, and find telephone numbers. Sales information, material on corporate research projects, and comparisons with competitor companies might be displayed, as might up-to-date corporate news: a chance for the company to explain its handling of the latest lay-offs or product launch.

More significantly, there will undoubtedly be links to the services provided by the human resources department, such as Ford's appropriately named (and frequently visited) "paystub online." The HR department is often the prime mover in setting up a corporate portal. It typically spends endless hours answering repetitive questions from employees. The move toward "cafeteria" benefits—a choice of various permutations of pension, health plan, holidays, and pay—brings lots of calls asking: "What happens if I. . . ." Many such questions are more efficiently answered by a computer than by a human being. This fact has encouraged companies to put their employees' personal records on a password-protected Web site and allow the staff to update them. In refined versions, staff can experiment with different combinations, answering the "What if I . . ." questions for themselves. The results can be even more dramatic than persuading customers to rely on online self-help. Even when staff could use the HR Web site only to update their records, Ford found that calls to the central help desk fell by 80 percent.[16]

Making the HR department more accessible and efficient is extremely important. After all, one of a company's main activities is looking after its employees. Even companies that do not think of themselves as particularly caring still have to consider salaries, pensions, health benefits, and training. The mundane tasks associated with these issues absorb time and resources, yet doing them badly will cost a company good people, who will become demoralized and leave in frustration. However impressive a company's performance, a badly administered health plan will drive key employees to leave. And however carefully a company plans its advertising campaign, disgruntled staff will wreck its image.

A successful portal must provide a mix of stuff that employees need to do their jobs and stuff they need for their lives outside work. In this, it must reflect corporate acceptance of the need to tolerate the way many employees now mix work with home life and vice versa. To persuade employees to look at the home page frequently, companies think up various cunning inducements. They know that they are often competing with the rest of the Web for their employees' attention, so they must keep the portal full of compelling content or employees may wander to eBay or Yahoo!. Motorola asked a cross section of sixty employees to develop ideas for its portal. Other companies post a list of employees with birthdays during the current week. Scient, an Internet consulting firm in San Francisco, has an area called "Do you want to scream at anyone?," where employees can complain about colleagues who send excessive e-mails. The site also shows the daily winner in categories such as "take a chill pill."

Portal pages such as these offer reach and build cohesion. Motorola sees its portal, designed by a Silicon Valley company called Epicentric, as a way to send a consistent message to its 140,000 employees and ensure alignment with corporate goals.[17] The pages are accessible not only to employees in the head office but also to people in distant subsidiaries, on the road, and at home. True, this wide reach can cause culture clashes: Scient's quintessentially Californian "stream of consciousness" site baffled its British staff.

But how far should portals go beyond offering in-house services and information? Should companies accept that every employee's work life and personal life are hopelessly entwined, and that it is simply not possible to tell intelligent and talented staff that they cannot shop from the office? "Knowledge workers' minds never call it quits for the day," explains one commentator. "We come up with ideas in the middle of the night, in the shower, watching Monday night football. Many of us work longer hours or take time on a weekend to jot down ideas or finish a project. On the flip side, the Internet allows us to take care of personal activities from the office. We do our banking and shopping on the Web. We send e-mails that aren't strictly work-related and check how our stocks are doing. We catch up on sports scores."[18]

Given this entanglement, why not make a virtue of the fact and persuade employees to make good use of the corporate portal? Thus the online services a company offers become an indicator of the extent to which it accepts that working life has changed. "A B2E portal reflects a new view of the relationship between an organization and its people," says Epicentric's cofounder, Oliver Mouto. "This isn't about anarchy, it's about shared control."[19]

It may also be about a new stream of corporate revenue. Increasingly, big companies want to offer their staff ways to buy their stock or their products. DaimlerChrysler's corporate portal offers both of those options—employees can order stocks or a company car online. Bank of America, going one step further, launched its portal in 2000 jointly with Amadeus, a big travel company that offers online booking and ticketing. Plenty of the bank's employees need tickets for company travel. And because a big bank already puts lots of travel business through a single provider, it can negotiate better deals for its employees' leisure travel too.

So the corporate work force becomes a market place. Big companies have always sold things to their employees, through the company store, say, or the company cafeteria. They have always accepted that their employees can pop out at lunchtime to buy a sandwich or the evening meal. Now, two things have changed. First, the company can offer all manner of products to its staff—or point them electronically toward others who can do so. That is an advertiser's dream: a stable group of people with regular pay and a known employer. Why not, for instance, offer a link from the page that informs employees of their vacation entitlements to a travel company? Why not charge local restaurants for the occasional advertisement? Why not link the pensions pages to banks and savings companies? There are, of course, awkward implications for privacy: Employers may want to know which pensions an employee bought. But convenience and staff discounts may overcome many people's fears on that score.

In addition, shopping on the corporate intranet accelerates the blurring of work and life. We will work from home and shop from work. Our employers will become agents and billboards and discount stores—together with whatever is their main line of business.

## E-mail: For and Against

S O THE INTERNET creates a means for managers in fragmented companies to rally their scattered troops. But the troops can also talk more readily with each other. The use of e-mail in particular is a decidedly mixed blessing. It can foment revolution; it can spark rows; it can even offer employees new ways to break the law or embarrass their employer.

E-mail is a particularly powerful tool for dissidents. Unhappy employees can use e-mail to spread harmful rumors and criticism. Thanks to the Internet, irate employees who once muttered behind closed doors can now send "flame" e-mails that everybody can read.

Distance workers, deprived of water-cooler gossip, may take such rumors more seriously than others.

One study of the use of e-mail as a political tool within an organization concluded that "the very characteristics that make it so powerful a tool for collaboration—the ability to send a message to many recipients simultaneously, to modify and forward messages from others, to respond immediately and publicly to a message—also make it highly suited to political manipulation and abuse."[20] The study described the use of e-mail in a number of universities to campaign against the university administrators by, for instance, sending out a "satisfaction questionnaire" to all faculty and distributing the results by e-mail.

Managers cannot easily control such campaigns—and if they are wise, they will head them off before they get going. One of the universities described in the study responded to an e-mail revolt by restricting access for everyone on the campus. That, clearly, is no way to restore morale. Instead, managers must regard mutinous murmuring online as a useful early warning of trouble. They should respond promptly with a clear statement of their strategy. They will have to accept that good communications flows two ways.

But politicking is not the only danger that office e-mail brings. Just as disruptive is unthinking anger. Michael Eisner, chairman of Walt Disney, argues that e-mail has increased the intensity of emotion within his company and has become the principal cause of workplace warfare. "With email," he notes, "our impulse is not to file and save, but to click and send. Our errors are often compounded by adding other recipients to the 'cc' list and, even worse, the 'bcc' list. I have come to believe that, if anything will bring about the downfall of a company or maybe a country, it is blind copies of emails that should never have been sent."[21]

The blind copy is a "software stiletto," asserts Michael Schrage, an academic at MIT's Media Lab. It is a way for someone to report a correspondence to someone else without the knowledge of the other writer. It is thus the perfect way to "shop a colleague." "If business ethics means anything to a firm," says Schrage, "it should surely disable the blind-copy field."[22] If it does so, corporate life is less spicy, but fewer careers are wilfully destroyed.

Some managers take a tough line here. They recognize that e-mail is a business tool to be used with care. It should never be employed to

resolve conflicts, either between employees or between staff and customers. That delicate job calls for a telephone call or a face-to-face
meeting, which can be followed up with a polite and neutral e-mail to
recap what has been agreed. Rosabeth Moss Kanter, in a recent book,
relates how renren.com, an Internet company based in Hong Kong,
came to ban e-mail for disagreements or strategic decisions. Michael
Robinson, the company's founder, received a copy of a string of testy
e-mails between one employee in Shanghai and another in Hong
Kong, arguing about some hardware equipment decisions. The row
was clearly getting out of hand. "I know you're both nice guys,"
Robinson told them, "and I know you both actually like each other, so
just get on the phone. They got on the phone, and within 20 seconds,
it was back to normal. They were very embarrassed afterwards."[23]
Conference calls can be tricky, but nothing is as tricky as e-mail.

As for negotiating by e-mail, that too is risky. Experiments by
Michael Morris, an academic at Stanford Business School, and a group
of colleagues have now demonstrated what many people instinctively
suspect: Negotiations are more successful if they are conducted, at
least in part, face to face rather than between strangers armed with
keyboards and screens. Together with Leigh Thompson of the Kellogg
Graduate Business School at Northwestern University and several
other academics, Morris studied mock negotiations that used only
e-mail and compared them with ones preceded by a brief getting-to-
know-you telephone call. The second type went more smoothly.
Other experiments found that electronic negotiations worked best
when the negotiators began by swapping photographs and personal
details or when they already knew each other.[24]

Kathleen Valley, a professor at Harvard Business School who has
also reviewed e-mail negotiation, is more skeptical than Morris and his
colleagues. "People lie more readily when they are interacting through
e-mail," she argues. "In addition . . . there's something about seeing the
entire exchange documented in black and white on a computer screen
that makes negotiators less flexible, less willing to get involved in the
kind of give and take that's normal in more personal communications."
She found that more than 50 percent of e-mail negotiations end in
impasse; only 19 percent end that way in face-to-face negotiations.[25]

Why is e-mail such a snare? Heidi Roizen, a Silicon Valley veteran,
thinks that part of the problem is that "most people are lousy typists—

and they don't think about the fact that an email lasts for ever." She has two rare advantages: She is an English major and a 90-words-a-minute typist. She finds that the durability of e-mail is one of its main advantages. It allows her to keep track of her dealings with the eight different companies on whose boards she sits: "It's instant record-keeping." But she scrupulously follows two rules to avoid misunderstanding: "Re-read each piece of mail before you send it, from the point of view of the recipient; and when in doubt, leave it overnight."[26] As every Victorian letter writer learnt, a night's sleep is the best filter to apply to a furious note.

## Controlling Communications

THE FREEDOM that the Internet gives employees is wonderful, but companies fear it. No wonder: They are vulnerable to much more than quarrelsome e-mails. Their employees may waste time; may clog up bandwidth; and may expose them to a variety of legal risks, from copyright infringement to libel.

Staff who download music at work or watch football games can clog up large quantities of bandwidth. They also waste huge amounts of time—at least as much as employees once spent goofing off. In the past, time wasting was visible to all. Now, a 2000 survey by SurfControl, a Californian company that makes screening technology, found that 18 percent of employees visited the Internet ten or more times on any given day for activities that have nothing to do with work. The company may have a vested interest in showing employers what their workers are up to, but its findings tie in with those of another survey, by Nielsen/NetRatings, that in January 2000, 53 percent of employees visited an entertainment Web site, 37 percent a financial services site, and 12 percent a porn site.[27]

Porn uses up lots of memory on corporate computers, to the fury of information technology managers who usually know exactly who is watching what and grumble when the system is clogged up with the unspeakable. One large British company was aghast to discover that its server contained 18,000 pages of porn.[28] Companies as diverse as Dow Chemical and Orange have sacked employees for looking at naughty pictures. If a female staff member comes into the room and catches a male colleague ogling the screen, she can claim sexual harassment, raising more than merely moral issues for businesses in the United States.

Plenty of bored office workers use e-mail as a way to circulate rude stories. In December 2000, a twenty-six-year-old British woman called Claire Swire briefly attained global fame when a friend forwarded a lubricious e-mail she had sent to a bunch of his friends. Proliferating at many times the speed of a chain letter, the e-mail soon reached hundreds of employees at top firms, including Clifford Chance, Linklaters, and Arthur Andersen. Some employees who forwarded it from Britain's Financial Services Authority were apparently threatened with dismissal for doing so. In many American companies, sending a smutty joke can get you fired.

No wonder companies impose restrictions. SurfControl sells screening technology that claims to be able to discern from skin tones whether a picture is naughty or not. More and more companies have an Internet access policy, and the vast majority use software to block some connections. A 2000 survey by the American Management Association found that 54 percent of large American companies monitored what their staff did on the Internet, and the proportion was rising.[29] Privacy at work has vanished even faster, thanks to electronic tracking, surveillance, and monitoring, than privacy in the world outside.

However, companies need to step carefully when they impose restrictions on Internet access. They obviously need to be sure that their employees do not land them in legal trouble, by breaking laws on copyright, libel, decency, or anything else. They need to keep time wasting under control. But they also need to accept that an Internet access policy is more likely to be accepted if not handed down from on high but constructed communally.

## A Sense of Belonging

GEOGRAPHICALLY DISPERSED, loosely attached to the company they work for, employees must more than ever feel part of a corporate community if they are to collaborate effectively. Companies will have to find ways to convey the same cultural message to staff on the payroll in the head office and to outsourced staff working in a call center in a distant country. The Internet will, in time, become the most effective mechanism to glue a company together in this way.

At present, it is still a blunt tool. Sending the same message is technically easy; getting everyone to understand the same point is altogether more difficult. Communication is not just about electronics but about the use of language, about shared experience, about a host of subtle cultural signals. To bind scattered workers into coherent and effective teams will take more than good software or the right bandwidth or the latest mobile gadget.

To build employee loyalty, managers need awareness and a light touch. Communication will be not just a top-down or even bottom-up exercise. It will also help to weld the dispersed work force together by encouraging members of the wider corporate community to form a web of smaller groups. Therefore, to communicate with their staff, companies must do more than send them periodic "let's chat" notes. They must become sources of useful information, ideas, and services, distributed online. They must use the Internet to give a common purpose to all those who represent them, whether chief executive or maintenance worker. Even more important, they must use it to provide employees with a sense of community so powerful that their best staff will not want to work anywhere else.

# Chapter 6
# Purchasing

O REGARD a company's purchasing department as an exciting place to work would have appeared eccentric not so long ago. Purchasing might account for between 50 and 80 percent of a company's expenditure, but the department that managed it was a corporate Siberia, one of life's dead ends, full of people chasing up invoices and calculating how many widgets the company bought last year.[1] No longer. These days, the folks who manage purchasing are the shock troops of the business-to-business (B2B) business, one of the areas of corporate life where new communications are causing the fastest transformation.

The reason is that purchasing managers can deliver something that not many other executives struggling to introduce Internet technologies into established firms can hope to show: real and rapid savings. Procurement is thus one of the early areas to demonstrate the Internet's potential benefits. As always, the long-term consequences will be much more extensive than the initial effects and will come only once significant organizational change has taken place.

When companies buy from other companies (or, even more, when organizations such as hospitals, universities, and government departments purchase supplies), they have electronic opportunities to save money in three main ways:

1. By aggregating dispersed purchases across the company and buying in bulk

2. By streamlining the whole process of purchasing

3. By seeking out new, lower-cost sources of supply

In order to achieve such savings, however, purchasing managers need a new approach. They must persuade line managers to accept a high degree of central discipline. The need for central discipline emerges as a recurrent theme with the exploitation of the Internet: in knowledge management, in managing customer relations, and in corporate culture. Achieving this will be hard. Most big companies have traditionally had a decentralized structure—and most employees associate the Internet with freedom, not constraint. But centralization is critical to the successful integration of Internet technologies into a company. And indeed, if managers at the corporate center have sufficient clout to enforce their will, these technologies offer them a way to put their stamp on activities that would once have been under local control. Ironically, a tool that appears to disperse authority will need centralization in order to work.

If purchasing managers can use the Internet effectively, then they win a great prize: a quantum leap in the amount of information they have both about their own company's activities and about what products and services are available for companies to buy in the market. As a result, power will shift from sellers to buyers, keeping prices in check as well as widening choices.

This chapter and the following one examine the ways that Internet technologies are helping to transform purchasing policies. The company of the future will use the Internet for two distinct goals: (1) to widen its range of potential suppliers and (2) to deepen its relations with existing suppliers. Through the Internet and electronic auctions, companies can hunt for fresh suppliers, make occasional purchases, and compare prices more easily and globally than before. But they can also use Internet technologies to build their relationships with old and trusted suppliers, reducing administrative costs and accelerating transactions. In the future, companies may separate these two functions, conducting them through different Web sites because they require such different approaches.

This chapter looks principally at the first approach: at purchasing itself, and particularly at the ways companies make nonstrategic purchases, those of supplies that do not usually go directly into the product itself. Here, the development of online catalogs gives purchasing managers new leverage over the vast range of items that many companies currently buy in an unstructured way. The coming of electronic marketplaces offers a way to widen the range of possible suppliers and to test prices. Chapter 7 goes on to explore the second approach—the implications of these developments and others for companies' long-term relationships with their suppliers. As in other areas, Internet technologies allow companies to increase their reach, but the more significant application is to deepen and strengthen existing relationships.

## How Companies Purchase

IN THE HEADY DAYS of the Internet stock-market bubble, corporate purchasing seemed to many investors a logical development, on a far larger scale, of business-to-consumer (B2C) purchasing. At the height of the boom, in 1999–2000, Forrester Research predicted that B2C commerce would grow from $20.3 billion in 1999 to $184.5 billion in 2004; B2B commerce would expand from $109 billion to $2,696 billion over the same period.[2] Excitable young M.B.A.s started up many new businesses on the basis of such optimism. One point, however, survives: The scope for applying Internet technologies to industrial purchasing is vastly broader than that for retailing. Corporate purchasing is a far more complex activity than retail purchasing. And precisely because electronic communications provide a framework around which a complex process can be reorganized, they offer tremendous promise to simplify it.

Roughly speaking, companies make two sorts of purchases. They buy direct materials that go into end products (such as parts or chemical feedstocks). For manufacturers, this is the larger category. As products move along the supply chain, different companies buy and sell them, adding value at every step. Because such products are vital to a company's output, businesses usually buy from a group of suppliers with whom they form close relationships. But all companies also buy a vast assortment of indirect materials, anything from carpets to lubricants to hotel bookings for traveling staff. Even in large manufacturers, this second category may account for as much as 40 percent of all purchases. Companies make these purchases largely on price and constantly look for new suppliers and better prices. But, even in this domain, reliability and trust also matter.

In both cases, corporate purchasing is a sprawling, decentralized mess. For instance, before it developed one of the world's earliest Internet-based purchasing networks in the mid-1990s, the giant General Electric operated with more than fifty different purchasing systems. Each of its 250-plus businesses had developed its own arrangements, often based on proprietary and inflexible electronic networks.[3] Where companies buy indirect materials, arrangements are even more chaotic.

Chaos aside, companies buy things in ways that are strikingly different from those consumers use.[4] The greatest differences are in direct purchasing. Individuals generally buy standard products, but most of the purchases that industrial companies make are for specially ordered components. An individual who buys an automobile may choose from a standard range of colors, trims, and accessories. But when a company builds an automobile, the seats, the dials on the instrument panel, and the windows are all custom-made to the buyer's specifications. Corporate buyers cannot surf the Web, looking for bargains in the serendipitous way that individuals may do.

In addition, the corporate decision to purchase parts or materials typically is very different from the individual's buying spree, where the decision to buy and the transaction are rolled into one impulsive moment. Corporate decisions are a matter of teamwork, not individual say-so. The decision to place an order occurs at a different time and place from the actual transaction. Purchases generally involve the negotiation of long-term contracts, specifying quality, price, and delivery characteristics. Such complexities, says Sam Kinney, one of the founders of FreeMarkets, a Pittsburgh company that runs electronic marketplaces, "eliminate the possibility that simple B2C business models could be successfully applied to business purchases."[5]

Indeed, many large companies have done direct purchasing online for years, although using inflexible and proprietary networks of the kind described later in this chapter. For that reason, the benefits of using the Internet become apparent more quickly in the second category, of indirect purchasing or general procurement.

Buying the vast array of miscellaneous items and services that a business requires to keep going is often a disorganized, time-consuming, and expensive affair. One consequence is that companies rarely know how much they buy of what from whom. Doing bulk deals with suppliers is therefore harder. "If you're really going to leverage the spend across divisions, you need to know what you're spending on what. Going after the data is the first priority. That's where e-procurement starts," says Kent Brittan, who runs supply operations for United Technologies (UTC), a company that owns a cluster of firms such as Pratt & Whitney (aircraft engines), Otis (elevators), and Sikorsky (helicopters).[6]

That knowledge, though, comes up against another problem with this kind of purchasing: the way it is authorized. Sometimes, the local building manager's signature is enough to authorize the purchase of paper towels for the company kitchen or carpeting for the finance director's office. Sometimes, the purchase requires the signature of the buying department.

Each approach presents problems. The first way tends to be extravagant and hard to track; the second, expensive to manage and infuriatingly slow. When the order is placed by the local manager in a big company that may use hundreds of suppliers, company purchasing policy becomes impossible to enforce. Nobody can track who buys how many pencils each year, or where, or at what price; or whether a rise in spending on pencils is the result of a rise in pencil prices or in corporate demand for pencils.

On the other hand, when the buying department does the ordering, the company spends money on squads of bored clerical staff. "Rogue" purchases proliferate as exasperated managers dip into the petty cash or bend the rules to acquire some office essential that has become stuck in the authorization pipeline.

All too often, the rigmarole involved in purchasing costs more than the items bought. When companies pause to look at these systems, they are aghast. Germany's SAP, for instance, realized that every purchase had to go through up to four levels of approval. UTC found that it was handling 200,000 invoices for 12,500 office supply items. Such complexity is typical, especially of indirect purchases. "Maintenance, repair, and operation typically account for 20 percent of a company's purchases but 80 percent of its orders," estimates Patrick Forth, a senior consultant with the Boston Consulting Group. "The cost of a purchase order is typically $100—e-procuring costs, $10."[7]

## Controlling Indirect Purchases

INTERNET TECHNOLOGIES make it much easier to control indirect purchases. But gaining that control will be no small matter: It will require imposing central guidelines and setting rules where few have existed before. That can entail a wrenching culture shift within a company. At the same time, it may mean devolving some authority that local managers have not previously enjoyed. Companies must rethink their sign-off systems on purchases. When terms and conditions have been negotiated in advance, a local manager can be given the power to approve sizable transactions. So centrally determined standardization in fact allows greater local empowerment.

Until companies staff supply management with some of their best people, they will find it hard to achieve the necessary shift in corporate attitudes. Yet in the past, the purchasing department has rarely been the place where star employees worked. When, in 1997, McKinsey consultants studied corporate purchasing, they found one chief executive who complained that the department in his company had become a dumping ground. "Purchasing is the home of engineers who can't add, accountants who can't foot, and operators who can't run their machines," he grumbled.[8]

Today, the quality is rising: At least two American state universities, Michigan and Arizona, now offer M.B.A.s in supply management. Some companies now install top executives to run their procurement departments. People such as Kent Brittan, who runs UTC's supply operations, have the corporate clout to attract good staff and to persuade this highly decentralized company to accept a degree of centralized discipline. Brittan has even brought in his own human resources staff to augment the "legacy" employees of UTC's purchasing department with people who know their XML from their MRP.

In addition, the UTC purchasing department has built its own elaborate Web site, with news, articles, employee profiles, a glossary of financial and engineering terms, and information on corporate training courses. Advertisements in the company's corridors and elevators invite people to click on to this corporate portal, which also offers a gateway to electronic purchasing. The challenging goal is to make the Internet understandable and interesting to the multitude of UTC employees who might still think of it mainly as something to play with at home.

On such Web sites, companies place a single catalog, listing products at prices that have been centrally negotiated with suppliers. Then the staff must be persuaded either to buy from the catalog or to explain why they want something different. Such standard catalogs are among the key innovations that the Internet makes possible. The Internet's low-cost, flexible technology makes them available to everyone in a company who has access to a browser and allows them to include illustrations and even videos showing how a particular part fits or a tool is used. Even small companies can afford them.

Transforming the management of indirect purchasing will become one of the most reliable sources of corporate cost savings. As Brittan puts it, "If you don't get at least 10 percent out, something's wrong."[9] Savings arise from several sources:

- Central negotiation yields bulk discounts.
- Coordinated purchasing saves administrative and inventory costs. Individual employees take over the data entry that previously would have fallen to corporate departments. For example, Oracle claims to have reduced the staff in its accounts payable department by one-quarter, no longer needing employees who did nothing but enter data from handwritten expenses forms.[10] To persuade the staff to submit their expenses claims electronically, Oracle took the drastic step of announcing that it would no longer pay claims made on paper. Other transaction costs are reduced if the Internet can link the buyer's computer system directly with the vendor's. Until 1999, SAP's offices bought locally. Now, employees log on to a standard catalog, click on an item, and fill in an online purchase order. The order is then sent electronically to a specific vendor with whom a price has already been agreed. The system confirms the delivery date and handles the billing, closing the whole deal. Thanks to automation and the resulting enormous saving in staff, SAP has cut its internal purchasing costs by 80 percent.[11]

- Companies can curb rogue purchases. At IBM, purchases outside the procurement system accounted for 30 percent of the
  total in 1995. Within five years of setting up a central catalog,
  that number fell to 0.6 percent of total purchases of more than
  $45 billion a year. If people are to accept such discipline, they
  need a system that is quick and easy to use: Unless the system
  makes sense and saves money, they will quickly learn ways
  around it. IBM served its people well when it cut the purchase
  process for office supplies from thirty days to one, renegotiat-
  ing its contract with Staples, a large office supply company, to
  speed delivery.[12]

Other points at which staff spend a company's money can receive
similar treatment. For example, companies can improve discipline and
at the same time make savings in processing the costs of expense
claims. Cisco Systems, for example, has an application called Metro
that compares an employee's spending on travel and similar expenses
with the corporate average. If employees typically spend about $250
on a night in a New Jersey hotel, but one person spends $350, the sys-
tem automatically flags the expense and asks the claimant to fill in an
explanation. A couple of auditors review all flagged claims: If they dis-
agree with an employee's explanation, then they e-mail that person
and his or her manager. The process both educates employees about
what they are expected to spend and enables managers to check out-
of-line claims.

How far can such standardized purchasing techniques extend?
Some companies wonder whether they can use them to streamline
their purchases not only of photocopier paper but of legal and
accounting services. To do so would call for ways of specifying professional services, no easy matter. Yet even this may turn out to be possible. SAP, for instance, is working to define different levels of consultancy services, its largest single purchase. If it can do so, then it will
start managing its consultancy purchases in the same way as it now
manages its purchases of PCs. It thus would establish a direct connection between managing materials purchasing in particular and managing outsourcing in general, a subject dealt with in more detail later in
this book.

## Product Procurement

S AVINGS can also be made in companies' purchases of direct materials. But they arise in different ways because companies have
always handled such purchases differently. "Rogue" purchases are not
a problem, of course: No plant manager pops out to buy a few thousand unauthorized motherboards. In addition, companies generally
buy materials and components from suppliers with whom they have
worked on the design of the product and entered into long-term contracts, so a standard catalog may not be useful.

Indeed, while online purchasing of paper clips and hotel-room
stays is a relative novelty, many large manufacturers were buying
online long before the Internet appeared on the scene. Back in the
1980s, big companies pioneered the use of electronic data interchange, or EDI, in their purchasing departments, to transmit purchase
orders and invoices from one computer directly to another. So on the
face of it, the introduction of Internet technologies into direct purchasing of the materials and parts that companies use to make their
products involves less upheaval. The main issue appears to be how to
adapt existing proprietary electronic networks to the Internet. However, as companies switch from proprietary systems to the Internet,
they come to see that the Internet's apparent similarities to their systems are misleading. In fact, the Internet enables quite a different relationship between companies and their suppliers.

Early electronic commerce, of a sort, often grew out of the purchasing department. In industries such as food manufacturing and car
making, where suppliers replenish in large volumes, EDI was popular.
EDI brought—and still brings—a number of benefits that the Internet
replicates: Sending an order electronically is inexpensive, fast, and
accurate because passing information directly from the buyer's computer system to the seller's eliminates the inaccuracies that manual
transcription may introduce. In addition, unlike some Internet-based
systems, EDI is secure. However, EDI has several limitations:

- It requires an expensive proprietary network built on costly
  private lines. That locks together those buyers and those

suppliers that can afford to invest in it, but keeps smaller ven-
dors away.

- It cannot adapt quickly when market conditions are changing.
  Because EDI merely conveys transaction information from
  point to point—from the buyer at the center to and from the
  several suppliers as fixed spokes—it is poorly designed for
  negotiation or for anything resembling an auction.

- It excludes the retail customer. EDI travels over private networks from big buyer to big supplier; an order sent over the
  Internet can go from my home PC to start production in the
  plant of a distant supplier.

- It requires the development of an additional proprietary network to link purchasing to what happens within the factory.

As long as EDI depends on proprietary networks, its benefits are
confined to big companies and their big customers. Only if it migrates
to the Internet are the drawbacks of expense and inflexibility overcome. For instance, Tesco, a big British supermarket chain with 830
stores around the world, is using the Internet to exchange purchase
orders and invoices with more than 500 small and seasonal suppliers
that—unlike 1,500 larger suppliers—are not connected to its EDI network. Previously, small companies had replied to orders with telephone calls, faxes, e-mails—or even letters. Now, Tesco can process
purchase orders with greater accuracy and less clerical work, and it
has a better view of what is happening where.

In order to realize the full potential of online links between buyers
and suppliers, however, another problem must be resolved: that of
common standards. And the experience of EDI suggests that arriving
at a solution may be slow and difficult.

In the early years of EDI, electronic documents could pass seamlessly from one company's computer system to another's only if each
system recognized the document for what it was. Initially, working
parties for individual industries devised standards for the documents
they exchanged. Because the working parties tended to represent the
whole supply chain, the standards were initially industry-specific; and
because they tended to be nationally based, the same industry might

have different standards in different parts of the world. That caused havoc for businesses such as transport companies, which might have customers in several different industries in different parts of the world. Only over a decade or so did international standards start to emerge.

A similar problem now faces Internet-based commerce. XML, described in chapter 2, is a sort of virtual EDI: It allows information to pass from one company's computer system to another's. But it still requires agreement on the structuring of the information. Otherwise, companies will have to continue engaging in what Harvey Seegers, head of the business unit at GE that is developing B2B applications in this area, calls "swivel-chair e-commerce," in which companies take the order from the Internet and re-enter it into their existing proprietary network.[13]

Once again, several separate industry groups have been developing common formats, some industry-specific and some more widespread. America's gas industry has developed guidelines for exchanging electronic documents over the Internet. The automotive industry has built an exchange through which hundreds of subscribers can trade, the essence of the exchange being common standards and a secure network. The World Wide Web Consortium (at www.w3.org) has done a vast amount of groundwork to set XML's basic rules. And RosettaNet, an independent, not-for-profit consortium, has agreed on standard electronic interfaces to allow companies in the electronic components and information technology industries to swap business documents and to use defined business processes globally.[14] In addition, a United Nations organization is working with OASIS, a standard-setting body, to come up with global, cross-industry standards.

When a body or an industry owns a standard, it acquires tremendous commercial power and rewards—as Microsoft's profitability, built on its operating systems, clearly demonstrates. The struggle to create dominant standards for Internet-based commerce is at the heart of the attempts to build electronic exchanges. The larger the group of industries requiring a common standard, the more arduous the negotiations. Yet, without common standards, the full benefits of Internet technologies to purchasers and suppliers will never materialize.

## Electronic Marketplaces

IF YOU HAD ASKED almost any industry guru at the end of 1999 how the Internet would transform online purchasing, the answer undoubtedly would have included a reference to electronic marketplaces, probably coupled with one to online auctions. One of the ways that early B2B development drew on B2C ideas was in the widespread assumption that companies would make use of commercial replicas of such ventures as QXL.com and priceline.com.

No wonder: As it happens, auction theory has become one of the most fashionable branches of economic theory. And the Internet allows all sorts of ingenious kinds of auction to run. In economics departments around the world, university professors dreamt up intricate ways in which prices for everything from cod to chemicals could fluctuate to reflect promptly variations in supply and demand, in just the way that prices do in money markets. Entrepreneurs and companies rushed to translate such ingenuity into start-ups.

By the beginning of 2001, perhaps 1,000 exchanges existed, offering to trade everything from salt to janitorial services. In metals alone, there were between 30 and 100.[15] Many marketplaces offered auctions of products that have long traded on real-world marketplaces, such as shipping capacity and minerals. Others set out to auction such novelties as advertising space. Thus several companies were founded to sell off spare slots on radio and television and in the print journals. Many were owned by entrepreneurs who hoped to attract buyers and sellers and charge them for providing an online meeting place. Others were the children of giant companies. Within just a few weeks in February and March 2000, a group of big car companies decided to launch an industrywide marketplace; a clutch of giant aerospace firms, including Boeing, Raytheon, and Lockheed Martin, announced plans for a marketplace for aerospace parts and services; a number of pulp and paper companies, representing about a quarter of the entire American forest-products market, unveiled an exchange trading in their materials; and fifty grocery businesses produced a scheme for a marketplace trading "noncompetitive products," such as equipment and basic materials.

The overall impression was of an extraordinary profusion of business models. No wonder a 2000 poll by AMR Research, which specializes in following such exchanges, found that many executives simply could not understand what these creatures were.[16] No wonder Peter Boit, head of e-commerce solutions for Microsoft, said dryly in late 2000, "People are still trying to figure out how this thing makes money."[17] Fair point: A 2000 report by AMR Research found that not one of the 600 exchanges it studied had reached even 1 percent of the overall trading volume of its industry.[18] Like the small regional stock exchanges of the early twentieth century, most soon withered away, casualties of the Internet shakeout of 2000–2001. Many vanished without even making the transition from PowerPoint presentation to customer service.

The main casualties among the exchanges have been those that entrepreneurs set up to serve a market niche. One problem was the founders' assumption that conducting business transactions, and especially making direct purchases, was much simpler than it really is. Even where they already exist in the offline world, public "spot" markets, quoting up-to-the-minute prices for materials and components, account for only a tiny share of business purchases each year. Perhaps 80 to 90 percent of all business goods and services are traded through long-term contracts, often lasting for a year or more.[19] These one-to-one deals are hard to bring to the Internet.

Lots of other, more minor problems have cropped up. For instance, markets have found that buyers and sellers are unenthusiastic about paying simply for the privilege of dealing online. Those exchanges set up to buy and sell advertising space show the nature of the problem: People use them to find the best price and then go offline to call the rep and do the deal.

One implication is that exchanges must work to create trust and to deliver reliably. For instance, only a few of the early public marketplaces launched in the United States were able to offer a payments mechanism, allowing buyers and sellers to complete the transaction online. Instead, companies buying on electronic marketplaces frequently have had to print out the details and then enter them into their internal computer systems. In the future, many exchanges may partner with banks to ensure liquidity and enhance trust.

Agreed-on standards are also essential, as in other areas of purchasing. Markets have had difficulty displaying comprehensive online catalogs because companies have no universally agreed-on way of describing products. "Just setting up a supplier's catalog to participate in one exchange is difficult enough," observes one commentator. "Product names and highly complex data descriptions used by a supplier must somehow be standardized and integrated with the taxonomy of the marketplace. But most suppliers will want to participate in several exchanges, and somehow all the different taxonomies will have to work together."[20]

As for the exchanges that groups of companies set up to coordinate buying—or selling—in their early stages, they are mainly about aggregating procurement. No wonder these exchanges worry competition authorities. Covisint, set up (and later spun off) by four of the world's biggest car companies, was initially stalled because of fears that it breached antitrust rules. But markets take two to tango. They must benefit both buyers and sellers to offer a durable improvement on what already exists. If the main aim of a marketplace is to allow one side of a transaction to clobber the other, it will fail.

## Restructuring Purchasing

BECAUSE electronic marketplaces offer a genuinely revolutionary way of doing business, they will eventually bear fruit. As with every novelty, it will take time and much experimenting to get the model right. Indeed, there will be many models, some of them hybrids: With the Internet, there need be no one-size-fit-all solution. Undoubtedly, the number of exchanges will diminish. In most industries a single electronic exchange will exist—or perhaps one per country, and then one per time zone, as is occurring with foreign-exchange markets and stock exchanges. These will be the comparison-shopping, new-supplier exchanges. A different kind of marketplace will connect an industry's regular suppliers and purchasers in the ecosystems that the next chapter describes. Sometimes the two functions may be present on the same exchange, sometimes not.

At FreeMarkets, the granddaddy of electronic B2B marketplaces, the founders believe that a one-off electronic auction can provide the foundation for long-term relationships, separating price testing and the quest for new suppliers from the long-term management of the supply chain. Kinney argues that "buyers typically use the auction to determine with whom to establish the market relationship, based on excellent price discovery. But, once the auction is over, production parts are approved and tooling is installed, the working relationship can run for years."[21] That "price discovery," when it works, is not to be sniffed at. In the first five years of FreeMarkets' auctions, its founders claim, buyers ended up paying on average 15 to 16 percent less than their previous purchase price.

Some did even better. When a study team from Cornell University asked David Farr, the chief executive of Emerson, an electronics firm, about the results of using FreeMarkets, he boasted that some suppliers had dropped their prices by as much as 50 percent.[22]

In fact, that boast probably says one of two things: Either the purchasing department had not been doing its job for many years, or the suppliers were intending to negotiate to their previous profit margin at the first possible opportunity. Even when they test prices in this way, many businesses may still want to preserve their carefully honed relationships with their proven main suppliers. Das Narayandas, of Harvard Business School, studied five suppliers whose customers went to FreeMarkets and put the work out to tender. Four out of the five customers "were back knocking on their [old] suppliers' doors three months later." The new suppliers had underestimated, and failed to match, the huge value of customization in the contract.[23] Price testing alone is rarely the key to building a successful supplier relationship.

Many companies find that price testing is complicated by the care needed to define the exact terms. The bidding process invariably is preceded by a couple of arduous months of prequalification, during which the company and would-be suppliers nail down every variable except price: quality, size, timing, ability to deliver, and so on. Even pricing must have ground rules: Does it, for example, include or exclude tax? The need to be rigorous about specification may be an advantage in its own right and may give a company better control over its purchasing program. Again, the process of price testing may in the long run deepen the relationship with existing suppliers.

What of the marketplaces set up jointly by large companies, such as the automobile industry's Covisint? Their principal value may well be to establish a common trading standard so that buyers and sellers can easily exchange information electronically. They will put together the sets of rules that XML requires to function properly. They will also simplify interchanges in other ways: "It's a convenience for suppliers not to have to build twenty interfaces," says Ron Wohl, head of applications development for Oracle.[24] Indeed, electronic marketplaces have their greatest potential in driving standards forward.

The most useful industrywide marketplaces for existing partners to transact more readily with each other may be those like Kewill.Net. That company was set up not by a bunch of youthful business-school graduates with a clever idea and a bright algorithm but by an established logistics company to provide small and medium-sized enterprises with facilities that only large companies had previously been able to enjoy. Member companies can make transactions, and they can trace and control goods, right down to the size of a carton, as they move along the supply chain. The portal—for that is what Kewill.Net really is—also offers such value-added services as the automated completion of export and import documents if a company is exporting or is buying goods from abroad.

Some individual companies will create their own private exchanges to purchase goods and track their whereabouts, inviting a group of suppliers to join them. Hewlett-Packard and IBM both run large private exchanges, in IBM's case, linking more than 20,000 suppliers and handling some 400,000 invoices a month.[25] The pioneer, though, is GE's Trading Partner Network (TPN), which has simplified and automated the procurement process for GE divisions, and grew from an Internet prototype launched in 1996. Its aims were the following:

1. To achieve uniformity. The TPN allowed GE to swap the diversity of systems that had previously prevailed for a simple, uniform purchasing mechanism. GE staff simply open a file for the contract they are working on, download the relevant drawings from TPN, and forward the request for quotes

to any number of suppliers. There are no codes or account numbers to remember. Suppliers can learn the exact date by which they must submit bids, get immediate confirmation that their bids have been received, and find out whether they have won the contract. The gains for GE Lighting, the earliest adopter of TPN, have been typical. That unit cut its bidding-process time from twenty-one days to ten.[26]

2. To attract new suppliers. Many companies using the TPN were small or foreign companies that could not afford EDI. These new participants made the process more competitive, resulting in lower costs for some goods. In some cases, prices dropped 20 percent.[27]

3. To reduce errors in the ordering process. Because employees no longer had to retype information from faxes into a proprietary purchasing system, GE Hydro decreased its purchase cycle time by about 60 percent and, like the Lighting unit, discovered new suppliers, especially outside the United States.[28]

GE now has even grander ambitions. All its big divisions run their own Web marketplaces. Through them, it buys a growing volume of its supplies—it hopes eventually to reach 70 percent—and is widening the geographic range of its purchases. By posting its requirements on the Internet, GE has attracted so much interest from Chinese manufacturers that it has had to develop new capacity to ship supplies from Shanghai.[29] GE has also opened its electronic trading facilities to other companies and now links more than 100,000 companies.

Electronic marketplaces will generally bring simplicity and breadth at low cost. Beyond that, they may provide benefits that different companies will rate differently depending on their individual circumstances. When AMR Research asked 250 American companies what they wanted from an electronic marketplace, it came up with a surprising result.[30] At the bottom of the wish list was auctions; at the top, product search capability.

This is a remarkable ordering of the functions that the Internet performs as a marketplace. It does two main things: (1) It allows prices to be set in new ways, and (2) it helps buyers and sellers of products and services to find each other, increasing choice. The second is the true killer application. Helping companies to find the lowest price is useful, but helping them find something they otherwise could not find at all is wonderful.[31]

## The Consequences of Purchasing Online

C OMPANIES will never buy everything on the Internet, but they will buy more and more, especially of those indirect purchases that give them so much trouble.[32] As they do, they will gain speed, consistency, efficiency, accuracy, and staff savings—all terrific benefits. Many companies will find it a revelation to see for the first time what they buy, from which suppliers, in what quantities, and at what cost. At present, some suppliers (Dell Computer is an example) offer this service to purchasing companies, whose own internal systems cannot measure what their subsidiaries in different parts of the world are buying.[33]

As always, to make the most of the benefits that Internet technologies offer, companies must adapt their organizational structure and their culture. "To an individual at home," says UTC's Brittan, "the Internet means freedom: to surf at night, after work, looking for a holiday trip to the South Seas, a pink bicycle, or rare stamps. The business-to-business Internet world wants the individual to order against a defined list of items whose price and delivery schedules have been prenegotiated by the company, using a common system. For most organizations, switching to this new way of life is—because of the decrease of freedom—a wrenching cultural change."[34]

And what of the broader effects? Given its accessibility and its global reach, the Internet will surely allow companies to source even more of their purchases abroad. It will drive globalization onward, bringing prosperity to the developing countries that have adequate telecommunications networks and adequate levels of literacy and organization to make use of it. The effect will be to hold down prices in the rich world for anything that can be sourced abroad. "Instead of importing inflation, you import deflation," says GE Capital's Charles Alexander.[35]

Overall, though, the most striking prospect is the change that will take place in the supply chain. Indeed, the bold vision of some trading platforms is to go beyond the supply chain and to assemble an entire industry into something altogether more radical: a network or—to use the most fashionable word in e-business—an ecosystem, the topic of the next chapter.

# Chapter 7
## Strategic Suppliers

THE REVOLUTION in purchasing departments will not stop there. It will engulf and reshape the whole corporate supply chain. Indeed, this is the heart of the change that Internet technologies are driving through business. As companies struggle to reduce inventory and to achieve just-in-time delivery, they depend more than ever on the efficiency of their suppliers—and on their own ability to manage them.

Over the years, companies have progressively stripped slack from the supply chain. The emphasis on just-in-time delivery and on reducing inventory means that if one supplier gets it wrong, then no shock absorber cushions the impact. Disruptions such as those that followed the terrorist attack on the World Trade Center in September 2001 can thus cause havoc. At the same time, customers grow ever more demanding. The Internet encourages this. As one observer notes, "By putting up e-commerce sites that take orders at the speed of light, companies are training customers to place orders at the last second and expect overnight fulfillment."[1]

Yet supply chains for large companies are now immensely complex. Materials, components, and services may flow through the company from many parts of the world. Some suppliers may serve many customers; some may compete with or buy from a customer as well as supplying it. In addition, the very concept of the supply chain is altering, as companies think of it as a "demand chain" through which product is pulled by the customer's need rather than pushed by the production department's decision. This change is the result of the dramatic increase in information about consumer demand all along the supply chain.

Even with good information, a supply chain can still deliver nasty surprises. Managing supply has always been a crucial part of a company's business, but now the penalties for mismanagement are greater than ever. Many high-tech companies that thought they had created state-of-the-art supply management systems still found, in the early months of 2001, that their balance sheets were crippled because of the unexpectedly ferocious slump in demand and huge consequent rises in inventory. Some sank under the burden. Yet the basic techniques they began to develop will continue to influence supply chain management in the future.

If key suppliers are to get it right, they must have far better information about what is happening at all points along the supply chain. That requires a view of key suppliers as partners to be trusted, not as irritations to be overcome. Suppliers need something more than a purchase order once a month, based on historical trends and a bit of pencil sucking. They must be able to share a retailer's understanding of swiftly changing market behavior, and to know something of what their fellow suppliers are doing. Happily, the Internet will help all that to happen—although, as always, the prior requirement is for companies to make the necessary cultural changes.

The key point is that the supply chain becomes a web, with each strand both supporting and relying on the others with which it intertwines. Without a reliable and trustworthy relationship with suppliers, the complex edifice falls apart.

This chapter looks first at the increasing pressures on companies to manage their supply chains more tightly and then at the ways information sharing fits into that task. It looks at the difficulties that information sharing can imply. Then it examines the ways two contrasting companies—Dell Computer and Ford—have organized their supplier relationships to reduce inventory and increase flexibility. Finally, it draws some broader lessons about the implications of strategic supply management for companies in the future.

# Managing Inventory

I
N DEALING WITH SUPPLIERS, companies frequently have several
aims, which they trade off against one another. They want lower
prices, better quality, more innovation, more reliable delivery. They
also want to pare to a minimum the inventory they have to hold and
pay for. The most immediate influence of Internet technologies may
be on the first and the last of these requirements.

Clearly the Internet offers buyers ways to strike sharper deals with
suppliers, serving as a tool for aggregating demand and for driving
down prices by searching for less expensive suppliers in distant and
low-cost parts of the world. But the relationship between buyers and
key suppliers is more than just a matter of price. Indeed, the overall
cost of making a purchase may include not just administrative and
transport costs but R&D, speed and convenience of delivery, and the
ability to boost or cut production swiftly.

Companies that lean too hard on price have always put at risk
their long-term relationship with their suppliers. In 2000, Daimler-
Chrysler, the big—and beleaguered—German automobile company,
tried to strengthen its position in the American market by persuading
its parts suppliers to cut prices by 5 percent. Several auto-parts suppliers decided to recall their truckloads of components from Chrysler
factories, and others simply refused to make the cut. How ironic:
Only four years earlier, Chrysler had won praise for creating an American *keiretsu* by encouraging its suppliers to propose improvements in
logistics and products and then splitting any subsequent savings with
them or giving them extra business as a result.[2]

The history of inventory management has often been one of the
changing balance of power between manufacturers and retailers. In
the 1980s, a manufacturer of, say, sports shoes could afford to accumulate inventory until shoe shops placed their orders. That inventory
served a useful economic function, which is now easily forgotten: It
allowed production to be spread evenly over time, thereby creating a
nicely efficient flow of output. And because shoe shops would unload
it at predictable times, the inventory did not represent too much risk.

Most of the risk lay with the shoe shop, which would have to cut prices if customers did not turn up.

Then, with the arrival of the just-in-time concept, retailers and distributors grew less willing to carry the costs and risks associated with inventory, so they shifted both back to their manufacturers. In turn, since the production process might take several weeks, manufacturers built up safety stocks in case of unexpected spikes in demand. In addition, the demand for greater choice and for incessant novelty increased the likelihood that some makes and models would not sell and would have to be discounted.[3]

Mistrust between companies and their suppliers, lack of information, and delays in the supply chain can easily aggravate inventory problems, in a way demonstrated by a simulation model that Peter Senge, who wrote a book on the subject, called the Beer Game.[4] A retailer selling a special beer notices an increase in demand and sends an order to the wholesaler, who in turn sends it to the brewery. But delays in brewing and delivery mean that by the time the order arrives, the retailer and the wholesaler have accumulated lots of unfilled orders—even though the original increase in demand was a one-off event. So they send in extra orders to cover the backlog and end up awash in beer that cannot be sold, at which point, unless retailer, wholesaler, and brewery realize their error, the whole process may swing into reverse.

The key to improving inventory management lies in providing better information, something that the Internet is extremely good at doing. "Inventory . . . is the physical embodiment of bad information," asserts Paul Bell, head of Dell's operations in Europe.[5] The prudent company must promptly disseminate throughout the supply chain all the information it has about changes in demand, and its interpretation of them. Suppliers can then be left to make their own decisions about how to respond.

Better information allows greater certainty. That in turn allows more accurate forecasting of demand, and thus lower inventories. As levels of information increase, so does certainty. But no company is ever likely to have good enough information to achieve absolute certainty and thus get rid of inventory entirely. Indeed, the experience of many U.S. high-tech companies in early 2001 was that even state-of-the-art technology might fail to predict sudden changes in demand, with ghastly consequences for inventory. The challenge for companies is to use information to balance the risks of such sudden changes against the costs of holding inventory.

In markets where demand fluctuates widely and rapidly, buyers cannot lose sight of these points. If they do, then they will move from just-in-time to just-out-of-stock and then, perhaps, to just-out-of-business.

## Exchanging Information—and Trust

THE INFORMATION that companies share with their suppliers typically takes three forms, says Hau Lee, director of the Global Supply Chain Management Forum at Stanford Graduate School of Business:[6]

1. Companies exchange information such as demand forecasts and sales data. These exchanges allow better planning. As in so many other areas where firms swap data electronically, companies quickly realize the need to define common standards for information such as point-of-sale and inventory data, so that each can interpret the other's material. Indeed, the discipline of common standards is fundamental if sharing data is to be meaningful. If a company wants to share quality information with a supplier working with several of its own divisions, then the definitions of what it is measuring and the scores given should be the same.

2. Companies exchange knowledge. Lee cites a customer-supplier relationship that has become a byword for intimacy but that used EDI long before the Internet mattered. When Wal-Mart's Florida stores ran out of mosquito repellent during a heat wave, the company discovered that Warner-Lambert, a subsidiary of Pfizer and the producer of the repellent, tracked weather forecasts to spot future peaks in demand. By sharing that knowledge electronically, both companies could do better.

3. Companies exchange the right to make decisions. Often, it is enough for one company in the supply chain to make the decision to move. For example, if Wal-Mart stocks more Pampers, then Procter & Gamble, which makes the diapers, and 3M, which supplies the sticky tapes, need not have three separate decision-making processes for a single product. So these companies developed a system that allows one company to decide for all three.

Such projects are called "vendor managed inventory," or VMI, and they require a striking degree of trust between a company and its suppliers. Of course, shrewd companies do not necessarily rely on trust alone. A variation of VMI is "jointly managed inventory," or JMI, which the parts division of Saturn, the car company, uses to ensure replenishment of dealers' stocks of parts and repair-completion rates for car owners. Saturn makes the decisions about the timing of restocking—but dealers must cope with angry customers if things go wrong, and dealers must pay up-front for parts. To spread the risk, Saturn has set up a centralized inventory system to locate parts quickly when a dealer unexpectedly runs short. If a part is not used within nine months, then the retailer can return it to Saturn for a full purchase-cost credit.[7]

Such combinations of incentives and assurances will bolster the exchange of trust that is the core of the evolving supplier network. When a computer company makes changes to the specification of a product, using software to alert all its suppliers, it must trust the suppliers to make the consequent changes in the components they produce.

Even greater trust is required to hand over the management of computer applications or a key database to another company. Long ago, of course, companies outsourced their links with customers to the mail and the telephone. Now, though, they may outsource not just the management of their servers and their networks but the provision of software applications and even the management of customer knowledge that underpins their entire business. With the emergence of application service providers (ASPs), some companies no longer own and maintain the software for their computer applications but buy it as they need it and have computer applications delivered from central-ized ASPs.[8]

Such outsourcing is quite different from buying electricity from a remote, specialist provider. After all, access to electricity is hardly a competitive advantage in the way that ownership of unique software may be. Allowing another company the responsibility for keeping your corporate secrets requires quite a different level of trust from allowing it to supply your power.

## The Benefits of Integration: The Dell Experience

THIS EVOLUTION of the supply network is easier for some compa-nies to accept than others. In spite of the difficulties facing the high-technology business, Dell Computer has experimented with new possibilities. The Internet is, however, only a tool: It does not solve all problems. Although sharing information is essential to integrating supply networks, it raises awkward issues of confidentiality and trust.

The central truth that companies such as Dell grasped early on is that shared information is the secret of an efficient supply network. In effect, Dell posts its actual manufacturing schedule on a private extranet—a walled-off bit of Internet—for suppliers. Suppliers benefit greatly when they can see their customers' production schedules and sales data because that information allows them to plan for the volume and timing of orders. They can react at once rather than wait for trickle down. This kind of information exchange was possible with EDI, but Internet-based networks allow such communications among many suppliers, big and small. Making information available simulta-neously along the supply chain turns the chain into a network.

The Internet allows a further refinement. Dell's suppliers know not only how fast Dell is using their components but also what fin-ished products customers are ordering. When a customer places an order by clicking on the company's Web site, the software immedi-ately feeds that order into the production schedule and informs the customer when the order will be ready to ship. Once the order is in the system, suppliers can see it coming and start making the appropriate parts. They can grab the information they need straight from Dell's systems and plug it directly into their own. Thus the Internet turns the company into a sort of portal—a semiprivate exchange—through which orders arrive for redistribution among suppliers.

This approach improves forecasting and so reduces the amount of inventory held all along in the supply chain. In the computer business, where prices change fast, inventory is potentially lethal. The average price of components, which account for 80 percent of the cost of a computer, drops by 1 percent every fortnight. So every day that can be cut from stocks saves computer manufacturers money. In addition, whereas most companies borrow money from the bank, use it to pay for the manufacture of a product and its storage until a customer comes along, and then sell the product, companies like Dell, with integrated supply chains, reverse that process. First, they take an order and (with retail sales) payment from the customer, then they build the product. The result is less need for working capital.

Dell increasingly passes on the information shared with its own suppliers to the second tier of companies that supply them in turn. Texas Instruments sells digital signal processors to Solectron, which incorporates them into motherboards that Dell buys. Dell has considered sharing some of the data that it already passed to Solectron with Texas Instruments too. Dell's ultimate goal is for all computer manufacturers that buy hard drives and all suppliers that produce them to make information about the market as they see it available anonymously on an electronic exchange. Establishing such an exchange would allow the whole industry a clear view of the balance of supply and demand. It would create a market as transparent as financial markets or as the marketplaces once found in country towns, where everyone could see exactly what was for sale, who was buying, and perhaps even how much buyers were paying.

The effect is to bind manufacturer and supplier tightly together. The manufacturer's infrastructure also becomes the suppliers'. Where once it might have taken two weeks for even quite an efficient company to pass information about its production program to its suppliers, now the information can be shared almost the moment it is available. Dell thus creates a triangular "information partnership" with its suppliers and customers by treating them as collaborators, who jointly find ways to improve efficiency right across the manufacturing process and share the benefits.

Working so closely with suppliers brings additional benefits. For example, it allows the speedier introduction of technological innovations. Every year, computer companies like Dell make well over a thousand evolutionary changes in the design of their products—creating what are really new models.[9] Without close liaison, that pace of change makes enormous demands on suppliers. Indeed, one software product automatically notifies everyone along the supply chain when a change takes place.

However, such openness raises many uncomfortable questions. Some of the information that companies share with their suppliers is stuff they would hate to see in the hands of competitors; some of it would knock down the share price if leaked to investors. Word of canceled orders travels fast and stock markets react swiftly. Companies must be certain that the benefits of closer collaboration outweigh and minimize such risks.

Moreover, once companies can get into each other's internal systems—as they must, for such arrangements to work—firms that supply several competing purchasers must have reliable "Chinese walls" to keep customers in separate compartments. Companies typically require that suppliers use different teams to work on their competitors' products and that the suppliers permit them to do random and unannounced security checks on their premises. But those precautions will not avoid a further difficulty: the supplier who uses the skills developed in its core competence also for a rival purchaser. So the more intertwined companies and their suppliers become, the more important a culture of trust will be.

## The Difficulties of Integration: The Automobile Industry

PLENTY of other companies in older industries would dearly love to emulate pioneers such as Dell. But the younger companies have some important advantages.

- They are less set in their ways. Dell began in direct sales, so it does not suffer the conflicts that plague most traditional companies.

- Most are one-product companies. Dell designed its assembly process around direct sales and has great flexibility to alter the design of a product to meet consumer demand. Established firms, with much more complex product lines, have difficulty integrating even their in-house supply operations, let alone those with myriad outside firms.

- Dell has remarkably few suppliers: 200 in all, with 30 companies accounting for about 78 percent of its total purchasing. Conventional large computer companies frequently have about 1,000 suppliers—in other words, they opt for width, not depth. Dell does the reverse.[10]

Not surprisingly, many older companies would love to pursue this kind of integration. Among the most enthusiastic are American automobile manufacturers. However, applying Michael Dell's bright idea to Henry Ford's legacy is not easy. Most cars are simply not built like Dell's computers. While Dell is organized around direct sales, American automobile companies have vast dealer networks.

This affects the whole relationship between manufacturer and customer. In Europe, most cars are built to order—which means customers have long waits to get exactly the right model and finish. But in the United States, most cars are built for stock. The customer therefore sees only what the dealer ordered two or three months earlier. Stocks of finished automobiles clutter the dealers' lots, tying up billions of dollars of cash—while customers still complain that they cannot find the car they really want. A dealer who guesses wrong needs to persuade customers to buy in order to move the stock and reduce the interest-rate burden. The consequent discounting wreaks periodic havoc with margins.

Dealers are not likely to disappear, although their role is changing. For buying a new car differs from buying a computer, and that influences the shape of the distribution channel. Brian Kelley, who came from GE to run e-commerce at Ford, says, "Most customers planning to spend $25,000 to $30,000 on a new product want to see and test it first. Besides, 80 percent of people who buy a new vehicle have an old one to trade in."[11] And cars need servicing from time to time. The initial challenge is therefore to find new ways to use dealers (see the discussion of channel conflict in chapter 3).

Ford's strategy is therefore different from Dell's and perhaps a more appropriate model for other established businesses. It uses the Internet to deepen relations with distributors as well as with suppliers. Like the high-tech companies, Ford has found that technology is no magic bullet: Its relationship with one of its principal suppliers, Firestone, went through hell and back in 2000–2001. Again, Internet technologies cannot prevent a relationship from turning sour. But they can provide tools to deepen a relationship that works.

Thanks to the Internet, Ford is rethinking its relationship with its distribution chain. For the moment, the vast majority of cars sold in the United States are still sold from the dealer's lot: 15.9 million in 2000, compared with a mere 300,000 sold by Internet "locate-to-order" methods, where the Internet helps a customer to track down precisely the preferred model. However, Forrester Research expects the second category to grow rapidly, to 4.4 million by 2006, while traditional lot sales fall to 11.7 million.[12] Ford, like other big car companies, therefore sees dealers evolving into delivery channels for online services such as FordDirect, which allows customers to configure, select, price, finance, and order a new car or truck through a Web site and then pick it up from a dealer.

Ford also hopes to use Covisint, and the common standards that the trading platform will create, to share its demand forecasts and inventory information with its suppliers. Ford wants to reach both the front line and those further along the chain: Indeed, the geographically more distant suppliers may gain most from the widening impact of the technology, which will bring them more and more accurate production and market data.

But Ford also knows that creating a network of this sort will be neither simple nor swift. Linking together not just the legacy systems within one company—hard enough, goodness knows—but the legacy systems of many companies, some of them very large, will be the challenge. The putative savings of between $1,000 and $3,000 a car will materialize only if Ford links all these disparate systems. "It will take years to play out," admits Kelley.[13]

And that is not the only challenge. The very nature of the production process limits Ford's ability to become more like Dell. For example, the color of a car is usually determined early in its manufacture, before the metal is even stamped. Eventually, automobile companies may have to refit their plants so that they can build cars more to demand rather than to sit on a dealer's lot. But when they do, they will hit exactly the same problems as those sports shoe manufacturers discussed earlier in this chapter. Without ways of smoothing out peaks and troughs in demand (a virtue of inventory), capacity utilization will decline and costs will rise.

The trick will be not only to offer different delivery times to customers at different prices but also to make the manufacturing process more modular and less sequential. For example, the basic platform will be built for stock and then speedily turned into the vehicle the customer orders. How much easier that is for a green-field operation in which a company starts a car plant from scratch, as Mercedes-Benz has done with the Smart car, a two-seater automobile of eccentric design built at a plant in Hambach, France. The plant, the staff, even most of the suppliers—all came fresh to the automobile business. Even the design grew out of an association with Swatch, better known for its inexpensive, cheerful watches.

As with Dell computers, Smart cars are built mainly to customers' orders. A customer can specify details on a terminal in the dealer's showroom, from which the order goes directly to the plant. As with Dell, too, the Smart's manufacture involves relatively few suppliers: seven companies supply 70 to 80 percent of the finished vehicle's volume and another sixteen supply a further 20 percent. Suppliers tend to be located nearby. The final assembly of the car takes just four and a half hours, far less time than in any other plant in the world, and the overall lead time is two to three weeks—compared with up to six months for some popular models of other European cars. Moreover, once assembled, the car can be transformed even faster: The clip-on side panels allow a dealer to change its color in an hour. One aim is to keep the customer in touch with the dealer, creating the sort of long-term relationship that many manufacturing companies now hope to achieve.[14]

It must be said that Smart cars have not been best sellers, perhaps because—in spite of their vaunted design—they are not inexpensive. Nor has DaimlerChrysler (which owns Mercedes and had other things to worry about in the late 1990s and early 2000s) introduced many

Smart concepts into the rest of its car making. However, modular processes such as those that the Smart car uses will be at the heart of the build-to-online-order process. Frank Piller, an economist at the Technical University of Munich who has studied the ways companies customize a basic product line (a process dubbed "mass customization" and discussed in chapter 3), offers a nice image: "You need modular production that fits together like Lego blocks."[15]

## Strategic Supply Management

BEFORE THE VOGUE for electronic marketplaces began, many companies had already begun to rethink their supply chains. The systems installed in the 1980s and 1990s, and EDI in particular, allowed big companies and big suppliers to work more closely together. Here, as in so many areas, the coming of the Internet brings a change of degree, reach, and cost—not a complete novelty.

For example, collaboration is simpler and extends readily over thousands of miles as more suppliers may now be on the far side of the globe. Internet technologies extend a company's reach, but even before they came along, the migration of low-cost production to Asia and Latin America meant that many products that wear a Detroit car maker's badge or a Californian computer company's brand were really the product of an elaborate international web of assemblers and suppliers. As the world becomes a single machine,[16] companies must not only work with suppliers with a different language, time zone, and culture—but also rely on them and trust them more than ever.

However, some of the key aspects of supply chain collaboration do not involve communications. Companies learn to undertake joint development and to share their quality systems with their suppliers. That requires identifying their own core skills and, above all, building trust. Add in the Internet, and such aspects acquire even greater importance.

Take outsourcing, an issue that predates Internet technologies but that is accentuated by them. Companies at the hub of a supply network must begin by asking themselves two questions: What are they best at? and How many suppliers do they really need?

In answering the first question, they will find that another firm would do many of their activities better. These tasks should be outsourced. Indeed, even those activities that they do as well as any other firm would often be better outsourced. Companies must focus all their creative energies on the areas that they do best. To see the consequences for the structure of the firm, turn to chapter 8. For the moment, note that the more companies outsource, the more they depend on their suppliers, who become as important to their survival as the firm's own departments used to be. When the supplier provides bad service, so does its customer company.

Answering the second question should lead companies to reduce the number of their suppliers and then choose a few as partners. The two go together. By reducing the number of suppliers to a manageable number, a company can forge a closer relationship with them—and ideally, also offer the advantage of larger and more consistent orders. A study of supply chain management by a group of consultants at McKinsey found that the companies that made the most effective reforms generally cut the number of suppliers by 40 to 50 percent. "They then select a few with which to work closely and play off the rest against each other."[17] A handful of "strategic" suppliers should be included in discussions of new product designs and in work with customers.

Thus with suppliers, as with customers, companies need to be selective. In both areas, the Internet offers a chance for strategic relationships to grow closer because the technology allows customers and suppliers to connect with each other's systems. The McKinsey study reported on the successes of several (anonymous) companies. For example, one large fast-food company reduced the number of its suppliers so that it could work closely with the remainder to improve their performance. The result has been several years of annual cost reductions of 4 to 5 percent—and also faster and more innovative product development.[18] An automotive manufacturer brought suppliers into the development process. In one case, a development team collaborated with a supplier to redesign an instrument panel, cutting the number of parts by 30 percent, the number of assembly steps and materials specifications by half, and the development time from years to months.[19]

Now, companies increasingly cooperate to share the costs of bringing new products to market and to reduce the uncertainty. Using suppliers to foster innovation has additional advantages: It allows a big company to cast a wider net, capturing good ideas generated in other businesses. Indeed, some evidence hints that the company may increasingly share development work with a supplier in another part of the world. For instance, a rapidly growing share of the inventors who register U.S. patents has co-inventors living in foreign countries.[20]

In the future, companies are likely to build more intricate relationship with their suppliers. They will want to glean almost as much information about their suppliers' practices as they would from one of their own subsidiaries. So companies now question their suppliers in ways that once would have seemed intrusive. The questioning, though, inevitably relates to the extent to which companies depend on some of their suppliers.

One of United Technologies Corporation's practices exemplifies the way such relationships are moving. UTC has been developing artificial intelligence tools to identify problems at suppliers' plants. At present, it sends inspectors to visit suppliers, routinely checking for problems such as inefficiency, poor quality, low maintenance, and excess inventory. But such inspections are inevitably rare and somewhat superficial. Soon, suppliers will fill in data directly, and software will audit their answers for inconsistencies that might reveal inaccurate supplier accounts. UTC will pinpoint problem areas automatically and, the company says, work with suppliers to resolve them. Why bother? "Lowering suppliers' margins is nice," says the company's Kent Brittan, "but it can't go on forever. The next big thing is to lower suppliers' costs and improve their lead times, delivery schedules, and so on."[21]

In an extension of this idea, the automobile companies have already begun to offer consultancy services to suppliers. They dispatch people with expertise in law, finance, and systems integration to talk with suppliers and help them to solve problems. The big company thus assumes a new role, and supply management becomes *supplier management*.

In the future, supplier management may increasingly extend beyond issues of product quality and service into areas of ethics and social responsibility. Big companies already want to know not just what the supplier is producing but how the product is being made. Environmental groups have put pressure on companies such as Nike and Reebok to establish guidelines that their suppliers in Asian countries must meet, guidelines not only about the health and safety of their employees and environmental standards but even about issues such as sexual harassment and equality of treatment for men and women. Just a short time ago, the notion that a company should concern itself with what its suppliers did about such issues would have amazed us. No more. In today's Internet-connected world, environmentalists and human-rights groups in one corner of the planet can quickly launch a global campaign against a corporate giant in another.

The way a company works with its suppliers defines its own moral stance. Too often there is ambiguity here. Many companies on the one hand demand high moral standards—often, it must be said, American standards that may jar in some countries—while on the other squeezing prices. Companies must decide what matters most and strike a balance between shareholder profits and how to achieve them.

## Spreading the Network

NOTHING will extend corporate use of the Internet faster than the supply network. Once big companies take or make orders only online, their customers and suppliers will quickly comply. The Web's open standards, easy accessibility, ubiquity, and global reach will all drive its use. As small companies discover its potential, they will become integrated into the supply network far more closely than in the past.

One striking effect will probably be on the business cycle. Since the late 1980s, American manufacturers have steadily reduced the value of the inventories they hold, relative to sales. This has saved money: One report estimates that the fall in inventory has saved U.S. companies some $10 billion a year—a cumulative $115 billion since 1988.[22] In addition, the transition to a just-in-time economy has implications for economic slowdowns. To judge by the slowdown of 2000–2001, they will become sharper but perhaps shorter. In the past, when demand grew more slowly, companies took months to adjust their inventories, prolonging the slowdown and amplifying a mild deceleration into a recession. Now, they cut immediately, sending powerful tremors right across the economy (and the globe).

As for the effect on corporate structure, that eventually will be to turn a company inside out. Companies will intrude into one another in all sorts of ways. The old boundaries that once defined a company will become less clear. The relationships that once existed among individual departments inside a firm now exist in its supply web. But while those earlier links were often of the hub-and-spoke variety, with lots of departments reporting upward rather than talking to one another, the links that the Internet allows, both within a company and outside it, will be more like a web. They can run sideways and diagonally as well as up and down.

So suppliers can converse with other suppliers at the same level as well as with customers and with their own second- and third-tier suppliers. What will be the potential of that? Nobody yet knows for sure. But if development and production grow more modular and less sequential, with more activities conducted simultaneously and collaboratively, then a web will be far more useful than a hub-and-spokes, let alone a chain. The potential for reorganizing the rhythm of supply and production is only just becoming apparent.

# Chapter 8
# Corporate Structure

WHAT SHOULD a company look like? In the early years of the past century, the Ford Motor Company thought that a wise company should own every stage of its entire production chain. It even bought a rubber plantation to ensure that it owned a source of the raw material for making tires, and fleets to ship its materials across the Great Lakes. But go back three centuries earlier, to the first joint-stock companies of all, and you find a quite different sort of creature: a bunch of people banding together for a single project—a perilous trading voyage to the East Indies, say—and disbanding when the task is done.

Will either of these models become the norm as companies work out how to integrate the Internet into their operations? Or will both flourish, together with lots of other new models? The key issue will surely be which model makes the best use of clever and creative people, turning their intangible assets into valuable, viable business plans and products in the ways that chapters 2 and 3 described. In an age of abundance of physical and financial capital, it is human capital that will be the rich world's limiting resource. The corporate structures that will do best will be the ones that best suit the brightest workers.

Some of the more imaginative forms the company of the future will take are discussed in chapter 10. But here, consider an effect that the information revolution is already starting to have. It is beginning to pick companies apart, to disassemble and reassemble them along new lines. No longer is a company a rigidly designed machine with parts that fit together in one way only. Now, corporate structure needs different metaphors. Companies will resemble constellations more than pyramids and be more Hollywood than hierarchical. Corporate structure grows diffuse and fluid, more kaleidoscopic in design. The patterns shift, and the component parts, sometimes locked tightly together, are at other times pried apart, like fabric held together with strips of Velcro. Franchises will be more important and will assume new shapes; so will alliances and partnerships with other firms. Horizontal integration will flourish as companies concentrate on doing what they best understand. New entrants—"plug-and-play" companies, which pull together a bunch of services provided by other firms—will spring up more quickly and increase competitive pressures.[1]

The changing costs of communicating and managing information are transforming the economic forces that underpin the integrated modern corporation. In the ominous title of an influential book on the subject, the arrival of Internet technologies means that many businesses will be "blown to bits."[2] Hardest hit will be the vertically integrated firm, but many businesses will find that what they thought they did best can also be done by unexpected new competitors, while the proposition they had scarcely noticed is where their true value lies.

One way to visualize what is happening is to think of the many parts that make up a company's business as pieces of a Lego kit. Managers now have potentially many more different types of blocks to play with. The challenge is to think creatively of new ways to put the new blocks together rather than assembling them in the ways they have always done in the past.

Internet technologies have other impacts on corporate structure. They reinforce the trend toward flatter, less hierarchical structures. They allow people in the middle of a business—the point at which its key competencies are most likely to lie—to communicate directly and easily with each other, even when they work in different business units or in different countries or in different languages and time zones. No longer does line management have to be the conduit. Ideas can travel more readily across normal reporting boundaries than via the hierarchy. For many people, the erosion of hierarchy will be painful: It destroys a source of power and status, truncating the old promotion routes. Companies must think carefully about ways to motivate long-term staff in the flatter firm without offending them or appearing to discriminate against them.

And what about scale? Will companies tend to be larger or smaller? Early views of the Internet's impact on corporate structure emphasized how the new technology razed barriers to entry and allowed small companies to compete on a more equal footing with big ones. Then came a host of giant telecoms and media mergers, culminating in 2000 with the takeover of Time Warner by AOL, the largest acquisition ever. Patently, the effects of the communications revolution on scale are not the same in every industry.

With rich, low-cost communications, the tasks of coordinating and managing a monster business certainly will become technically easier. And some of the characteristics of new markets lead to concentration. But these are not the most important considerations. The real test of size, as of every other aspect of corporate structure, will be its impact on recruiting and on making the most of scarce talent. If good people prefer small companies over large ones, then big firms must emulate the small to retain the staff they need. If big is boring, then the best employees will go, regardless of the economy's ups and downs.

Whether the best people want to work for giant corporations or for themselves is likely to change over time. People's preferences are shaped at least partly by experience. A long period of prosperity and security, such as the one the United States enjoyed in the 1990s, will make good people more eager to become free agents, amassing clients rather than working for a single big boss. A bout of recession and economic and political insecurity may alter that for many. For companies, too, an era of tight labor markets encourages ingenious ways to rent scarce talent by, for example, becoming the best client of a star employee who takes the free agent route. When times are slack, companies can more easily persuade the best to join the payroll. Outsourcing, similarly, may swing with fashion and the economic climate: Fragment services into too many small pieces, and the inevitable result will be trouble, with no clear responsibility for actual delivery. Ownership gives control and security of supply.

The influence of technology is to widen the range of choices available to companies and to their best people. The economic barriers to becoming a free agent or to outsourcing a division are now lower than ever. That is not, in itself, a reason for making the change—but it removes a substantial reason against doing so. The choice becomes clearer; opportunities abound to ask fundamental questions about the ideal structure that a particular business requires in order to thrive.

## The Changing Economics of the Firm

THE COMMUNICATIONS revolution alters the economic pressures on companies in many ways. It changes the external pressures that encourage concentration within an industry into a few large firms, and it changes the internal costs of running a business. The effect will not be the same in every industry. In many, starting up a business will become easier, as will remaining small and profitable. But the underlying economics, for some time to come, will encourage scale.

In a world of networks, a powerful winner-take-all effect operates. People use AOL's Instant Messaging service because lots of other people also use it; they sign up with the cell phone network that most of their friends belong to; they use eBay because it is the largest online retail auction and so they are more likely to find what they want. Large networks are disproportionately more valuable than small ones. Networks—such as cell phone networks—may interoperate, but at a cost; and so the government often has to step in, as with cable television or banks, to retain competition and to curb the natural pressures of scale.

In some markets, another factor kicks in: increasing returns to scale. It costs millions to create new drugs, software, movies—but then just pennies to make each extra copy. High fixed costs and tiny variable costs give such industries enormous potential economies of scale. Creating a new computer game may take months, but once it exists it can be distributed online at no cost at all. In markets that can combine increasing returns to scale with network effects, big players score a double win: Each extra sale not only reduces average production costs but also increases product values to other users.

The huge success of Microsoft's Windows in the 1990s showed just how profitable and powerful these winner-take-all effects could be. But nothing is forever. New challenges to Microsoft's hegemony—not just its legal troubles but also the rise of Linux, of Java, of mobile devices that do not incorporate Windows—suggest that no company is too large to be spared the threats from changing technologies.

At the same time, other changes make life easier for new entrants. One of the main messages of this book so far is that the Internet alters the basic economics of running a business. Properly used, it can chop the transaction costs of collaborating and paper shuffling and invoice processing. Yet these transaction costs (and the search for ways to minimize them) have been one of the main forces shaping companies throughout the industrial era.

That idea goes back some seventy years, to 1932, when a twenty-one-year-old professor named Ronald Coase gave a lecture to students at the School of Economics and Commerce in Dundee, Scotland. Five years later, in 1937, the lecture became a paper, "The Nature of the Firm." This work won Professor Coase, now a professor emeritus at the University of Chicago's law school, the Nobel Prize for economics in 1991.[3] But Coase has lived long enough to see the dawn of a neo-Coasian era, in which his work has moved from the economic journals to new popularity as a way to explain the impact of changing technology on corporate boundaries.

If the market's success is striking bargains and setting prices, then, Coase asked, why does it not dominate all economic activity? Why doesn't each person, at each stage in the production chain, work as a solo profit center, just as a farmer once hired a laborer by the day and sold produce to a trader who sold it on a market stall? The answer, argued Coase, is imperfect information and the importance of minimizing transaction costs: the costs of searching for the right deal, of negotiating the right contract or terms, and of coordinating processes such as producing and marketing.

A company can either buy materials, parts, and services in the marketplace, or it can produce and own them itself. A supplier will probably charge a lower price, but against that, the company will have to spend time and money searching for the right partner, negotiating the price, agreeing on the terms, and drawing up a contract. Such costs do not show up in the price that a company agrees to pay when, for example, it arranges for another firm to manage its car fleet or host its Web site. But they are costs nonetheless, consuming management time and attention, and the more a company uses a succession of short-term contracts, the higher those costs may be.

Many transactions therefore take place within a company. Instead of endless on-the-spot bargaining, a firm effectively makes a succession of long-term contracts: an agreement, for instance, to pay an employee a certain sum of money at monthly intervals in return for obeying, within limits, the instructions of a manager. The worker may willingly forgo the chance of bumper earnings in some years for the security of a regular wage. Such deals turn out to be better ways to recruit and deploy a well-educated work force than the sort of daily auctions of the impoverished and unskilled that were once used to recruit dock laborers and are still used to hire agricultural workers in some parts of the world. Long-term relationships with workers bring other benefits, especially important in companies that depend mainly on complex human skills and ingenuity for their competitive advantage: Often an employee may not make a profit for a company until after several months or even years of employment.

Coase quotes a phrase from Dennis Robertson, a British economist of the early twentieth century, who spoke of firms in relation to the market as "islands of conscious power in [the] ocean of unconscious co-operation like lumps of butter coagulating in a pail of buttermilk."[4] Companies adhere, like the butter, only when it is more efficient to coordinate activities that way than to do so among independent entrepreneurs in the buttermilk pail that is the open marketplace.

For much of the past 120 years, the butter effect has been on the rise. Indeed, the changes in communications and the declining cost of managing information throughout most of that period have increased, not diminished, returns to scale.

Companies have grown larger and more complex. One in every ten of the companies in the Fortune 500 in 1994 was founded in the single decade of the 1880s. The reason is partly the fall in the cost of managing information. When Alfred Chandler, the grandfather of business history, looked at the birth of big corporations in the decades after 1880, he pinpointed information as the crucial factor. Until then, most companies were partnerships—a structure that had hardly changed since Elizabethan times. The big corporation that sprang up in the late nineteenth century was a completely new kind of economic institution, producing and marketing goods on an unprecedented scale for national and international markets, and requiring a new kind of structure. This kind of "managerial, integrated corporate enterprise" was possible because of the nineteenth century's communications revolution, built on the railway, the steamship, the telegraph, the cable, and a unified standard for time.[5]

Even in the final decade and a half of the twentieth century, the largest companies were growing increasingly large and complex. In 1999, the average annual revenue of the fifty largest public companies in the United States was about $51 billion, 70 percent higher than it had been fifteen years earlier, even after allowing for inflation. More than fifty public companies employed more than 100,000 workers; in the mid-1980s, only eighteen did so.[6] These vast empires, sprawling across continents, would have been completely beyond human control had it not been for the fall in the cost and the improvements in the reliability of electronic communications.

Now, though, the fall in the costs of communicating and of acquiring information is having a more diffuse effect on companies. Costs of acquiring and using information are declining: The search for the best price, the best product, the best buyer grows easier and less expensive as applications of the Internet grow more sophisticated. Companies therefore face a more evenly balanced choice about how much to concentrate on what they are good at and how much to buy other goods and services from outside.

Because almost everything can be inexpensively outsourced, it is possible to go from idea to product in nine months. Many Internet start-ups—not just the high-tech ones—are, as it were, plug-and-play companies. Many small firms can now access services that were previously affordable only to big companies. At the simplest level, a small company no longer needs to employ an accountant, a typist, or a telephone operator; instead, it can use accounting software, a word processor, and voice mail. No longer are small businesses excluded from dealing directly with big buyers who use EDI; they can scour the world for customers on the Internet as inexpensively as any giant can.

But what is possible will not necessarily be the path that every company chooses. Indeed in some industries, especially in those with lots of increasing returns and network economies, the typical company will grow larger, not smaller. However, the evenly balanced choice will create competition between a company's internal facilities (such as its human resources department) and external service providers (such as search firms). Internet technologies now make arm's-length transactions easier to set up, monitor, and control.

## Outsourcing

OFTEN, the biggest changes that Internet technologies bring are not headline-grabbing innovations but new efficiencies in existing business models. Over time, the results may be just as revolutionary. Take three examples: outsourcing, franchising, and alliances. For different reasons, all now become more important forms of corporate organization.

Outsourcing is hardly a new concept. Clothing companies have used it for years, dividing in various ways the tasks of designing, manufacturing, and retailing clothes. One of the most experienced outsourcers in Europe in the second half of the twentieth century, Britain's Marks & Spencer, sold only its own brand goods, made for it by suppliers who worked for it mainly or entirely. It managed its suppliers so that, provided they did exactly what it wanted, they could always run an adequately profitable business. Because almost all the suppliers were in Britain, they knew the market as well as Marks & Spencer and so they could contribute to product innovation. Proximity allowed Marks & Spencer to communicate easily with its suppliers and enjoy quick delivery times. Sadly, the company eventually became overpriced and uncompetitive, and lost its way. Outsourcing is not a panacea or an alternative for astute management.

Internet technologies, however, do give outsourcing a new lease on life. Not only do they allow much closer coordination between a company and its contractors; they also allow the outsourcing of corporate functions that once would have appeared to be core.

To understand "modern" outsourcing, consider Nortel Networks, a Canadian company that specializes in building high-performance Internet networks. At the end of the 1990s, Nortel decided to move from vertical integration, owning many stages of the production process, to what it dubbed "virtual" integration. It therefore sold off fifteen manufacturing facilities around the world that made products such as printed circuit boards. Large manufacturers such as Solectron,

SCI, and Sanmina bought the plants, which were already selling to Nortel and now signed new long-term supply agreements with the company.

Like so many high-tech companies, Nortel suffered terribly in 2001 from collapsing sales and excess inventory. However, like others, the influence of its pioneering business structure is likely to outlive its financial troubles. The contract manufacturers to which it outsources a great deal of work have a far larger turnover than Nortel alone and can therefore enjoy greater economies of scale in highly price-sensitive businesses. The contract companies can also afford to keep track of the fast-changing manufacturing technology of the particular components they produce and to invest heavily in the components' development. Nortel, previously having spread its resources across many different products, had risked being left behind.

The switch to virtual integration also gave Nortel flexibility: If a large order arrives from a particular part of the world, production easily can be arranged nearby. Most important, by retaining the highest-value part of the manufacturing process at a number of "systems houses" worldwide, staffed with people skilled in industrial and test engineering, virtual integration allowed the company to specialize in what it does really well.

The reorganization also changed the way Nortel deals with its suppliers. In the days when Nortel owned most of its suppliers, an order might take up to three months to fulfill. Now, orders for some products take mere days. Using an in-house Internet exchange, the company can circulate an order instantly to a galaxy of sixty potential suppliers. Chahram Bolouri, president of global operations, says that he now devotes most of his time to recruiting and keeping high-quality talent to manage the supply chain, and to ensuring that everyone along the chain is kept constantly up-to-date about the company's plans.[7] The company thus concentrates on what it does best rather than merely on what it could do as well as any other similar business.

Rich communications make outsourcing more efficient and attractive. In some industries, this may perversely reinforce a trend toward concentration: A few large global manufacturers—which may draw on thousands of suppliers and sell to hundreds of buyers—will supply a whole industry. One model is the aircraft industry, where world production of large civil aircraft today is in the hands of two airframe companies and three engine manufacturers, with many customers and many more suppliers. Such a trend, a potential corollary of the decline of vertical integration and rise of outsourcing, would be likely to take hold in manufacturing, an industry in which many services must cater to local tastes and inspire trust in local buyers. But companies such as GE Financial Services increasingly "manufacture" financial products such as store cards that local companies then market under their own brands.

In other industries, though, outsourcing will help new entrants to gain a foothold. Many of the new consumer-electronics firms, such as Palm and Handspring, ship many thousands of gadgets but do not own a single factory. Their success is built upon the growth of those same contract manufacturers, such as Flextronics and Solectron, that sell to Nortel. Once, a company that aspired to be big in consumer electronics had to build and run a vast plant, using cheap labor in some corner of Asia. Now, because contract companies will manufacture for anyone, even the smallest start-up can sell devices made on the same production line as those of Sony or Panasonic. The rise of the contract manufacturer has thus dramatically lowered the barriers to entry into the business and so helped to transform it.

Thanks to Internet technologies, companies are now beginning to go further, outsourcing core corporate functions rather than just the peripheral elements of a business. Payroll operations have long been outsourced, but now the entire accounting function could be handed over to an outside company. As Juha Laaksonen, chief financial officer of Fortum, a Finnish energy company, says, "Before immediate electronic access, outsourcing accounting would have meant delays in receiving the numbers from the accounting company. But once it is possible for a company to connect directly to the accounting company's system, the CFO and other people in the department can have immediate access to the numbers, just as if they were in-house. This will also mean that a CFO can randomly check that everything is on track." He believes that the only core financial functions that a company really needs to have in-house are strategic corporate financing, performance management, and skills in mergers and acquisitions. Everything else can be done outside.[8]

When companies ask themselves which activities to outsource, the answers will not always be obvious. The "Coase audit" will sometimes produce unexpected results. The basic principle that a company should outsource everything that is not essential to its competitive advantage requires some qualification. For instance, companies must think about the availability of talent they have at their disposal and how they can best deploy it. They need to consider issues such as reputational risk: A supplier's unreliability or unethical behavior can damage a company's brand. And they should think about the risks entailed in putting commercially sensitive information into the hands of an outsourcer that may also work for a competitor. The key point, though, is that the decision can now be made on basic business principles; questions of cost and of technical feasibility matter less and less.

## Franchising

THE FRANCHISE is a well-established way to give many small businesses the benefit of a common brand, common training, and common production methods. For the new entrepreneur, joining a franchise is safer than starting out alone because it involves doing something that many others have successfully done before. The business is proven. And the franchiser saves on capital costs—useful when capital is expensive. So franchising is an inexpensive and speedy way to scale up a good idea.

However, franchising has big limitations. Most obviously, it is extremely rigid: a McDonald's hamburger or a leg of Colonel Sanders's KFC may look or taste subtly different, depending on whether it is made for the palates of São Paulo or Seattle, but the differences are marginal. There are local variations in the taste of Coke (as the aficionado can discover by visiting the World of Coca-Cola in Atlanta), and a branch of McDonald's in Prague will serve Czech beer. However, the fundamental experience—the environment, the furniture, the service style, the decor—is universal. That is not surprising. The brand that is the basis of a franchise demands consistency. Another limitation: New ideas tend to flow in one direction only—from the head office to the restaurant. These limitations may explain why many of the most successful franchises are rather downscale: A one-size-fits-all cup of coffee must not only be exceedingly easy to prepare in a foolproof way; it must taste the way the mass of humanity expects a cup of coffee to taste.

Now, with the help of the Internet, franchises can acquire new characteristics. Innovation can spread more easily from the bottom up, as best practice discovered in one restaurant can be rapidly deployed around the world. A future franchise might set wider bounds to the freedom of each new store. It might look more like a geographically dispersed cooperative or a medieval guild than a hierarchical organization with ideas mainly handed down from on high.

A possible template is the Great Harvest Bread Company, a bakery based in Montana with about 140 outlets. It aims to "combine the fun of doing it yourself with the quick learning that comes with being part of a community."[9] One part of the plan is a franchise agreement that puts much looser limits on owners than most do. In the first year, new owners serve an apprenticeship; after that, they work within a few operating guidelines, with plenty of freedom where the company does not see any case for limiting it. The franchise agreement says nothing, for instance, about service quality or cleanliness—assuming, no doubt, that an eager owner does not need to be told that a successful store must be clean and offer good service.

Even more interesting is the emphasis on creating a community of owners who learn from each other. "We spend nearly all of our operating budget on things that cause us to connect one owner with another and thereby cross-pollinate the best thinking in the system," the bread makers boast.[10] They encourage owners to share bread recipes and promotional tips. After all, the owners are a perfect example of a "community of interest": a group of entrepreneurs who do not compete but are all much the same size and all in the same business. Given plenty of freedom to experiment, they often find that what works in one local market also wows another.

## Alliances

I F OUTSOURCING and franchising are two ways of tying together more-or-less separate businesses, alliances are a third—although usually temporary. Again, alliances are not new. In one of the most famous European examples, back in the 1980s, Matra, a French defense company, came up with the novel idea of a big, square car but had no expertise in automobile marketing or distribution. It took the idea to Renault, and the result was the Espace, the first "people carrier," which made good profits for Matra and developed a new market in people carriers for Renault.

At the least, the Internet will make alliances more common, partly because they are a way to connect suppliers in a corporate ecosystem. It will also make the management of alliances easier, by improving the trust and the communications that are so essential. An ecosystem will require a magic ingredient to make the difference between mere coherence and wild success. Alliances that allow managers to share information and ideas comfortably between companies in an atmosphere of openness are the ones most likely to flourish.

Even before Internet technologies had become important, the popularity of alliances appears to have been growing rapidly. Counting alliances is not easy: Whereas mergers, like marriages, are legally defined and so easily recorded, alliances are more like love affairs in their transience and many variations. But one writer estimates that they accounted for about 10 percent of the revenues of America's 1,000 largest firms in the early 1990s and double that by 1997.[11]

Most new alliances seem to be driven by the need to break into foreign markets. Outside the United States, nearly all alliances are cross-border ones. In businesses where local knowledge is particularly important, such as retailing, cross-border partnerships are essential. Other new alliances are frustrated mergers. Sometimes, they are attempts to circumvent the restrictions that government competition and antitrust policy impose; sometimes, ways to dodge the rules that governments often use to keep out foreign ownership by preventing cross-border mergers in businesses such as airlines, television, and telecommunications. All these businesses, built around networks, would otherwise establish a few global giants. Indeed, the huge Star Alliance, which includes Lufthansa and United Airlines, began as a series of loose arrangements to share codes and direct passengers to partners' flights but now looks more like a quasi-merger, with shared executive lounges and pooled maintenance facilities but limited sharing of customer information and frequent-flier points.

Another kind of alliance allows companies to spread risks, dipping a toe into a new market without losing a lot of money. Forming alliances also allows a company to poke a finger in many pies to see which one tastes the best. Alliances may aim to minimize several different sorts of risk, but one common sort is technological. Here, alliances have allowed pharmaceuticals companies to pick the brains of smaller biotechnology companies: In almost a decade, between 1988–1990 and 1997–1998, the number of biotech alliances among the top twenty pharmaceutical firms rose from 152 to 375.[12] Alliances of this sort, allowing companies access to rapidly developing new technologies, also leave open the possibility of moving on if something better comes along. Equally important, they allow big companies a way around the sad fact that many of the bright scientists whose ideas they most need do not want to work each day for a corporate titan.

Of course, companies do not form alliances only with other companies. More and more, their search for innovation creates links with universities and government-funded research bodies. Some of these links work better than others: Academics do not always respond well to companies' demands, and companies sometimes suffocate good research. But universities have become an increasingly important source of new corporate ideas, for business plans, for new technologies, and for innovative products.[13] One model that seems to work well is that of the MIT Media Lab: Companies pay to sponsor it but cannot tell the Media Lab what research to do. Researchers come up with off-the-wall ideas and basic research that the sponsors are free to commercialize. Corporate sponsors thus neither dictate nor get sole ownership of the ideas that emerge.

In its days of feverish innovation, the Internet created lots of strange alliances, as new online companies sought to create novel bundles of products to sell. Thus Streamline, an Internet home-shopping service, would deliver its customers a cup of coffee and a video. The first came from Starbucks, the second from Blockbuster. In that alliance, a new company put together the products of two well-known brands. More logical is the Amazon approach: See how many alliance partners' products you can stretch a well-known brand across, using the Internet to direct shoppers easily to their offerings.

Brand extension is always tricky, even online. Streamline was one of the dot-com deaths of fall 2000; Amazon is becoming part of Wal-

Mart. But forming alliances remains an inexpensive way for companies to experiment with packages of products, to determine whether customers will buy more if they are offered a bundle than if they are offered individual products one at a time.

In no situation is collaboration more important and more difficult than when two companies with different corporate cultures (and perhaps different nationalities) are trying to work seamlessly together. Whereas connections in the alliance partners have tended to run from the top people down to the staff, in the future many lines of communication will directly connect staff at many levels in each pair of allied firms. All the tools that help to enable collaboration within companies can also help to bind alliances together. They will be the Velcro that allows companies to form and reform in the clusters that are likely to be the hallmark of future corporate relationships.

## Structures for Innovation

THE INTERNET unleashed an extraordinary wave of innovation. It is not just the basis of new products, many of which doubtless remain to be discovered and exploited. With its collaborative power, it also improves the process of innovation, making it easier for inventive people in a company to work together—and to watch what innovators in other businesses are doing. As a result, new ideas may arise internally or may increasingly come from a network of companies, each working on a different part of the project.

The process of innovation itself is changing, becoming more diffuse, now occurring at many points throughout a company or an industry. It is also more likely to be a half-accidental evolutionary improvement in a product than the deliberate outcome of research and development in a laboratory. Some of the most vibrant innovation is occurring not in manufacturing but in service industries, and especially in individual business units, where people run an operation and understand what is needed.

Companies must organize themselves to capture, channel, and finance new ideas. This can be difficult for big, established companies, where it is harder to innovate and harder still to exploit innovation.

There are good reasons for that. Gary Hamel, a management guru, complains that they listen poorly, that one person often controls the internal market for capital, and that many companies have a strong aversion to taking risks that makes them excessively conservative. And that is not the whole story. In addition, markets for brand-new technologies are often small and chaotic, with lots of recently devised products vying for customers. The instinct of a big company is to concentrate instead on proven technologies and business models that produce a reliable cash flow. That is why the dot-com revolution was spearheaded mainly by completely new companies, such as Amazon.

Undoubtedly, companies require structures that allow the emergence of new technologies. But those same structures must also enable incremental improvements in processes and products. Indeed, this is often the point at which significant value can be added. Moreover, once it is clear that innovation is largely about refinement and process, it becomes essential to collect ideas from people who are actually doing the job at the moment rather than confining the search for new ideas to a separate part of the business. So companies must find ways to draw good ideas from the majority of their employees rather than simply from a few creative spirits in R&D. Some companies are good at listening to suggestions; many others are not. "The last bastion of Soviet planning is your own organization," says Gary Hamel. "Ideas have to fight their way up. In Silicon Valley, the average venture capitalist gets 5,000 unsolicited business ideas a year."[14]

Of course, lots of those prove to be flops. But if companies want to increase the flow of ideas, they need innovation in their process of innovation. So some experiment with electronic equivalents of the suggestions box. For instance, Wal-Mart employees earn cash rewards for submitting ideas to cut costs or enhance service, and their ideas are transmitted throughout the corporate network, partly through the company's internal magazine. CAP Gemini Ernst & Young, the global management consultancy, has tried to mimic the developers who band together to write new software by creating what it calls an "open source" strategy for innovation. The consultancy has installed an "Innovation Intranet," based on proprietary software, to monitor, archive, and analyze ideas. The software periodically flags the ideas that interest most people so that they do not languish on the virtual shelf.

That is important: People will soon stop generating ideas if the company does not seem interested in their views. Often an idea advances because a director likes it or because the person who comes up with it is a good communicator. If companies have transparent structures for evaluating ideas—even something as simple as peer review—then their employees are more likely to contribute them. As with customers, so with their staff: Good companies may want to ensure that they have several channels of communication.

Important, too, are the incentives to contribute. These may not necessarily be financial, or at least wholly financial. The lesson of the development of open source software is that inventive people may want recognition even more than cash.[15] Companies can develop ways to give creative people nonfinancial rewards. Just as firms need to look at where they add most value to the consumer, they must also look at the points where they add most value to the employee and then build on these.

In-house incubators give greater authority to the bright idea. Many incubators are revamped versions of old R&D departments but aim to act faster and to generate a stream of new ideas for the whole business. For example, at Spaarbeleg, a small division of Aegon, a Dutch insurance company, any employee who comes up with a good idea can assume responsibility for its development. Ideas that the division's top management team likes can be developed quickly and then passed across to Aegon.[16] Another example of an in-house "skunk works" is Boeing's Phantom Works, which is a "tool for sucking knowledge out of different parts of the huge company and squirting it into a business plan."[17] Scientists and engineers from different parts of Boeing come into this unit on three- or four-year assignments before returning to operating businesses.

Both of these arrangements work because senior management backs them. For example, Boeing's bosses see the Phantom Works as a central part of the strategy to drive the business forward. This championing is essential: Good ideas, whether they come from individuals or from incubators, go nowhere unless they can make the difficult next step from brainwave to business proposition. A McKinsey study argues that companies should think of themselves as "opportunity-based" organizations, and that managers should see their corporation not as a portfolio of business units but as a portfolio of "opportunities to create value."[18] The trouble is, large companies tend to be built around formal structures—of career paths, of accountability, and of decision making. Value-creating projects have an awkward way of cutting across formal boundaries and of needing to plunder resources from other departments. As is so often the case, true change is likely to call for corporate reorganization in order to be effective.

In spite of their problems with generating innovation, big companies may sometimes do so less wastefully and more durably than venture capitalists. Europe's dot-coms were mainly spin-offs of blue-chip companies such as France Télécom and Vivendi Universal. Europeans bewailed the absence of venture capitalists. But Silicon Valley, though more vibrant, wasted more investors' money in pursuit of the new. When innovation can take place within existing corporate structures, it may be less exhilarating, but it may also have a stronger future.

## Structures for Entrepreneurship

COMING UP with new ideas is, in a way, the easier part of innovation. Turning them into successful business propositions is the harder. Here, the challenge for established companies is to harness the entrepreneurial energy of their own people.

Part of the trouble is that many entrepreneurial people simply do not want to work for big firms. These people chafe when companies refuse to take big risks or insist on keeping too large a share of the rewards of success. But often, the snag is that the new venture simply does not sit comfortably beside what a company is already doing. It does not gel with the existing portfolio, say, or it threatens to cannibalize an established and profitable market. A new business model may bring staff problems if new employees, with different expertise and different views on rewards, work just down the corridor from existing staff.

One common strategy is to create an independent subsidiary to experiment with new ideas. Yet this strategy may also deprive the parent company of the energy that the new business generates. "That's why I tell companies to take all the juice and put it in one place," says Forrester Research's George Colony.[19] But a separate subsidiary, depending on who heads it, may be free to take a new technology or business model in unexpected directions. Sun Microsystems created JavaSoft in 1996, an independent subsidiary to develop and market products based on Java technology. Sun continued to concentrate undistracted on its high-margin server business. Meanwhile, JavaSoft quickly spotted the fact that Java's commercial potential lay in areas such as cell phones and network appliances rather than (as Sun originally thought) as a challenge to Microsoft's grip on PC operating systems.[20]

Increasingly, large corporations act, in effect, like investment trusts, taking stakes in promising new young businesses, or like venture capitalists, nurturing and advising start-ups. Intel and Nokia, for example, both have what are essentially internal venture capital funds. However, the pioneers here are the pharmaceutical companies. To harness the entrepreneurial ventures of small independent biotechnology companies, they generally build alliances, giving the biotech firms access to cash, marketing, and distribution in return for a call on their intellectual property.

One version of this approach, easiest to apply in a company whose business is research and development, is to turn staff into entrepreneurs. This is the strategy that Bell Labs, AT&T's former research division, pursued when it was spun off in 1997. Bell set up the New Ventures Group to handle technology that did not fit into the company's current business lines, to help researchers to develop financial plans, and to attract venture capital.[21] As Arun Netravali, head of Lucent Technologies (as Bell Labs subsequently became), puts it, "If you try to nurture that new thing in the same organization, with that same set of people who are today managing fairly substantial businesses using older technology, it becomes very difficult for this new thing to get much attention."[22] The scheme provided a halfway house for those Bell Labs employees who had come up with good ideas but who might not think of themselves as entrepreneurs.

By 2001, Lucent had become yet another innovative high-technology company in dire straits. However, its pioneering ideas, like those of its peers, are likely to influence many less turbulent companies. In Lucent's case, its New Ventures Group had identified two dozen projects by fall 2000. Lucent Technologies had chipped in some $225 million and raised $150 million in outside venture capital. Not every project was a winner: Two did not make it even to the spin-off stage.

Three had been brought back into the parent company, and one—Talarian, an Internet company—had gone public.

Along the way, Lucent learned two important lessons. First, it needed a group of young business-school graduates who also had the technical expertise to help evaluate ideas and develop them into workable business plans. These "entrepreneurs-in-residence" might also join a new venture as chief executive or chief operating officer to get it off the ground. Second, it should not try to finance its new ventures alone. Its early, quite understandable, instinct was to keep total ownership of proprietary ideas. But the group soon realized that outside venture capitalists brought added benefits that more than compensated Lucent for relinquishing part of its stake. For one thing, they had experience in launching start-ups; for another, they had wonderful contacts. Best of all, their reputations were such that having their names on the investor list could raise the chances of success.

Another version of corporate venture capitalism was developed by Reuters, the global media business. John Taysom (who persuaded Reuters to take a stake in Yahoo! in 1995, when the Internet company was still a start-up on the Stanford University campus) set up Reuters's Greenhouse Fund. The fund also has stakes in some seventy businesses, including such interesting companies as Infoseek and VeriSign. In 2001, Taysom and a senior colleague planned to lead a management buyout of the fund. Up to then, however, the fund had backed projects that could potentially benefit Reuters in the form of appropriate new technologies. For example, one of its investments, Digimarc, developed a product to watermark sports pictures on the Web to prevent copyright infringement.[23] The fund has always encouraged its offspring to share and collaborate. More than twenty of the seventy or so companies in its investment portfolio deal with one another. Indeed, three worked together to develop and launch Dynamai, an Internet caching technology.

Just as important as sharing ideas may be sharing talent—maximizing the use of human capital and minimizing the use of financial capital. Small companies may be exciting places to work for a while, but they rarely offer much opportunity for career development. So when a large company brings a number of small ones together under its wing, it not only overcomes one of the problems with being large, but it may also offset some of the disadvantages of being small. Big companies can create some of the sense of working for a small group by forming well-structured teams. In addition, they can offer employees some of the potential benefits of scale, which may be the opportunity to work abroad in other offices, greater job security, training and education programs, or even the simple advantage of not having to explain to outsiders what your company does.

## Market or Function?

ONE OF THE OLDEST dilemmas of organizational architecture is whether to build around functions or markets. In the past, large companies have usually opted for function, mainly because that arrangement best achieves economies of scale. So there is a purchasing department and a sales department, a research department and a finance department. Managerial skills typically reflect these divisions: The salesperson is a different breed from the finance boffin.

When it was easier to communicate internally upward or downward than inside to outside, companies found that functional division had big advantages. Now, that is changing. In most companies, some sort of functional dividing lines will persist. But a psychological effect of emphasizing function is to create a business in which production matters more than the customer and supply more than demand. The divisions that produce the product or service push it out to the customer; the customer does not pull what he or she requires out of a responsive organization.

Some companies have therefore moved to an organization based around market instead. In 1999, Microsoft replaced a technology-based organization with a customer-based one. Other technology companies, such as Hewlett-Packard and Sun Microsystems, soon did the same, as did AT&T and Harley-Davidson. All set out to give the global customer a single point of contact. In such "front-back" organizations, the lead comes from the people who deal directly with customer segments. They pull from the back the products or services the customer wants.

Lots of companies talk about putting the customer first; few have an organizational structure that really does so. The aim must be to create a culture in which the whole organization becomes more sensitive to what its customers want and to changes in their requirements. Ideally each group in a company thinks of other groups as their customers when it hands on a task or a product. By making feedback much more immediate, corporate intranets help to implement this thinking.

Indeed, without communications systems that allow the customer-facing part of the business to talk easily to every other division, the task of putting the customer first is almost impossible. But even with such systems in place, this transformation is enormously difficult, and it often requires a monumental cultural shift toward sharing information and communicating between a firm's divisions. Companies with territorial and secretive cultures will find that shift extremely painful.

Multinational companies face a different version of this problem. There, tension has long existed between managers responsible for an individual region or country and managers responsible for an individual brand or product line. That bifurcation is giving way—albeit slowly—to a trend toward treating the regional manager as a sort of hotel keeper and local emissary and giving primary responsibility to global section heads. When PricewaterhouseCoopers surveyed 400 chief executives in 1997, it found that only 39 percent had reduced the influence of geographical leaders.[24]

The sheer ease of global communications will drive this process forward. In the words of one study, companies need to treat foreign subsidiaries as "peninsulas rather than as islands"—as extensions of the company's strategic domain rather than isolated outposts.[25] They may sometimes be able to use subsidiaries to incubate new business ideas that will work outside the home market. But they will also handle centrally many tasks that regional chieftains formerly needed to control.

At Oracle, for example, several functions, such as IT, legal affairs, and marketing, that once reported to the country management now report centrally. All the financial people around the world report to the group's chief financial officer, Jeff Henley, whose office is in Redwood City, south of San Francisco. Making such a strategy work requires ferocious determination at the top. "There was tremendous ill will when we took marketing away from the country managers," Henley recalls. But Oracle argues that such centralization is essential to gain speed, productivity, and coherence. "You have to ask which things can be globalized. There is very little difference in how our software should be marketed and sold around the world. People often say, we're different. It's not true: they *do* do things differently, but it's not necessary."[26]

Not every company will agree. Some will feel that if local people lose too much authority, the company will sacrifice an ability to respond to the particular tastes and needs of local customers. For communications can also offer a way for big companies to behave in local markets like sensitive small ones. This benefit is perhaps clearest in consulting and advertising. In both businesses, the middle-sized national business has more or less gone, bought by huge multinationals, whose only rivals are small local boutiques. With a corporate intranet, a consultancy can, for instance, have a team of experts on energy based in the United States or in Britain. When a customer in Italy needs advice, the team can provide it, and the Italian office can add nuances of the local market. That allows the firm to compete efficiently with national companies, which might have to pay heavily to get such expertise locally, especially if it were not needed full time.

With devolution, as with outsourcing, Internet technologies remove the cost barriers that once drove choice in a particular direction. The sophistication of communications will allow more of a company's operations than ever before to be managed directly and daily from the corporate center. The balance of advantages is therefore much more even. Companies will make decisions about devolution on business grounds, not because cost or technology forces the issue.

## The Shape of Future Companies

AS THE COASE EFFECT works through companies, reducing the costs of collaboration and communication and increasing the rates of innovation and knowledge deployment, the shape of the firm will evolve. Change will come gradually, not dramatically: This will be evolution, not revolution, and therefore more durable. Moreover, the Internet will not be the only force driving change. Others, such as globalization and the constant search for talent, will also have a continuing impact.

The company that emerges will be a looser structure than today's, with fewer hierarchies and tiers of management. It may sometimes undergo the same transition as a Hollywood studio, which once employed everybody from Lana Turner to the sound technicians. Today, the studio is more like a finance-house-cum-marketing-department. Studios have retreated to their core role: To make a movie, they now assemble teams of the self-employed people and small businesses who are today's stars and technical support.

The Internet will push other industries in a similar direction. Companies will find it easier to outsource or to franchise. They will use communications to develop deeper relations with suppliers, distributors, and many other partners that might once have been vertically integrated into the firm. Some companies will end up as aggregations of smaller firms, bound together by corporate culture and communications. Some will manage projects, as Bechtel and Schlumberger do, assembling teams of specialist businesses, some on their payroll and some not. When the project is over, the teams will disband, to reform with some different players for the next project. Like the manufacturing process itself, company structure will become more modular.

An implication is that corporate structures are becoming more heterogeneous at exactly at the same time as power at the center—over standards, systems, and the like—is growing stronger. The company is becoming simultaneously more centralized and more diffuse and open. Internet technologies will enable the company of the future to choose the appropriate structure in much more flexible ways. The Lego blocks can be assembled, disassembled, and reassembled indefinitely. Corporate leaders constantly will have to manage the tension between centralization and decentralization. But at the core of the structure will be freer transfer of information between communities, teams, divisions, and companies.

As assemblers and coordinators of business processes, established companies will thus play a different role from today's. Their strengths will lie in their ability to assemble projects quickly and nimbly; in their coordination skills and technologies; in their brands; and above all, in their ability to attract and retain the best people. The management of human capital will be the key skill for running a successful business in the years ahead.

# Chapter 9
# Leading
## and Managing

T O RUN a company well calls for a rare mix of skills. It requires breadth of vision and attention to detail, toughness and compassion, patience and alacrity, charm and audacity, good health, good sense, and good luck. Most of today's effective corporate leaders should do well in the company of the future because leadership and management will remain essential skills. Internet technologies will not alter that, but they will change the balance of skills that companies need at the top.

Already, running a large company is a complex, exhausting task for several reasons:

- Technical change is relentless, and managers must keep abreast of it and understand its implications. Discontinuous change is especially tricky because it forces companies to operate differently, not just better.

- Information, whether an earnings forecast or a nasty rumor, is more instantly ubiquitous, accessible, and uncontrollable.

- Capital markets expose companies to speedier and more arbitrary discipline.

- Globalization has sharpened competition and spread corporate interests and stakeholders far and wide.

In the coming years, corporate leaders will continue to anticipate and respond to change—but not change merely for the sake of revolution.

Incessant disruption distracts, unnerves, and produces few results. Peter Brabeck, chief executive of Nestlé, argues that the best sort of change involves "just constantly challenging people to be better, day by day, bit by bit."[1]

However, the injunction of GE's Jack Welch to "control your destiny or someone else will" reminds managers to watch constantly for change and differentiate between manageable and uncontrollable changes. Managers may not always control discontinuous change, although if they benefit from it, they may well revolutionize the business, as Michael Dell revolutionized the business of selling computers. But every manager can continuously improve how the business operates.

In everything, managers must remain nimble. They must make decisions—preferably good ones—fast and wisely, as noted in chapter 2. They must adjust swiftly and appropriately. In reality, plenty of big companies still resemble the Bell System in 1962, which its then chairman, Frederick Kappel, described as "a damn big dragon. You kick it in the tail, and two years later it feels it in the head."[2] Only seismic shocks, such as takeover bids, can speed the process, and those may destroy more value than they create.

The greatest challenge, however, is maximizing a company's access to talent and intellectual capital. Executives must therefore excel at spotting and recruiting talent, handling the complexities of rewards, and managing clever people around the world. Here, corporate needs pull managers in two directions. On one hand, collaboration and teamwork matter more, so companies must find ways to motivate and reward good team players. On the other, companies also require the occasional star, who may earn more than the chief executive. Running a business may resemble managing a sports team—a group of competitive superstars who need coaching collectively but who also know exactly what their individual talents are worth in the market. Phil Jackson is the modern model: a good basketball player and a great basketball coach, once of the Chicago Bulls (and Michael Jordan) and now of the Los Angeles Lakers (and Shaquille O'Neal). Both are champion teams with extremely valuable players because Jackson understands how to persuade the stars to play as a team.

That is why executives must also use a company's best people frugally. As good people become a company's most valuable asset, the company must manage them just as skillfully as it does its physical and financial assets. That means creating opportunities for collaborating and exchanging ideas and then turning good ideas into prompt action. Because time and talent are the two scarcest resources in any business, executives must waste neither.

## Managing Communications

MANAGING CHANGE calls for world-class communications skills, and Internet technologies give companies and chief executives new and more versatile tools for communicating: John Chambers, president and chief executive of Cisco Systems, estimates that he uses e-mail or voice mail—tools that did not exist a few years ago—for at least 90 percent of his communication with employees.[3] However, if corporate leaders use these tools to talk to employees around the world, then they must understand how different cultures respond to pep talks. What invigorates American ears may irritate the Brits and vice versa (just try transporting cricketing metaphors one way across the Atlantic or baseball idioms the other way).

To guide a company through trauma, leaders must perform well not just in the privacy of the boardroom but in public, too. They must be engaging speakers, sharp thinkers, and compelling characters on a telephone conference call to analysts or in a Web cast or a chat room with customers, and via satellite to journalists halfway around the world. That requires mastering the art of connecting with several different audiences at once—a skill in the politician's repertoire—and across media.

To some extent, perhaps, such tools are like drawer space: The moment you have it, you fill it up. The superabundance of messages probably results from the simple fact that more people now have more ways to communicate with still more people. Indeed, to rise above the noise, communicating with investors, suppliers, partners, customers, employees, trade unions, and the government, already constitutes a greater part of a corporate leader's job than it did a generation ago. Wayne Sanders, chairman and chief executive of Kimberly-Clark, the giant paper manufacturer, recalls spending about a day a month communicating with investors and the public when he first took the job in 1989. Now, he spends a day a week. Large investors want continuous access to a corporate leader; multiplying media outlets want the same but preferably in clever sound bites and tailor-made suits.[4]

A corporate head must manage publicity just as skillfully as a politician and devote as much care to the internal as to the external audience. That may create new roles within a company, for publicists and media managers explaining corporate strategy to staff rather than to the world at large. It may also transform the role of middle management from "keepers of information" to "communicators of information" on behalf of a company's leaders.

Such communications duties challenge even the best of executives. Many business leaders, though, face the extra burden of travel. Sanders has wisely passed that burden on to his second in command, Thomas Falk. He logged an ear-popping 160,000 miles of corporate travel in 2000, the equivalent of six times round the world, visiting the 40 countries in which the company has factories and the 150 or so in which it has sales.[5] Such passport marathons, which make hefty demands upon executives' time, health, and home, partly reflect how the relative roles of the head office and regional divisions are altering. Internet technologies may reduce the need for routine travel (to review a monthly report with a colleague, say), but they may increase the value of a personal visit (to key accounts, for example). Simply put, showing up in person communicates loudly.

## Managing Change

DO COMPANIES need leaders or managers? The answer, of course, is both—but leadership matters more because company bosses inevitably spend much of their time coaxing people to work in new ways. If they lead well, then people may even wax enthusiastic about tasks that they never expected to enjoy. A classic example of inspired and inspiring leadership is the explorer, Ernest Shackleton, whose expedition to the South Pole failed when his ship struck ice. For an entire winter, he devised ways to raise the morale of his crew, stranded on an ice flow, in what most leaders might consider an extreme change-management program. After a weekly evening get-together, one of the surlier members of the crew recorded in his diary that he had just experienced one of the happiest days of his life.[6]

Good leaders know that human diversity calls for a pragmatic, inventive approach. "Leading people is rather like a game of chess, with many different pieces all going different ways," says one who has led a health care business. "Some go forward in a straight line, some jump about, some can go almost anywhere, but all have to be managed in order to reach the goal."[7] This diversity is even more apparent when a company's operations span several countries or continents. To drive change in a culturally heterogeneous company is a monumental endeavor; to drive it in a multinational is a superhuman task. The strains of external complexity exacerbate those of internal diversity and complicate negotiations in different cultures with politicians, regulators, and law enforcement officials.

The importance of communications skills has heightened the profiles of some corporate leaders over those in the past. Hero-leaders may take a company through difficult or disruptive times, as Jack Welch did at GE and Jacques Nasser has done at Ford. Maybe equally impressive figures will emerge from the technology collapse and the uncertainties bred by recession and the tragedies of September 2001. But the dot-com fashion for "extreme leadership" and "insanely great" ideas was just that: a fashion. In time, hero-leaders leave, and when they go, the organization suffers. Companies need structure and good management to develop a life that can survive and grow without the hero.

A hero-manager, who can lead even an indifferent staff through hell and back, may be a useful person in a time of change. Organizational change is difficult to achieve: A 1999 survey by the consultancy A. T. Kearney of almost 300 senior executives in European companies found that they rated only 20 percent of their change programs successful. A further 63 percent resulted in some change but failed to sustain it. The remaining 17 percent achieved nothing at all.[8] Revolutionary change, uncomfortable as it is, calls for obsessive persistence, such as that of Henry Ford, who tried to start his car business several times before it actually took off.

So companies need people at the top who can lead change and people at every level who can manage it. Otherwise, initiatives go nowhere.

Some companies clearly excel at change: They institutionalize their knowledge into their culture and into performance assessment. They use outside consultants more prudently than other companies, hiring them mainly to work with senior managers or to develop specialist capabilities. These firms regularly inform their staff of what they are doing, and create incentives for inventive cooperation. Because such companies learn as they go, they find change easier to sustain.

Compared with firms where leadership is weak, companies with powerful leaders must manage succession and intergenerational transition with special care, because the capital markets vote, so to speak, on announced or even rumored successors. Further, most of the leaders who are currently steering companies through change "grew up" in the days before the Internet—or even the home PC. Such leaders will struggle to bring about a revolution, and so the real revolution will occur when the next generation of managers, totally at home with the potential of Internet technologies for business, take the lead.

But most companies, most of the time, need another skill: a coach-manager, who can enable a group of skilled individuals to perform their jobs quite independently. The key qualities in extracting value from the Internet are not technological but profoundly human skills, such as the ability to create trust, to communicate, and to build strong teams. Much of the focus on the ways the Internet has been changing business has been on technology. In fact, people are what matter most.

## Managing Alliances

COMPANIES rarely act alone these days and will do so even less often in the future. More of their activities involve alliance partners for outsourcing, marketing, innovating, or simply exploring new technology or foreign lands. Some alliances are loose agreements to collaborate on a project; others are full-blown joint ventures.

However, the success rate of alliances, measured in strategic and financial terms, hovers around 50 percent.[9] That beats the rate for mergers and takeovers, but strong management can clearly improve it further. So the ability to manage alliances becomes a key executive skill, and one that does not emerge naturally from the familiar corporate hierarchy. Indeed, it involves more consent and mutual respect and less command and control.

Managing an alliance well differs significantly from managing a takeover (buy another company, aim the hatchet at the right place, and then rebuild the morale of the survivors). Running an alliance is, in the nice phrase of Firoz Rasul, chairman and chief executive of Ballard Power Systems, a Canadian pioneer of fuel cells, "like getting married. You have to understand each other's expectations. And even then, you have to work very hard to keep the excitement going."[10]

Like marriages, alliances work well only when based on trust. Partners can write only so much into the contract. Indeed, one expert argues that an alliance must deliver more than a simple transaction such as licensing could do, and that added value depends on responding harmoniously and effectively to unanticipated events and market shifts. The partners must be able to depend upon each other to adapt appropriately to new circumstances.[11]

Two companies with plenty in common can more easily establish trust. Unfortunately, opposites still attract: Companies more often pair off with partners that take a different approach, understand a different country, or run a different business. Allies may measure success in incompatible ways, or they may fret that they are donating too much of their precious intellectual property to the other firm.

To build trust, a first step is to define objectives and agree on ways to measure progress toward them. That means a company must know from the start what it hopes to gain from a partnership. However, a company must also accommodate its partner's needs, giving as well as taking. Vantage Partners, a company spun out of a Harvard University think tank that specializes in negotiation, teaches companies to write down a procedural contract and to define the responsibilities of each team, so that senior managers in the partner firms do not constantly demand more than the people in the trenches can deliver.[12] Another approach is to appoint internal "champions" with responsibility for the success of the alliance and to insist that the partner company do the same.

Technology can underpin trust by allowing alliance partners instant access to each other's systems (if that has been agreed). If a company can check at any time how a partner or a supplier is doing, it may feel more reassured. But if trust does not exist in the first place, no amount of technological wizardry or paper contracts can create it. Only in the presence of trust will an alliance be founded on good will, which in turn will sustain the relationship when one company does something the other dislikes or does not understand. In the words of Peter Boot, alliance expert at Dow Corning, one of the most experienced managers of alliances in the business: "You have to be disposed towards the most benign interpretation of the strange signals you get from time to time. You have to interpret them innocently."[13] That is just the sort of advice a good marriage counselor might give—together with an injunction to spend plenty of time with your partner. Not surprisingly, alliance managers entertain one or other of their corporate partners almost every night of the week. So among the prerequisites for good alliance management are a good digestive system and a tolerant spouse.

## Managing Collaboration

THE LEADERSHIP SKILLS needed to manage alliances are also ideal for handling internal joint ventures. Indeed, these ventures are just as important as alliances because many of the new business propositions that companies launch cut across entrenched departmental lines. One division's innovation may be useful to another; one department may want to cross-sell to another's customer; the department on the eighth floor may need a person who understands its computer system and want to borrow someone for a few weeks from the department on the fourth floor.

To exploit the full benefits of internal collaboration calls for an emphasis on sharing knowledge and other resources. It also calls for the imaginative use of the peer-to-peer contact that Internet technologies so strikingly facilitate. In the pyramid-shaped companies of the twentieth century, most communication traveled up through one divisional manager to the top, and then back down through another divisional manager. In the weblike corporate structures of this century, communications will be as likely to travel sideways, across normal reporting boundaries, as up or down.

Yet plenty of managers still behave as though they were the warring barons or quarreling princelings of medieval Europe. In the first half of the 1990s, for instance, Motorola's culture was one of one of tribal warfare, with chieftains more determined to stymie each other than to serve customers. Executives built up personal empires and refused either to share the limelight with colleagues or to jeopardize their bonuses by working for the benefit of the whole group. The key problem was a view that individual managers could not both lead and cooperate.[14]

Of course, today's managers (as Motorola now knows well) must do both. For starters, that requires collaboration at the top to set the tone for what happens lower down. Top executives must lead at least some of the working parties and projects that pull different departments together. One study of companies that work well across business units found that senior managers typically put substantial energy into promoting collaboration. For example, when customer managers at IBM have difficulty getting access to the resources they need from other divisions, they can go directly to one of the company's 250 top executives for help.[15] A collaborative company's culture will train the managers of business units to think of themselves as stewards, not owners, of their resources, responsible for ensuring that the people who report to them are deployed to their best advantage right across the organization.

Effective collaboration of this sort also calls for pay and incentive structures and a system of promotion criteria that rewards sharing and teamwork as well as individual effort. Establishing those is difficult because measuring collaborative skills is harder than measuring contribution to the bottom line. At IBM Europe, for example, the size of the stock-option grant awarded to leaders of customer segments is based on their overall contribution to the company. To determine that, a personnel committee polls the employee's colleagues about such nonquantifiable factors as an ability to spot opportunities, a commitment to developing subordinates, and a willingness to share resources for key projects.[16] That system may suit IBM, but many other companies might worry about giving so much weight to collaboration. They should look carefully at their eventual goals and decide whether in the long run collaboration suits them better than competition, or vice versa. Striking the right balance will always be extremely difficult, and that balance will vary from one company to another.

Some collaboration may be ad hoc and transient. But managers will need to run many other cross-departmental ventures rather like external alliances and apply many of the same rules and techniques. That means being clear about the joint goals and how they will be measured, fostering trust, and having well-defined lines of responsibility for the success of the project. Especially in the early years, when the new collaborative possibilities of Internet technologies are becoming embedded in a company, the process may need to be more formal than it will eventually become.

Because sharing involves such contradictory behavior, one study advocates an approach that it calls "T-shaped management," practiced by a new kind of executive who "breaks out of the traditional corporate hierarchy to share knowledge freely across the organization (the horizontal part of the 'T') while remaining fiercely committed to individual business unit performance (the vertical part)."[17] That sounds like an impossible ideal, but careful structuring may help companies to approach it. For instance, Siemens, the German engineering company, sets up small teams of young managers from several different parts of the business to solve a problem facing one of the business divisions. Team members work together for about a year to draw up recommendations, and the experience not only trains them but also builds friendships across units.[18]

No company seems to have given as much thought to T-shaped management as BP, the British energy giant. BP gives every manager of its business units two jobs. In addition to running the unit, these managers devote between 15 and 20 percent of their time to activities that share knowledge—and people—with other units. The company argues that meetings of peer groups helped to sort out the thorny staffing issues that cropped up after its acquisition of Amoco and allowed BP more or less to complete the integration of the two groups within three months. Brainstorming by managers from different units has proved a good way to spot new business opportunities. And peers may be the people best placed to criticize and coach one another.

BP is aware that there is a limit to the benefits of institutionalizing such networks. A bit of bureaucracy may turn the ad hoc into the sustainable; a bit more may bring rigidity. The company thinks that managers' superiors should keep away from peer-group meetings, to generate the right mix of "robust confrontation and collegial support."[19]

It has also discovered that knowledge-sharing meetings can easily waste managerial time: Too many peer-group meetings may produce lots of argument but not much useful action. "We found that people were flying around the world and simply sharing ideas without always having a strong focus on the bottom line," says John Leggate, who ran several cross-unit networks in the early 1990s.[20]

Managers in the company of the future will undoubtedly have to learn the skills to be T-shaped: One of the main economies of scale that big businesses will enjoy in future could well turn out to be not the volume of their purchasing or production but the breadth of their knowledge and their ability to pool it. So effective collaboration may be just as significant a competitive strength to the company of the twenty-first century as vertical integration was to the giants of the twentieth century.

## Managing at the Head Office

WHEN THE COMPANY becomes a network, what skills does it need at its core? Companies have long debated how much power to localize and democratize rather than monopolize at the head office. In the 1990s, the decentralizers were winning because they could cut big costs. For example, a study of organizational change in 450 large European companies by Warwick University Business School between 1992 and 1996 found that 32 percent had a high degree of decentralization at the start of the period and 61 percent at the end.[21]

During delayering, many companies move from grandiose head offices into more modest digs. Percy Barnevik, former chairman of ABB Asea Brown Boveri, famously pronounced, "I believe you can go into any traditionally centralized corporation and cut its headquarters staff by 90 percent in one year."[22] Chief executives saw it as a matter of macho pride to shake bodies out of corporate HQ. A survey of eighty-nine multinationals, two-thirds American and one-third European, found that 85 percent had reorganized their headquarters at least once during the course of the 1990s.[23] More than half of these reorganizations had cut staff; many had moved staff to business units or had outsourced activities. As a result, head offices shrank, and the headquarters of the best-run businesses seemed to shrink the most: The survey found that well-managed firms were particularly likely to employ 2 percent or fewer of their total head count in the head office.[24]

In the future, the axe-man approach will surrender to a more thoughtful one: Many corporate leaders will want a head office that is small but strong, and that provides only those services that add value to the corporation as a whole. Its responsibilities will be those where corporate leaders believe that they are most able to add value. Specifically, it will:

- manage the strategy process; indeed, some see headquarters as ideally "the embodiment of corporate strategy"[25]
- develop leadership and recruit key people
- undertake the functions that are part of a corporation's existence as a single legal entity, such as raising capital and publishing accounts
- make policy, including setting overall performance targets
- provide services where there are economies of scope or scale, as in management training
- lobby government and deal with broader corporate responsibilities for the environment and social responsibility
- handle corporate brand management
- manage internal and external communications

In all these areas, companies replace people doing processing jobs with specialists and strategists. The managers who focus on the tasks that most add value to the organization will stay at the top. No longer, of course, must they run such facilities from a particular building. A company may scatter its top team geographically but connect it electronically. After all, top executives can now participate in the decision-making process anywhere on the planet. Douglas Daft, chief executive of Coca-Cola, travels 80 percent of the time, and says, "The headquarters office is where I am."[26] Other company leaders are equally mobile.

Ironically, one important effect of new communications will be to enhance authority at the center. Senior managers will find that Internet technologies give them tools of unprecedented power for enforcing common standards and centralizing some activities. "To have a truly global company, you need to get everyone to agree on the way you do billing or purchasing," says Oracle's chief financial officer, Jeff Henley. "We have sixty country subsidiaries. You can't globalize if you don't standardize the way you do business."[27] Nowhere does that wise advice apply more strongly than in information technology. Companies find that a dozen or two different e-mail systems tend to spring up in various departments, with huge costs in terms of expert time, money, and reliability. Unless they standardize, they save nothing.

Top managers will set rules and standards that will apply to every unit. Another example is the drive by the heads of corporate purchasing departments to reap economies of scale. At United Technologies, Kent Brittan, in charge of supply management, is installing databases of all that sprawling group's purchases not just on the office-stationery-and-carpeting side but by production units. That will allow him unprecedented scrutiny of what the group buys where and eventually may bring new coherence and economy to the group's purchasing policies.[28]

Standards are vital if networks are to operate efficiently. For instance, if a multinational company's common language is English, its staff around the world has a way to communicate easily. But standards are also important in the sense of common policies. Companies will protect themselves from reputational risk by setting global standards for health, safety, treatment of the environment, and approaches to sensitive social issues, such as the workplace rights of women and trade unions.

Developing appropriate standards is therefore both immensely important and immensely difficult. Some senior managers regard it as a task for which they themselves should take responsibility; others argue that if competing standards already exist internally, then their companies should seek out and adopt the best practice. The important point is that standards are likely to pervade a company only if they have the unequivocal backing of its leaders. Once a company's senior managers set standards, they must react quickly to any breaches. An immediate slap on the wrist must follow the moment someone begins to stray, unless that variation is part of an experiment agreed on at the top. Standards waste money if some people ignore them.

But good standards rarely need enforcement, once the initial bugs are out and they become integrated into the company. And the true hallmark of good leadership is to be sufficiently flexible to allow creativity and ingenuity to spring up within a firm framework. Standards must encompass what a company does but not suffocate it. Good leaders must balance structure and flexibility.

## Managing Talent

G IVEN that intelligent people are the most valuable resource of the company of the future, executives must systematically attract and deploy them well. That job will become harder. Like the purchasing department, the much-despised "human refuse department" may at last become recognized as one of a company's strongholds.

Competition for the most talented people, even within the firm, will intensify. In a curious inversion of Marxism, power is swinging back from capital to labor—or at least, to labor with scarce skills.[29] It will therefore become even more important for managers to be skilled coaches, able to spot potential early and to nurture it. Good employees will feel loyal to a manager who has given them that vital first break. Loyalty will be a company's main defense against becoming dragged into frequent talent auctions. The peril with recruiting stars who already know their market value is that they extract from a company every penny they are worth—and more. Only if a company can find nonfinancial ways to attract them will they be willing to leave a bit behind for the shareholders.

What might such rewards be? The admiration and respect of their peers will matter. So will the satisfaction of working side-by-side with other first-rate people. Good people tend to like working for a company with a collegial atmosphere of intellectual stimulus and self-confidence. They also like working for a well-managed company, where the elevators are not endlessly broken and the support staff is capable. And they will want to work in a congenial geographical location: People might take a pay cut to work in Paris for a year or two but probably not to move to Pittsburgh.

Even with rewards like these, some managers will have to pay a few key superstars more than they earn themselves. Executives in investment banks and television networks have long grown used to the sensation that causes—not, for most managers, a pleasant one. Others will learn to live with it in the future. They might find it instructive to talk to one of the many sports coaches who have started a second career as a management trainer. A coach must persuade a soccer team of millionaire prima donnas to work together. The players are better paid than the coach is, and the players, not the coach, shine in the limelight and get the endorsement deals. Yet the players, if they are wise, know that a good coach can ensure that team effort pays off for all of them. And the coach must be the sort of person whose greatest reward from employment is the satisfaction of seeing people grow and succeed.

In most businesses, though, stars will be less important than teams. The most widespread revolution in the workplace will come from the rise in collaboration and the decline of hierarchy.[30] Traditionally, companies have been organized around individual competitiveness. The view has been that if each employee surpasses the others, the company will benefit. So promotions, pay, power, and possession of the prize parking space have always been the outcome of fierce competition among employees. Corporate hierarchies have encouraged this behavior because every step up the ladder is narrower. The further you climb, the fewer the positions to fight for.

But managing alliances and collaboration requires a quite different approach. For one thing, ladders will shorten, and so the challenge will be to find ways to motivate employees other than through promotion. That in turn creates problems for pay. Most companies (and other organizations too) talk about paying differently for different performance but in reality attach a bigger financial reward to a grander title. They have performance-related promotion rather than performance-related pay. Staff and managers alike seem to accept this system more easily. Without so many rungs to climb, however, they may have to accept wider pay differentials among people who do similar jobs.

Rewarding a team is tricky. Incentives must encourage both collaboration and individual effort. Offer too little payback for individual effort, and the best people will go. But team rewards do not have to be based on the old Communist collective-farm principle of giving the same to everyone, no matter what their effort. One option is to pay individuals different basic salaries, to reflect excellent individual performance, but to link all bonuses to group performance. This approach is not without problems: The most competitive people may well depart, feeling underpaid. But it has one advantage: The group begins to notice the people who do not pull their weight and reacts to them, so that the manager does not have to be the only person to crack the whip.

Inevitably, different companies in different countries will need different approaches for their global teams. It is important to be clear about the right balance. The Internet will enable a "what-fits" approach rather than a "one-size-fits-all" solution. Some businesses need lots of individual talent and compensation structures to match. Many more will need to teach their employees to work well together, collaborating rather than competing—or rather competing with other teams rather than with one another. All will know that their success depends on being able to get the best human capital on offer—without having to pay good people so much that there is nothing left for the shareholders. That will mean managing the business so that its best people get more out of working for it than they would if they set up shop on their own.

## The Future at the Top

I N A PERIOD when technological change appears to be shaping the corporate future, business leaders may find it difficult to remember that they actually shape their company's destiny. Technology is a tool—sophisticated, versatile, and powerful in the case of the Internet, and capable of dramatically altering long-established patterns of cost and competitive advantage. But the success with which technologies are exploited depends primarily on good leadership and management. It is people skills that will ultimately determine how successful the company of the future is.

High among those essential skills is the ability to communicate. Since the Internet transforms communications, leaders need to be able to use it skillfully, together with other tools such as television and the press. They must be able to communicate with several different audiences—inside and outside the company, in different countries and cultures—a task made all the harder by the seamless nature of the mediums that carry their words. Yet effective communications are one of the main underpinnings of trust. Increasingly, a corporate leader, a company's brand, and the customers' feelings about the company are all interconnected.

Within the company, corporate leaders now have unprecedented tools for carrying the influence of the center to every far-flung corner. In theory, everything from global press relations to finance and marketing can be centrally run. Certainly, top managers should set parameters: standards for ethical behavior, for instance, and for technology, knowledge management, and corporate culture. After that, the more inventiveness and creativity that can bubble up from the bottom, the better. Striking this balance will be complex but vital.

Given the importance of a company's people, managers must excel at handling talent and choosing the right mix for the right stage of company development. And having selected that talent, leaders must solve the conundrum of rewarding it sufficiently to win loyalty but not so lavishly as to enrage the rest of the staff and impoverish investors. No wonder vision, bravery, wisdom, and persistence are the qualities every leader needs to build the company of the future, much as they were in Ford's day.

# Chapter 10
# The Company
# of the Future

MOST PEOPLE overestimate the effects of change in the short term, underestimate them in the long term, and fail to spot where change will be greatest. Nowhere is this judgment truer than with new technologies. The Internet stock-market bubble, like the bubble in railway stocks in the nineteenth century, reflected overestimates and misjudgments of the potential impact of new communications. And as with railways, the Internet bubble burst, leaving lots of empty hands but an infrastructure that survived—and changed the world. There will be evolution rather than revolution, and it will take many years to work through. Recall that even though the telephone was first used commercially in the 1870s, telephone banking did not spring up until the 1980s. Consider that the Internet had been in commercial use for a mere seven years by the time recession struck. Profound change rarely comes fast.

Over the next quarter century, though, the Internet will help to transform companies, although the transformation may be too subtle for people to notice much while it happens. It will be most striking, at least in the medium term, in companies providing services: financial, travel, medical, educational, consultancy. Many manufacturing businesses will grow more like service industries: They will cater to the individual customer's tastes, for instance, and create a continuing relationship to ensure they get repeat purchases.

These changes will occur in established companies as they build the Internet into their existing processes. Largely gone is the view of the late 1990s, which saw the Internet as a freestanding technology and a basis for freestanding businesses; so is the notion that the Internet, in and of itself, may be a technology that generates lavish profits. Some pure Internet plays will survive as viable businesses, but they will not be where the impact of Internet technologies is greatest. The main revolution will involve enabling established companies to do familiar tasks in new ways, and then to do new tasks in increasingly familiar ways. Those changes may or may not prove profitable—they will certainly raise productivity and sharpen competition—but companies will have no more choice over whether to deploy the Internet than they had over whether to deploy the telephone. Internet technologies will offer managers much more scope to define their company in the most efficient way; they will not, however, undertake that job on managers' behalf.

The biggest changes inevitably will be those that go with the grain of what is already happening. Internet technologies will thus reinforce outsourcing, a trend that has been in progress for at least two decades. They will further reduce inventory, a move that began long ago with just-in-time lean production. They will bolster globalization, allowing companies to manage overseas operations and connect with foreign suppliers in more intricate ways. They will highlight the emphasis on the customer that so many companies strive to achieve. They will accentuate the need for talented and inventive people, who will have an even sharper idea of their financial worth on the world market for human capital. They will enable the flat structures of modern businesses to operate more effectively and make them even less hierarchical.

Indeed, one of the truly remarkable things about these technologies is the extent to which they reinforce trends already under way. This reflects the fact that many of the things they do are not entirely new: Proprietary electronic networks have long allowed large companies to do what smaller firms can now emulate. But such networks, and packaged software applications such as ERP, tend to be cumbersome and expensive, forcing companies to accommodate them. By comparison, the Internet is flexible, accessible, inexpensive, and ubiquitous.

And there is more to come. Some Internet technologies that promise profound changes are only in the early stages of application. They include peer-to-peer applications (variants of Napster); applications that rate the relevance of information by the frequency with which others use it (as Google, the search engine, does); and, indeed, XML and its variations, which allow seamless document exchange. All these clearly have great potential to change the way companies work, yet we may not see those changes until well into the first decade of the twenty-first century—or even later.

Sometimes, an accumulation of modest differences adds up to an immensity.

As this book has argued, the astonishing fall in the cost of communicating knowledge and information has the power to transform knowledge management (chapter 2). So has the development of new tools for collaboration, giving people new ways to share ideas and information. However, not only must access to knowledge be as free and open as possible, but senior managers must decide how to filter and structure that knowledge. Only then will they be able to apply it to make good decisions, a task that will grow harder as the flow of new information becomes ever more relentless. If the center does not first impose structure, the true benefits of an open culture will be lost. Here, as in many other applications of Internet technologies, the center's power to set standards and structure grows more important, not less: The Internet may be a tool of democracy, but in knowledge management, effective democracy requires self-restraint.

In the future, Internet technologies will give companies new control over their relations with their customers (chapter 3). The Internet will not just widen reach, allowing companies to reach new markets; more important, it will provide ways to deepen existing relationships. Here, as in many other areas, the development of a culture of trust will do the most to deepen the relationship. In addition, companies will develop more sophisticated tools to identify their most profitable customers, to retain them, and to sell them extra products. They will find subtle ways to price discriminate, for example through developing two familiar concepts, loyalty schemes and clubs.

Given the importance of creativity and new ideas to corporate success, companies must work harder than ever to recruit and retain the right staff (chapter 4) and to create a corporate culture that encourages loyalty and effective collaboration (chapter 5). With recruitment, as with customer management, identifying those people likely to contribute most to corporate profitability and concentrate on retaining and developing them will be critical. With staff, as with customers, acquisition costs will encourage companies to care about retention, because profits per worker take time to accrue.

One of the earliest and most visible effects of Internet technologies is on purchasing (chapter 6). Here, a genuinely new business model has arisen: the electronic exchange, which will take several forms but will be built around a single standard that will allow different industries and different companies within an industry to transact freely with one another. In networks and in marketplaces, applying centrally determined standards is one of the keys to realizing value. In purchasing within individual companies, central discipline will also be essential if companies are to benefit from savings and from new suppliers.

More far-reaching will be the impact on the management of supplier networks (chapter 7). Here, the key will be the power of Internet technologies to make information available simultaneously to many different points in a system. The transformation of the supply chain into an ecosystem will bring the biggest rewards when the whole production process can become more modular, so that different stages that once took place sequentially can now occur simultaneously. That change will speed production, reduce output, and increase the flexibility with which companies can respond to changing customer tastes.

In the past, the costs of transferring information have been one of the main factors determining the structure of the company (chapter 8). Now, that is far less true, and the consequence is that companies can make decisions about whether or not to outsource some process or to decentralize some authority in terms of the business case alone. The pressure to outsource will grow, partly because it will leave companies free to concentrate on what they do best rather than on what they merely do well. It will grow, too, because talent is scarce: Some of the brightest and best may choose to be free agents rather than wage slaves. However, when business is slack, employees may be less enthusiastic about going it alone; and outsourcing will have drawbacks when companies are eager to keep direct control over their quality of service and the reputation of their brands.

The benefits of Internet technologies depend not on their wizardry alone (which, in the coming years, will seem remarkably ordinary and natural, just as the phone does now). Companies will reap the full benefits only if they have appropriate structures and cultures. Creating those calls for skillful leadership (chapter 9). Leaders must be able to cope not only with change, disruptive and continuous, but also with the pressures on decision makers to digest a ceaseless torrent of new data—a task that the next generation of managers will be better able to do. Leaders must be good at communicating both with the outside world and with their own people, and able to withstand the sense of managing in a fishbowl, visible to all. They must be as adept at making business decisions as at managing public opinion and issues, such as the environment and corporate social responsibility. Running a big company will remain one of the world's most complex and demanding tasks.

Internet technologies may eventually have dramatic effects on some areas where relatively little has yet happened. Three have particular potential: (1) companies' ability to monitor and time their financial transactions; (2) companies' relationships with stockholders and the wider community; and (3) perhaps even the predominant form of corporate organization.

## The Real-Time Company

AS COMPANIES integrate all their corporate operations electronically, their senior executives will gain an important advantage: a clearer view than ever before of the state of the business from hour to hour. That should enormously shorten their response time to changing market conditions. If they also make some of that corporate information publicly available, customers, investors, and regulatory authorities should receive fewer nasty surprises.

Precise and timely information itself can drive efficiency and always has. Before the international telegraph became available, British merchants, gambling blind on what was needed in Australia, a month and a half away by fast ship, flooded the country with boots or mirrors or fencing. The telegraph reduced the resulting gluts and scarcities.[1] In the same way, companies, and therefore the economy, will now adjust more quickly to changing demand, be it boom or bust. Other instability remains: Investor behavior and exogenous shocks such as technological change still will drive economic cycles. And corporate adjustments, coming swiftly, may be cumulatively more violent than before.

But companies will move to just-in-time increases or reductions in their inventories and work forces.

Ironically, given its subsequent financial woes, Cisco Systems piloted this panoramic management style in the late 1990s with the concept of the "virtual close": Each day the company can read its exact earnings per share, revenues, expenses, and margins by every single product right around the world. In the early days of the virtual close, a procession of corporate bigwigs—many of them chief executives and chief financial officers wanting to revamp their financial processes and compress the normal reporting cycle—beat a path to Cisco's door.[2] In those days, Garry Daichent, Cisco's vice president of worldwide operations, liked to boast, "We can close the books every twenty-four hours. I could run it every two minutes if I wanted to. It means that we should never surprise Wall Street."[3]

Never say never. Yet the fact remains that Cisco's powerful tool has enormous potential for improving management. No longer need a problem malinger unnoticed for three months before it darkens the quarterly accounts. In addition, executives can drill down and review the productivity of the week by product, by region, or by customer. So no longer do orders suddenly materialize in the reports in the final days of the month, skewing the figures and clouding judgment about needed capacity.

If a company can generate immediate information in this way, then should it publish in a steady stream some of the numbers that now reach financial markets every quarter or every year? Publishing annual accounts will remain a good discipline, but some numbers could appear on the corporate Web site at the end of each day, a move that the accountancy profession might (profitably) encourage. And what other activities might in the future move away from their current stately cycle around the calendar? Do employees need to be paid once a month, or could they receive a constant trickle of pay into their bank accounts? Might government eventually insist that it receive tax revenues, from corporations or even from individuals, day by day rather than a quarter or a year at a time? Spreading out some of these large and lumpy payments would have the same sort of benefits as improving inventory control: It would allow money to flow more evenly and efficiently, avoiding some of the peaks and troughs that make monetary management tricky for central bankers.

## Collaborative Governance

O NE OF THE unsatisfactory aspects of corporate governance in countries such as the United States, Britain, Australia, and Canada is the dispersion of shareholdings. In most companies, many shareholders have relatively small holdings, and the rules protecting shareholder privacy make it almost impossible for them to locate and communicate with one another. It is therefore extremely difficult for them to impose their views on an unsatisfactory management. This is particularly true for individual investors, who in the United States hold about 40 percent of the equity in large corporations. One result is a low level of participation in corporate governance by individual shareholders. Into this vacuum have increasingly stepped politicians and protesters, eager to make companies more socially and environmentally accountable.

The Internet is a powerful tool for protest, allowing disgruntled consumers, unhappy environmentalists, and social protestors to unite, anywhere on earth, against a company. From Seattle to Prague to Gothenburg, direct activists have discovered in the world's most globe-spanning technology the ideal medium for organizing global protest. Because protestors can watch any part of a company's operations, or those of its suppliers or even its suppliers' suppliers, a company will need the same seamless vigilance.

More manageable are the difficulties posed by the shortcomings of corporate governance. For here, the Internet promises to allow shareholders, especially individuals, to exercise their powers more effectively. Already, shareholders have begun locating one another online in new ways and collaborating in cyberspace—cautiously, to avoid breaking the law. When United Companies Financial, a publicly traded company, began to collapse in 1999, a couple of shareholders started posting notes on the Yahoo! message board to try to find out what was happening inside the troubled business. When one of them asked people using the message board to identify themselves and fax him evidence of their shareholdings, he found that the board's posters and readers jointly held an astonishing 40 percent of the stock. The shareholders formed an action group. As it turned out, they were too late to rescue the company. Aaron Brown, one of the two activists, believes that the Internet played a crucial role in the rescue bid: The main mistake, he reflects, was not to organize six months earlier.[4]

Such collaboration may well grow more common, especially if the law finds ways to accommodate it. Certainly, more and more companies (and indeed the Securities and Exchange Commission) now monitor message boards and chat rooms, looking for early signs of shareholder activism. But even in normal times, when a company faces no acute crisis, the Internet may allow shareholders to play a more useful role in corporate governance. One way or the other, the market will keep them accountable.

In the United States, investors have for several years been able to vote proxies by touch-tone telephone or on the Web, using services provided at proxyvote.com. Large companies use this service extensively, although most other corporations have been slower to sign up. Online proxy voting has the potential to alter the nature of shareholder influence.

For example, once a voter checks an online box on the proxy form, software can transmit that shareholder's identity number and vote automatically in accordance with all the management's recommendations. The same software could easily allow the shareholder not to follow the management blindly but instead to take the voting recommendations of a specialist adviser. Already, pension and mutual funds employ such advisers—companies such as Proxy Monitor and Institutional Shareholder Services—to study all proposals that corporations put to shareholder vote and then to recommend how to respond. For individual shareholders, such an adviser could be a favorite financial journalist or Greenpeace or an agent that followed the voting strategy of a governance activist fund, such as LENS or the California Public Employees' Retirement System(CalPERS). CalPERS is one of several large investors that already posts some of its votes in advance so that people can free-ride on its analysis of complex issues such as stock-option proposals.

Shareholders as a group might hire advisers, for which the corporation would pay on their behalf, to make independent voting recommendations and even to make proposals, such as nominating independent directors. Mark Latham, an independent consultant who has described such a scheme, suggests that these adviser agents might be called "corporate monitoring firms."[5]

The most serious danger with such a development is probably that the software that voters can use to assign their proxy votes to the Sierra Club could equally well be used to sell the votes to the highest bidder. Vote selling of that sort would allow the management to regain control of the company and must be outlawed. Apart from that issue, though, the software would give shareholders new power to influence corporate governance. Already, incidentally, a rather similar mechanism is being used in a company called FOLIO*fn*, set up by Steve Wallman, a former SEC commissioner, to create a variation of a mutual fund in which investors continue to own their stocks and to vote proxies from their holdings.

Another step that tips the balance between corporate owners and managers is the amendment in 2000 of state corporate law in Delaware (which covers almost all of America's public companies) permitting companies to hold their annual general meetings online, with no requirement for any physical location or presence. The choice of whether to hold a "virtual" meeting lies with the board of directors. Some shareholders are uneasy with the online route: For example, the AFL-CIO, the umbrella body for U.S. trade unions, feels that the annual general meeting is the only opportunity that shareholders have to engage directly with company executives. However, shareholders attending virtual meetings must be able to participate and vote while the meeting is taking place. Because many investors—even large ones—may find it hard to be physically present at every meeting of a company in which they hold stock, this change may well increase participation. An analyst or institutional stockholder will now be able to take part and vote from a laptop.

One probable consequence will be less predictable outcomes of shareholder meetings.[6] Companies will be unable to forecast what proportion of shareholders will revoke their proxies during a meeting in order to cast "live" votes as a contested issue appears on their computer screens. Last-minute announcements by management during a meeting—or points raised by shareholders—may swing votes. With a traditional physical meeting, companies can predict the outcome of most votes days in advance. If shareholders use online meetings to play a more active role in corporate governance, then that certainty will be gone. All of this reinforces the importance of "good" standards at the center that are spread throughout the company and its network of suppliers, as firms will be held more accountable by their share-holders, customers, and capital markets.

## The Shape of Tomorrow's Company

WHAT THEN will it look like, the company of the future? Perhaps the question should be cast more broadly: Will the joint-stock company remain the most appropriate vehicle for most commercial activity? Much of the variety that characterized corporate ownership structures half a century ago has gone or is vanishing: Mutuals and partnerships become public companies, state-owned enterprises are privatized, cooperatives disband. The upshot is an increasing conver-gence around the joint-stock company. Not since the start of the industrial age has a single form of ownership been so dominant.

One important reason for this dominance has been the need to find new ways to reward a company's most valued employees. In the long stock-market boom, top talent wanted equity. Happily, that desire coincided with a widespread view that the best way to persuade managers to look after the interests of a business's owners was to align their interests by giving them options on corporate stock. So the own-ers—stockholders—felt that they had an interest in rewarding valued executives with some dilution of equity.

The retreat of stock prices may change that; so may the realization of the harmful distortion in company profits that stock options have caused. Disillusion with stock options, on both sides of the table, will increase. But the basic conundrum will remain: How can the owners of a company adequately reward their best people? Indeed, if the cap-ital is largely human, does it make sense to talk of "owners" in the same way as it did when the capital was largely physical, and created with the owners' funds? In some "companies"—football clubs, for instance—all that is really happening is a securitization of the ex-pected earnings of a talented team. When, for instance, Goldman Sachs was floated, was that really so different?

This is, then, not the world of Karl Marx but its mirror image: a world where the workers—or, at least, the most talented workers—are the true capitalists. The question becomes: What form of organization is most likely to encourage these capitalists to share their wealth and to use it for the common good? The answer may turn out to be much more various than today's uniformity allows. Some talented people will want to work for themselves; some will want to work in itinerant teams or partnerships; some will want the stability of large companies; some may rediscover the virtues of the mutual or the cooperative as appropriate structures for sharing the returns from joint effort.

Some of these new structures may look extraordinarily like the commercial organizations of the preindustrial era. Both the East India Company and the Hudson's Bay Company were set up to manage particular projects in the way that many companies of the future may be. Some companies will look like Hollywood studios and operate as bankers and talent brokers: Think of Ford, buying Volvo and Jaguar and recruiting BMW's star executive to knock the new business into shape.[7]

Some industries will still depend on physical capital. The oil industry, for example, will always need lots of extremely expensive equipment—as well as clever people who know about extracting oil. But even companies with large physical plant costs are changing. Some may increase their emphasis on managing a series of interconnected projects, much as a company like Schlumberger or Bechtel does already. Yet the important thing for such companies will be to retain a group of people who have long experience in the core business: finding oil, building bridges, engineering roads. These embedded competencies are the heart of such a business. Placing too much emphasis on the self-contained project—putting too many people there only for the duration of the task—creates a "Velcro" company that quickly loses its raison d'être.

Might some companies in the future look more like universities?[8] Those venerable institutions, dating back to the Middle Ages, have always been in the human-capital business. They have demonstrated a durability matched by precious few other institutions, and they are still flourishing today. Not only are there far more universities, and students, than ever before in history, but plenty of big companies, including Motorola and McDonald's, have established their own "universities."

The university offers a common brand, the provision of central services, and vast experience in knowledge management. It employs, on a variety of terms, individuals contracted to supply it with some or all of their intellectual capital. Many of them increase their stock of intellectual capital by transferring it to others: Most teachers learn from their students as well as from their research. Some universities are, of course, state-owned, but the really successful ones—the global brands—are almost all private institutions.

The key characteristic that the Internet will implant in tomorrow's company will be that of lateral communication. Old pyramids will go; new webs will replace them. At every level in a company, contact with others at the same level, but in different locations, divisions, or subsidiaries, will grow easier. Messages, orders, plans—all will no longer need to travel up through the hierarchy, across, and back down through the layers to their destinations. Instead, they will skip sideways, cutting out the chain of command.

For many old-generation managers, this change will be uncomfortable. Their role in controlling the flow of information within a company will diminish. Their staff will be able to talk to one another more easily—and will do so, whatever restraints the company tries to put on the use of the corporate intranet. Members of the teams, which will be so marked a feature of the new landscape, will be loyal to one another but not necessarily to the managers who direct them. The new corporate communities that spring up will not automatically have the blessing of the boss.

As companies acquire more fluid shapes, forming and reforming around talent and ideas, the economy may enter a new period of industrial instability. However, that will probably occur when, happily, financial stability returns after the inflationary gyrations of the twentieth century. The time that combines instability in industrial organization with financial stability will resemble that earlier period of communications revolution, the mid-nineteenth century. Then, too, there was a ferment of new ideas in corporate structure as society struggled to evolve ways to channel innovation and to share wealth. How curious an irony it would be if the company of tomorrow turned out to look extraordinarily like the company of the day before yesterday.

# Notes

## Chapter 1: Management, Information, and Technology

1. Quoted in Martin Brookes and Zaki Wahhaj, "Is the Internet Better than Electricity?" (London: Goldman Sachs, 2 August 2000).

2. For a fascinating midcentury view of the long-term impact of automation, see L. Landon Goodman, *Man and Automation* (London: Pelican Books, 1957).

3. Pam Woodall, "Untangling E-conomics: A Survey of the New Economy," *The Economist,* 23 September 2000, 10.

4. Ibid.

5. Survey by Fleet Capital of 300 chief financial officers of middle-sized American manufacturing firms, quoted in *Manufacturing News,* 22 December 2000, <http://www.manufacturingnews.com>.

6. Quoted in Thomas L. Friedman, "Internet Entrepreneur: Act Small, Think Global," *International Herald Tribune,* 10 March 1999.

7. Daniel H. Pink, *Free Agent Nation: How America's New Independent Workers Are Transforming the Way We Live* (New York: Warner Books, 2001).

8. See <http://www.opennet.net/DualControl/industrialrevolution.htm> for an account of America's relatively late entry into the office revolution.

9. JoAnne Yates, "Business Use of Information and Technology during the Industrial Age," in *A Nation Transformed by Information: How Information Has Shaped the United States from Colonial Times to the Present,* ed. Alfred D. Chandler, Jr., and James W. Cortada (Oxford: Oxford University Press, 2000), 111. Much of the information in this section is taken from her fascinating essay.

10. "Industrial Revolution Resulted in More Complex Business Operating Requirements," OpenNet Corporation, 1998, <http://www.opennet.net/DualControl/industrialrevolution.htm>.

11. "Electronic Computing Systems Provided Support for High Volume Transaction Processing of Situations with Relatively Static Classification Requirements," OpenNet Corporation, 1998, <http://www.opennet.net/DualControl/index.html>.

12. "New NAM/Ernst & Young Index Charts Status of E-Commerce Growth," press release, 8 March 2001, <http://www.nam.org>.

13. *The reNEWed Economy: Business for a Dynamic Europe* (Brussels: Union of Industrial and Employer's Confederations of Europe, 2001), 10.

14. "Business in the Information Age: International Benchmarking Study 2000," <http://www.ukonlineforbusiness.gov.uk/Government/bench/International/bench2000.pdf>.

15. "New NAM/Ernst & Young Index Charts Status of E-Commerce Growth."

16. "Statistics Denmark" and "Statistics Finland," quoted in *A New Economy? The Changing Role of Innovation and Information Technology in Growth* (Paris: OECD, 2000), 59. Available at <http://www.oecd.org/publications/e-book/9200031e.pdf>.

17. Jess Blackburn, Dell Americas, e-mail to author, 6 June 2001.

18. Arno Penzias, *Digital Harmony: Business, Technology & Life After Paperwork* (New York: HarperCollins, 1995).

19. *A New Economy?*, 61.

20. Charles Grantham claims to have coined the term; see *The Future of Work: The Promise of the New Digital Work Society* (New York: McGraw-Hill, 2000).

21. "B-to-B Buyers to Move Online Despite Market's Slow Digital Commerce Growth," Jupiter Media Metrix, 5 March 2001, <http://www.ir.jmm.com/ireye>.

22. The term, used in this sense (it has been around since 1935), was coined by James F. Moore in *The Death of Competition: Leadership and Strategy in the Age of Business Ecosystems* (New York: John Wiley & Sons, 1996), 15.

23. P. Taylor, "Electronic Revolution in the Retailing World," *Financial Times,* 3 September 1997.

24. The company as film studio is a powerful image that several authors have discussed, including Joel Kotkin and David Friedman in "Why Every Business Will Be Like Show Business," *Inc.,* March 1995.

25. Pink, *Free Agent Nation.*

26. Grantham, *The Future of Work.*

27. Frances Cairncross, "Inside the Machine: A Survey of E-management," *The Economist,* 18 November 2000, 6.

28. Yankee Group, quoted by Michael Maerz of Etrieve, personal communication with author, 26 June 2001.

29. Cairncross, "Inside the Machine," 9.

30. Erik Brynjolfsson, Lorin Hitt, and Shinkyu Yang, "Intangible Assets: How the Interaction of Information Technology and Organizational Struc-

ture Affects Stock Market Valuations," working paper, MIT, Cambridge, MA, July 2000. See <http://grace.wharton.upenn.edu/~lhitt/itqo.pdf>.

## Chapter 2: Knowledge, Decision Making, and Innovation

1. Baruch Lev, "Knowledge and Shareholder Value," January 2000, <http://www.stern.nyu.edu/~blev>.

2. Karl Erik Sveiby, *The New Organizational Wealth* (San Francisco: Barrett-Koehler, 1997).

3. "A Price on the Priceless," *The Economist,* 10 June 1999.

4. See <http://www.sll-6.stanford.edu/speakers/leifer/presentation/sld 018.htm>.

5. Tools that help to map unstructured information include <http://www.webmap.com>, <http://www.map.net>, and <http://www.antarcti.ca>.

6. John Seely Brown and Paul Duguid, "Balancing Act: How to Capture Knowledge Without Killing It," *Harvard Business Review* 78, no. 3 (May–June 2000): 73–80.

7. Ibid., 73.

8. Described at <http://agents.www.media.mit.edu/groups/agents/projects/>.

9. Russell Eisenstat, Nathaniel Foote, Jay Galbraith, and Danny Miller, "Beyond the Business Unit," *McKinsey Quarterly* 1 (2001): 54–63.

10. Ben Schiller, "Tapping Remote Knowledge," *Net Profit,* February 2000.

11. Brown and Duguid, "Balancing Act," 80.

12. "New Wiring," *The Economist,* 15 January 2000.

13. Ibid.

14. Ray Hurst, "Dispersed Experts Collaborate On-line," *Net Profit,* March 2000, 12–13.

15. Quoted in Paul McDougall, "Groove Networks' Software to Aid in Collaboration," InformationWeek.com, 30 October 2000, <http://information week.com/810/groove.htm>.

16. Christopher Ireland, "The Gist: Intuitive App Lets Team Collaborate Without Missing a Beat," *Wired* 9.02, February 2001, <http://www.wired.com>.

17. Laszlo Mero, *Moral Calculations: Game Theory, Logic, and Human Frailty* (New York: Copernicus, 1998), 198.

18. John S. Hammond, Ralph L. Keeney, and Howard Raiffa, *Smart Choices: A Practical Guide to Making Better Decisions* (Boston: Harvard Business School Press, 1999), 3.

19. *A New Economy?,* 32.

20. Rosabeth Moss Kanter, *Evolve! Succeeding in the Digital Culture of Tomorrow* (Boston: Harvard Business School Press, 2001), 222.

21. *A New Economy?,* 44.

22. Ibid., 47.

23. Ibid., 54.

24. Durward K. Sobek II, Allen C. Ward, and Jeffrey K. Liker, "Toyota's Principles of Set-Based Concurrent Engineering," *Sloan Management Review* (Winter 1999): 76–83.

25. Alan MacCormack, interview by author, Cambridge, MA, September 2000.

26. Robert Axelrod and Michael D. Cohen, *Harnessing Complexity: Organizational Implications of a Scientific Frontier* (New York: The Free Press, 2000).

27. James Barron, "Something for Nothing," *CIO Magazine,* 15 October 2000, <http://www.cio.com/archive/101500_something_content.html>.

28. Quoted in Eric S. Raymond, *The Cathedral and the Bazaar: Musings on Linux and Open Source by an Accidental Revolutionary* (Cambridge, MA: O'Reilly, 2001), 176.

29. Susanne Hauschild, Thomas Licht, and Wolfram Stein, "Creating a Knowledge Culture," *McKinsey Quarterly* 1 (2001): 74–81.

30. Ibid., 77.

31. "Patent Wars," *The Economist,* 8 April 2000.

32. James Gleick, "Patently Absurd," <http://www.around.com/patent.html>, published in the *New York Times,* 12 March 2000.

33. Quoted in "Patent Wars."

34. Kevin G. Rivette and David Kline, *Rembrandts in the Attic: Unlocking the Hidden Value of Patents* (Boston: Harvard Business School Press, 2000).

35. Thorold Barker and Dan Roberts, "The Cost of Forgetting Inventions," *Financial Times,* 24–25 June 2000.

36. Kevin G. Rivette and David Kline, "Discovering New Value in Intellectual Property," *Harvard Business Review* 78, no. 1 (January–February 2000): 66.

## Chapter 3: Customers and Brands

1. Both studies are cited in Walter Baker, Mike Marn, and Craig Zawada, "Price Smarter on the Net," *Harvard Business Review* 79, no. 2 (February 2001): 123.

2. The emphasis on the Internet as a tool for price discrimination is the idea of Andrew Odlyzko.

3. A visual image of this effect is the chart in Frederick F. Reichheld, *The Loyalty Effect: The Hidden Force Behind Growth, Profits, and Lasting Value* (Boston: Harvard Business School Press, 1996), 39.

4. "Ryanair's Results Surge, Helped by the Internet," *International Herald Tribune,* 26 June 2001.

5. Cairncross, "Inside the Machine," 43.

6. Interview with Maurice Geller, *Nasdaq Magazine,* January 2001, 16–21.

7. John Fiore, interview by author, Boston, MA, September 2000.

8. Ward Hanson, interview by author, Stanford, CA, September 2000.

9. Rolf Jensen, *The Dream Society: How the Coming Shift from Information to Imagination Will Transform Your Business* (New York: McGraw-Hill, 2001).

10. B. Joseph Pine II and James Gilmore, *The Experience Economy: Work Is Theatre & Every Business a Stage* (Boston: Harvard Business School Press, 1999).

11. Michael J. Wolf, *The Entertainment Economy: How Mega-Media Forces Are Transforming Our Lives* (London: Penguin Books, 1999).

12. A good discussion of Internet branding is to be found in Jeffrey F. Rayport and Bernard J. Jaworski, *E-Commerce* (New York: McGraw-Hill/Irwin Marketspace, 2001).

13. L. Jean Camp, *Trust and Risk in Internet Commerce* (Cambridge, MA: MIT Press, 2000), 37.

14. Hanson, interview by author.

15. Quoted in John A Murphy, *The Lifebelt: The Definitive Guide to Managing Customer Retention* (Chichester: John Wiley & Sons, 2001), 20.

16. "Managing Customer Relationships: Lessons from the Leaders," a report published by the Economist Intelligence Unit with Andersen Consulting, New York, NY, 1998.

17. Camp, *Trust and Risk in Internet Commerce.*

18. Tim Jackson, "In Praise of Amazon," *Financial Times,* 1 August 2000.

19. Frederick F. Reichheld and Phil Schefter, "E-loyalty: Your Secret Weapon on the Web," *Harvard Business Review* 78, no. 4 (July–August 2000): 105–113.

20. B. Joseph Pine II, Don Peppers, and Martha Rogers, "Do You Want to Keep Your Customers Forever?" in *Markets of One: Creating Customer-Unique Value through Mass Customization,* ed. James H. Gilmore and B. Joseph Pine II (Boston: Harvard Business School Press, 2000), 53, 57.

21. C. K. Prahalad and Venkatram Ramaswamy, "Co-opting Customer Competence," *Harvard Business Review* 78, no. 1 (January–February 2000): 81.

22. "Weld Royal, Web Marketing's New Wave," *Industry Week,* 11 June 2000.

23. Frederick F. Reichheld, *Loyalty Rules! How Today's Leaders Build Lasting Relationships* (Boston: Harvard Business School Press, 2001).

24. The term seems to have been coined originally by Stanley M. Davis in *Future Perfect* (Reading, MA: Addison-Wesley Publishing, 1987).

25. Heidi Anderson, "How Reflect.com Turned Browsers into Buyers," 21 December 2000, <http://www.Clickz.com>.

26. Matthias M. Bekier, Dorlisa K. Flur, and Seelan J. Singham, "A Future for Bricks and Mortar," *McKinsey Quarterly* 3 (2000): 78–85.

27. Avid Motjitbai, interview by author, San Francisco, CA, September 2000.

28. Himesh Bhise, Diana Farrell, Hans Miller, Andre Vanier, and Adil Zainulbhai, "The Duel for the Doorstep," *McKinsey Quarterly* 2 (2000): 33–41.

29. Ibid.

30. Ranjay Gulati and Jason Garino, "Get the Right Mix of Bricks and Clicks," *Harvard Business Review* 78, no. 3 (May–June 2000): 107–114.

31. Richard Metters, Michael Ketzenberg, and George Gillen, "Welcome Back, Mom and Pop," *Harvard Business Review* 78, no. 3 (May–June 2000): 24–26.

32. Iain Carson, "Meet the Global Factory," *The Economist,* 20 June 1998, 17.

33. "Managing Customer Relationships."

34. Quoted in Ray McKenzie, *The Relationship-Based Enterprise: Powering Business Success Through Customer Relationship Management* (Toronto: McGraw-Hill Ryerson, 2001), 58.

35. George Colony, interview by author, Cambridge, MA, September 2000.

## Chapter 4: Recruiting, Retaining, and Training

1. Kanter, *Evolve!,* 198.

2. Bruce Tulgan, *Winning the Talent Wars: How to Manage and Compete in the High-Tech, High-Speed, Knowledge-Based, Super-Fluid Economy* (New York: W. W. Norton, 2001), 37.

3. Woodall, "Untangling E-conomics," 29.

4. "Germany Desperately Needs More Technical Graduates," *Manpower Argus,* September 2000, 3.

5. Woodall, "Untangling E-conomics," 29.

6. Sherwin Rosen, "The Economics of Superstars," *American Economic Review* 71, no. 5 (December 1981): 845–858.

7. Robert B. Reich, *The Future of Success: Work and Life in the New Economy* ( New York: Alfred A Knopf, 2000).

8. Reichheld, *The Loyalty Effect,* 100.

9. Bronwyn Fryer, "Novell's Eric Schmidt: Leading through Rough Times," *Harvard Business Review* 79, no. 5 (May 2001): 116–123.

10. Thomas Neumann, interview by author, Walldorf, Germany, September 2000.

11. Mike Mazarr, "Hiring," *TrendScope,* September 2000, <http://www.trendscope.net>. Reprinted by permission of the publisher.

12. Peter Cappelli, *The New Deal at Work: Managing the Market-Driven Workforce* (Boston: Harvard Business School Press, 1999).

13. Peter Cappelli, "A Market-Driven Approach to Retaining Talent," *Harvard Business Review* 78, no. 1 (January–February 2000): 103–111.

14. Ben Schiller, "Online Recruitment Is Just the Job," *Net Profit,* February 1999, 14.

15. Survey of fifty Fortune 500 companies by Recruitsoft/Logos Research, quoted by Peter Cappelli in "Making the Most of On-Line Recruiting," *Harvard Business Review* 79, no. 3 (March 2001): 140.

16. Chuck Salter, "There's a War for Talent Going On, and We're Right in the Middle of It," *Fast Company,* December 1999.

17. Pink, *Free Agent Nation.*

18. See Cappelli, "Making the Most of On-Line Recruiting," for examples.

19. Cappelli, "A Market-Driven Approach to Retaining Talent," 104.

20. Ibid., 107.

21. Egon Zehnder, "A Simpler Way to Pay," *Harvard Business Review* 79, no. 4 (April 2001): 53–61.

22. "What Do Employees Really Want? The Perception vs. The Reality," Korn/Ferry International in conjunction with The Center for Effective Organizations, Marshall School of Business, University of Southern California, 2001.

23. Kanter, *Evolve!,* 222.

24. Tulgan, *Winning the Talent Wars,* 12.

25. Ibid., 60.

26. Cappelli, "A Market-Driven Approach to Retaining Talent," 111.

27. John Coné, telephone interview by author, September 2000.

28. Richard Wellman, telephone interview by author, March 2001.

29. Rainer Zinow, interview by author, Walldorf, Germany, September 2000.

30. Rob Koehler, telephone interview by author, February 2001.

31. Coné, telephone interview by author.

32. Wellman, telephone interview by author.

33. Ibid.

34. Don Tapscott, David Ticoll, and Alex Lowy, *Digital Capital: Harnessing the Power of Business Webs* (Boston: Harvard Business School Press, 2000), 173.

35. Matt Murray, "As Huge Companies Keep Growing, CEOs Struggle to Keep Pace," *Wall Street Journal,* 8 February 2001.

## Chapter 5: Communities and Corporate Culture

1. Department of Transportation statistic quoted by Michael Maerz of Etreive, personal communication with author, 27 June 2001.

2. Michael Powell, "Gift of the Gab or Driven to Distraction?" *International Herald Tribune,* 30 June 2001.

3. "Gridlock Eats More Hours, Survey Shows," *New York Times,* 8 May 2001.

4. Niall Ferguson, *The House of Rothschild: The World's Banker, 1849–1999* (New York: Viking, 1999).

5. Eric Laurier and Chris Philo, "Meet You at Junction 17," unpublished study, Glasgow University, quoted in "The Long Commute," *The Economist,* 17 December 1998. The garden office is where this book was written.

6. See <http://active.boeing.com/companyoffices/ethicschallenge/cfm/initial.cfm>.

7. William Nuti, interview by author, London, September 2000.

8. Chittur Ramakrishnan, interview by author, Munich, Germany, September 2000.

9. Jon Katzenbach and Douglas Smith, *The Wisdom of Teams: Creating the High-Performance Organisation* (London: Harper Business, 1994).

10. Michael Mazarr, "Working in Very New, Very Old Ways, Part 3," *TrendScope,* January 2001, <http://www.trendscope.net>.

11. Eisenstat, Foote, Galbraith, and Miller, "Beyond the Business Unit," 54–63.

12. Mark Lurie, personal communication with author, New Orleans, LA, February 2001.

13. Louise Kehoe, "Rise of the e-Office," *Financial Times,* 14 February 2000.

14. Eric Schmidt, interview by author, San Francisco, CA, September 2000.

15. Bipin Patel, Director of Management Systems for Ford Motor Company, personal communication with author, 29 June 2001.

16. Bipin Patel, Director of Management Systems for Ford Motor Company, personal communication with author, May 2001.

17. Wendy Green, "Business-to-Employee Portals: Improving Company Cohesion and Employee Efficiency, Creating Better Culture," *TrendScope*, June 2000, <http://www.trendscope.net>.

18. Ibid.

19. Eric Ransdell, "Portals for the People," *Fast Company*, May 2000, 366.

20. Study by Celia T. Romm and Nava Pliskin described in Nicholas Carr, "Organization: The Politics of E-mail," *Harvard Business Review* 76, no. 2 (March–April 1998): 12.

21. "Why the Pen Is Mightier than the Mouse," commencement address to students at the University of Southern California, republished in the *Financial Times,* 27–28 May 2000.

22. Michael Schrage, interview by author, San Francisco, CA, September 2000.

23. Kanter, *Evolve!,* 183.

24. "Negotiating by E-mail," *The Economist,* 6 April 2000.

25. Regina Fazio Maruca, "The Electronic Negotiator," *Harvard Business Review* 78, no. 1 (January–February 2000): 16–17.

26. Heidi Roizen, telephone interview by author, March 2000.

27. "Surfing the Web at Work," July 2000, <http://www.surfcontrol.com>.

28. From an anonymous conversation with a senior executive of the company.

29. See <http://www.amanet.org>.

## Chapter 6: Purchasing

1. Timothy L. Chapman, Jack J. Dempsey, Glenn Ramsdell, and Michael R. Reopel, "Purchasing: No Time for Lone Rangers," *McKinsey Quarterly* 2 (1997): 30–40.

2. From <http://www. forrester.com>.

3. Nikki C. Goth, "Bringing Extranets to Life—Case Study: GE's Trading Process Network," *Red Herring* supplement, fall 1997.

4. Sam Kinney, "An Overview of B2B and Purchasing Technology: Response to Call for Submissions, Federal Trade Commission," FreeMarkets, Inc., Pittsburgh, 22 June 2000, <http://www.freemarkets.com>.

5. Ibid.

6. Andrew K. Reese, "e Marks The Spot," *iSource,* June 2000, <http://www.isourceonline.com>.

7. Patrick Forth, interview by author, Cambridge, MA, August 2000.

8. Chapman, Dempsey, Ramsdell, and Reopel, "Purchasing."

9. Kent Brittan, interview by author, Hartford, CT, September 2000.

10. Cairncross, "Inside the Machine," 19.

11. Ibid., 32.

12. Ibid.

13. Quoted in Michael Vizard, "GE Extends PwC Partnership, Opens Exchange," InfoWorld.com, 20 February 2001, <http://iwsun4.infoworld.com/articles/hn/xml/01/02/20/010220hnge.xml>.

14. A good description of these moves is in Steve Scala, "Business-to-Business Integration: Participating in Supply-Chain Initiatives and Business Exchanges," GE White Paper, July 2000, <http://www.gegxs.com/downloads/b2b_integration_wp.pdf>.

15. Ruhan Memishi, "B2B Exchanges Survival Guide," *Internet World Magazine,* 1 January 2001.

16. See <http://www.amrresearch.com>.

17. Memishi, "B2B Exchanges Survival Guide."

18. "The Container Case," *The Economist,* 19 October 2000.

19. Ibid.

20. Memishi, "B2B Exchanges Survival Guide."

21. Kinney, "An Overview of B2B and Purchasing Technology."

22. Patrick M. Wright and Lee Dyer, "People in the E-Business: New Challenges, New Solutions," working paper 00-11, Center for Advanced Human Resource Studies, School of Industrial and Labor Relations, Cornell University, New York, November 2000.

23. From unpublished research, described to author in conversation, Cambridge, MA, September 2000.

24. Ron Wohl, interview by author, Redwood Shores, CA, September 2000.

25. Nicole Harris, "Private Marketplaces May Hold the Key to Net Commerce," *Wall Street Journal,* 19 March 2001.

26. Goth, "Bringing Extranets to Life."

27. Ibid.

28. Ibid.

29. Charles Alexander, GE Capital, interview by author, London, September 2000.

30. See <http://www.amrresearch.com/>.

31. For a good summary of this argument, see Tim Jackson, "When Choice Beats Price," *Financial Times,* 17 October 2000.

32. Glenn Ramsdell of McKinsey is probably not far off with his guess that big companies will meet about half their purchasing requirements online by 2005. See "The Real Business of B2B," *McKinsey Quarterly* 3 (2000): 174–184.

33. Joe Marengi, telephone interview by author, September 2000.

34. Kent Brittan, telephone interview by author, February 2001.

35. Cairncross, "Inside the Machine," 35.

## Chapter 7: Strategic Suppliers

1. Bryan Stolle, then chairman and CEO of Agile Software, quoted in Bronwen Fryer, "Competing for Supply," *Harvard Business Review* 79, no. 2 (February 2001): 25.

2. Jeffrey H. Dyer, "How Chrysler Created an American Keiretsu," *Harvard Business Review* 74, no. 4 (July–August 1996): 42–56.

3. These developments and possible strategies to deal with them are described in Frederick H. Abernathy, John T. Dunlop, Janice H. Hammond, and David Weil, "Control Your Inventory in a World of Lean Retailing," *Harvard Business Review* 78, no. 6 (November–December 2000): 169–176.

4. Peter M. Senge, *The Fifth Discipline: The Art and Practice of the Learning Organization* (New York: Doubleday 1990).

5. "All Yours," *The Economist,* 1 April 2000.

6. Hau L. Lee, interview by author, Stanford, CA, September 2000.

7. Hau L. Lee, "Creating Value through Supply Chain Integration," *Supply Chain Management Review,* September–October 2000. See <http://www.scmr.com>.

8. Annette Fantasia, "Decoding ASPs," *Harvard Business Review* 78, no. 6 (November–December 2000): 33.

9. Fryer, "Competing for Supply," 26.

10. Cairncross, "Inside the Machine," 36.

11. Brian Kelley, telephone interview by author, February 2001.

12. See <http://www.forrester.com/ER/Research/Forecast/0,1586,340,00.html>.

13. Kelley, telephone interview by author.

14. For a good description of the Smart's supply chain, see Remko I. van Hoek and Harm A. M. Weken, "Smart (Car) and Smart Logistics: A Case Study in Designing and Managing an Innovative De-integrated Supply Chain," Erasmus University, Rotterdam.

15. Frank Piller, interview by author, London, September 2000.

16. Title used in an interesting survey of manufacturing by Iain Carson, *The Economist,* 20 June 1998, 1–18.

17. Chapman, Dempsey, Ramsdell, and Reopel, "Purchasing."

18. Ibid.

19. Ibid.

20. *A New Economy?*, 61.

21. Kent Brittan, telephone interview by author, February 2001.

22. U.S. Department of Commerce, Economics and Statistics Administration, *Digital Economy 2000* (Washington, DC: GPO, June 2000).

## Chapter 8: Corporate Structure

1. A phrase coined by Ward Saloner of Stanford Graduate Business School.

2. Philip Evans and Thomas S. Wurster, *Blown to Bits: How the New Economics of Information Transforms Strategy* (Boston: Harvard Business School Press, 2000). A similar argument is made more briefly in John Hagel III and Marc Singer, "Unbundling the Corporation," *McKinsey Quarterly* 3 (2000): 148–161.

3. Bob Tedeschi, "Divining the Nature of Business," *New York Times,* 2 October 2000.

4. D. H. Robertson, quoted in Ronald Coase, "The Theory of the Firm," *Economica,* November 1937.

5. Alfred D. Chandler, Jr., "The Information Age in Historical Perspective," in *A Nation Transformed by Information: How Information Has Shaped the United States from Colonial Times to the Present,* ed. Alfred D. Chandler, Jr., and James W. Cortada (Oxford: Oxford University Press, 2000), 15.

6. Matt Murray, "As Huge Companies Keep Growing, CEOs Struggle to Keep Pace," *Wall Street Journal,* 8 February 2001.

7. Chahram Bolouri, telephone interview by author, September 2000.

8. Kaija Pöysti, personal communication with author, May 2001.

9. See <http://www.greatharvest.com/philosophy.htm>.

10. Ibid.

11. John Harbison and Peter Pekar Jr., "Smart Alliances: A Practical Guide to Repeatable Success" (San Francisco: Booz•Allen & Hamilton/ Jossey-Bass, 1998), 1.

12. "Hold My Hand," *The Economist,* 13 May 1999.

13. MIT's Sloan School of Entrepreneurship has an excellent program described at <http://entrepreneurship.mit.edu/>. In its eleven-year history, the center has contributed to the start of more than seventy-five new companies.

14. Gary Hamel, interview by author, London, December 1999.

15. A point made by Kaija Pöysti.

16. Ibid.

17. "Building a New Boeing," *The Economist,* 12 August 2000.

18. Eisenstat, Foote, Galbraith, and Miller, "Beyond the Business Unit," 56.

19. Colony, interview by author.

20. G. William Dauphinais, Grady Means, and Colin Price, *Wisdom of the CEO: 29 Global Leaders Tackle Today's Most Pressing Challenges* (New York: John Wiley & Co., 2000).

21. Robert Buderi, "Lucent Ventures into the Future," *Technology Review* (November/December 2000).

22. Ibid.

23. Kanter, *Evolve!*, 124–131.

24. Dauphinais, Means, and Price, *Wisdom of the CEO*, 137.

25. Julian Birkinshaw and Neil Hood, "Unleash Innovation in Foreign Subsidiaries," *Harvard Business Review* 79, no. 3 (March 2001): 132.

26. Jeff Henley, interview by author, Redwood Shores, CA, September 2000.

## Chapter 9: Leading and Managing

1. Suzy Wetlaufer, "The Business Case Against Revolution: An Interview with Nestlé's Peter Brabeck," *Harvard Business Review* 79, no. 2 (February 2001): 114.

2. Dauphinais, Means, and Price, *Wisdom of the CEO*, 136.

3. Murray, "As Huge Companies Keep Growing, CEOs Struggle to Keep Pace."

4. Ibid.

5. Ibid.

6. Margot Morrell and Stephanie Capparell, *Shackleton's Way: Leadership Lessons from the Great Antarctic Explorer* (London: Nicholas Brealey, 2001), 194.

7. Helen Taylor Thompson, "Taking People with You—Leadership in the Healthcare Profession," in *On Work and Leadership: A Selection of Lectures Organised by the Royal Society for the Encouragement of Arts, Manufactures and Commerce* (Aldershot, England: Gower Publishing, 1999), 115.

8. "An Inside Job," *The Economist*, 15 July 2000.

9. David Ernst and Tammy Halevy, "When to Think Alliance," *McKinsey Quarterly* 4 (2000): 47–55.

10. "Hold My Hand," *The Economist*, 15 February 1999.

11. Jordan D. Lewis, *Trusted Partners: How Companies Build Mutual Trust and Win Together* (New York: The Free Press, 2000), 4–6.

12. "Trust Us," *The Economist*, 26 August 2000.

13. "Hold My Hand."

14. Lewis, *Trusted Partners*, 187.

15. Eisenstat, Foote, Galbraith, and Miller, "Beyond the Business Unit," 54–63.

16. Ibid.

17. Morten T. Hansen and Bolko von Oetinger, "Introducing T-Shaped Managers: Knowledge Management's Next Generation," *Harvard Business Review* 79, no. 3 (March 2001): 108.

18. Ibid., 110.

19. Ibid., 114.

20. Ibid., 109.

21. This study was financed by PricewaterhouseCoopers.

22. Quoted in "Getting a Head," *The Economist,* 7 July 1999.

23. Robert J. Kramer, *Organizing for Global Competitiveness: The Corporate Headquarters Design* (New York: The Conference Board, 1999).

24. Ibid.

25. David Young and Michael Goold, "Effective Headquarters Staff: A Guide to the Size, Structure and Role of Corporate Headquarters Staff in the UK," report, Ashridge Strategic Management Centre, London, July 1999.

26. Cairncross, "Inside the Machine," 10.

27. Jeff Henley, interview by author, Redwood Shores, CA, September 2000.

28. Brittan, telephone interview by author.

29. Idea from Lewis Neal and covered at length in Stan Davis and Christopher Meyer, *Future Wealth* (Boston: Harvard Business School Press, 2000).

30. An idea from Kaija Pöysti.

## Chapter 10: The Company of the Future

1. Geoffrey Blainey, *The Tyranny of Distance: How Distance Shaped Australia's History* (Sydney: Sun Books, 1966), 224–225.

2. H. Darr Beiser, "Cisco Chief Pushes 'Virtual Close,'" *USA Today,* 12 October 1999.

3. Garry Daichent, interview by author, San Jose, CA, September 2000.

4. See <http://www.eraider.com>.

5. Mark Latham, "The Internet Will Drive Corporate Monitoring," *Corporate Governance International,* June 2000.

6. A point made by Jesse A. Finkelstein in "Stockholder Meetings in Cyberspace: Will Your Next Meeting Location Be a Website?" <http://www.rlf.com/2130749a.htm>.

7. The ideas in this paragraph are from Hamish McRae.

8. Hamish McRae's intriguing idea.

# Index

Accenture, 32, 95

acquisitions, 35–36, 184. *See also* mergers; takeovers

Aegon, 167

airline industry, 49, 60, 103, 124, 159–160

Alexander, Charles, 130

alliances, 40, 162–165, 180–182

Amazon.com, 34, 57, 59, 164

American Airlines, 103

America Online (AOL), 154

AMR Research, 125

annual reports, 9, 198

antitrust rules, 126

AOL. *See* America Online (AOL)

application service providers (ASPs), 138–139

ARPANET, 34

A. T. Kearney consultants, 179

auctions, 124, 127

automobile industry, 3, 135, 138, 141–145

Barnevik, Percy, 185

Beer Game, 136

Bell, Paul, 136

Bell Labs, 169

Bell System, 176

Bid4geeks, 89

*Blair Witch Project, The* (film), 53

Blockbuster, 164

BOC, 57

Boeing, 96

Bolouri, Chahram, 159

Boot, Peter, 182

BP, 184

Brabeck, Peter, 176

brands, 51–54. *See also* franchising

Brittan, Kent, 117, 119, 130, 147, 187

Brown, Aaron, 199–200

Brown, John Seely, 28, 101

Brynjolfsson, Erik, 19, 20, 71

Burger King, 83

"Buy, Don't Build," 39–40

Camp, L. Jean, 54, 58

Cannondale, 62–63

CAP Gemini Ernst & Young, 166

capital

  human capital knowledge managers, 74, 90

  intellectual, 44

  organizational, 20

  physical, 203

capitalism, 40, 202

Cappelli, Peter, 76, 80, 81, 83

Cascade Engineering, 83

catalog shopping, 62, 65, 119
cell phone service, 57
centralization, 172–173
Chambers, John, 49, 177
Chandler, Alfred, 156
change
    corporate structural, 151–154
    cultural, 28
    effects of, 193
    in look of future companies,
        151–152
    managing, 177, 178–180
    production, 149
    results of, 21
    structural, 19–22
changing jobs, 76
channel conflict with customers,
    63–66
Charles Schwab, 63
Cisco Systems, 120, 198
Coase, Ronald, 155
Coase effect, 173
Coca-Cola, 51, 53
collaboration, 34–37, 145. *See also*
    alliances; partnerships
    software for, 36
    tools, 28
Colony, George, 68, 168–169
commitment, 99–100
communications, 98, 179, 190–191.
        *See also* intranets
    of company's mission, 96–100
    controlling, 109–110
    effects of revolution in, 153,
        186–187
    exchanging information with
        suppliers, 137–139
    managing, xi–xii, 177–178
    and outsourcing, 159–160
    technologies, 2–3

companies of the future
    changes in look of, 151–152
    collaborative governance, 199–202
    corporate structure, 173–174
    human resources management,
        89–90
    knowledge management, 45–46
    management/leadership, 190–191
    real-time companies, 197–198
    shape of, 202–204
    structural changes, 20–22
Coné, John, 86, 88
consultants/consulting services, 7,
        147, 173, 179
consumer-electronics firms, 160
coordinated purchasing, 119
corporate culture, xi
    changing aspects of, 102
    communicating the mission,
        96–100
    creating, 91–94
    e-mail, for and against, 106–109
    IBM's, 93
    intranets, 102–106
    sense of belonging, 110–111
    shifting work force and, 94–96
corporate headquarters, 185–188
corporate memory, 26
corporate structure
    alliances, 162–165
    building the right, xi
    changes to, 151–154
    changing economics, 154–158
    decentralized, 114
    for entrepreneurship, 168–171
    franchising, 161–162
    for innovation, 165–168
    market versus function, 171–173
    outsourcing, 158–161
    shape of future, 173–174

corporate training, 84–89
Covisint, 126, 128, 143
credit card companies, 58
cultural change, 28
customer clubs, 58, 60
customers
    brands and, 51–54
    click-through behavior of, 48
    data on, 54
    delivery/channel conflict, 63–66
    learning about, 54–56
    loyalty of, 61
    mass customization/content for,
        61–63
    monitoring activities of, 55–56
    organizing for focus, 66–68
    recruitment/retention of, 59–61
    relationship management, 19
    self-service, 49–51
    spotting profitable, 56–58
    targeting needs of, 48–49,
        52–53
customer segments, 67
customer service, online, 50


Daft, Douglas, 186
Daichent, Garry, 198
DaimlerChrysler, 105, 135
Davis & Co., 35
decentralized structure, 114
decision making, ix–x, 37–39
    decentralizing, xii
    improving efficiency of, 6
    tools for, 25
decision making skills, 38–39
delivery of products
    and channel conflict, 63–66
    just-in-time (JIT), 133, 136, 137
delivery of services, 61

Dell, Michael, 2, 142, 176
Dell Computer, 2, 12, 44, 78, 83,
    139–141
Department of Labor, 71
distribution chains, 143
Dollar General, 65
dot-coms, 1–2, 39, 53, 59, 164
Duguid, Paul, 28, 101
Dynamai, 170


East India Company, 203
easyJet, 40
eBay, 89–90, 154
economies of scale, 154
Economist Intelligence Unit, 67
Egon Zehnder International, 81
Eisner, Michael, 107
e-lancers, 89
electronically delivered training,
    85–89
electronic data interchange (EDI),
    30, 121–123, 139
electronic marketplaces, 124–126
Eli Lilly, 61
e-mail, 16, 98, 101, 106–109
employees, xi. See also talent
    as assets, 176–177
    competence of, 25
    corporate investment in, 19
    databases on, 31–32
    future of human resources
        management, 89–90
    incentives for ideas, 43–44
    loyalty of, 109, 111
    mobile, 94
    outsourcing talent and, 82–84
    paying, 198
    recruiting, 73–74, 75–78
    retention of, 79–82

employees *(continued)*
  sharing expertise of, 32
  storing data on, 74
  time-wasting by, 109–110
  tracking spending of, 120
  training, 84–89
  unskilled, 72
entertainment industries, salaries in, 72
Epicentric, 103
e-procurement, 117
ERP, 194
ethics, 96–97, 107
Eureka, 33
European dot-coms, 168
Eustace, Clark, 25
exchanging information/trust with suppliers, 137–139
*Experience Economy, The* (Pine and Gilmore), 52
expertise, locating, 29–34
Extensible Markup Language (XML), 30–31, 123, 128, 195

Falk, Thomas, 178
Farr, David, 127
filtering of information, 35, 46
Fiore, John, 50
Firestone, 143
First Chicago Bank, 58
Folio*fn*, 201
Ford, Henry, 3, 142
FordDirect, 143
Ford Motor Company, 35–36, 97, 103, 151
Forrester Research, 143
Forth, Patrick, 117
Fortune 500 companies, 156
franchising, 161–162

free agents/freelancers, 2, 79, 89. *See also* outsourcing
FreeMarkets, 127

games, online, 77
game theory, 38
Garana, Henry, 44
garbage in, garbage out principle, 38
gas industry, 123
Gates, Bill, 30
GE Financial Services, 160
GE Medical, 100
General Electric (GE), 16, 116, 123, 128–129
General Motors (GM), 33
Gleick, James, 44
globalization, 5, 72, 194
global team building, 28
Google, 195. *See also* search engines
Gossieaux, Francois, 101
Great Harvest Bread Company, 162
Green, Michael, 99
Greenhouse Fund, 170
Groove Networks, 36–37
Gross, Bill, 99

Hamel, Gary, 166
Hanson, Ward, 49, 50–51, 54
head office, management at, 185–188
Henley, Jeff, 172–173, 187
Hewlett-Packard, 128
hierarchies, 98, 189
Hippel, Eric von, 43
hiring principles, 77–78

Hormats, Robert, 5
Hotmail, 53
Hudson's Bay Company, 203
human resources management, 74,
    79–80, 89–90, 104
Hypertext Markup Language
    (HTML), 30

IBM, 10, 32, 93, 120, 128, 183
IDtown.com, 62
incentives
    for attracting talent, 188–189
    for customers, 58
    for employee retention, 81
    for ideas, 43–44
    nonfinancial rewards, 167
    rewards for ideas, 46
    for sharing customers, 68
    stock options, 183
    to suppliers, 138
incubators, 167
indirect purchases, controlling,
    118–120
information
    access to, 6
    accumulation of unstructured,
        26–27
    benefits of better, 136–137
    customer, 55–56
    exchanging with suppliers,
        137–139
    sharing with suppliers, 140
information and communications
    technology (ICT), 11
in-house incubators, 167
innovation, 13, 39–41, 43,
    165–168, 195
intangible assets, 24–25
intellectual capital, 44

intellectual property rights, 23,
    41–45
Internet
    catalog sales, 119
    extracting value from, 180
    influence of on companies of the
        future, 193–194
    as marketplace, 129–130
Internet technologies
    accumulating customer data using,
        54
    barriers to successful use of, 70
    benefits of, 13–16, 196–197
    brands and, 52–53
    communication, 97–98
    consequences of online
        purchasing/purchases, 130–131
    controlling indirect purchases
        with, 118–120
    for decision making, 36–37
    future of, 195
    innovation using, 40–41
    job hunting with, 76
    networking with, 29–30
    outsourcing, 158–159, 160
    purchasing policies and, 114, 196
    statistics on usage of, 4
    structural change and, 19–20
    success strategies using, 20
    as tool, 2
    training programs, 85
interviews, job, 77–78
intranets
    development of, 13
    Eureka, 33
    managing human resources with,
        104
    recognizing importance of,
        100–101
    uses of, 102–106

inventory
  jointly managed, 138
  management of, 135–137, 140,
    147
  vendor managed, 138

JavaSoft, 169
Job, Peter, 39
job interviews, 77–78
job market, 72
job switching, 76
jointly managed inventory, 138
joint-stock companies, 202
just-in-time (JIT) delivery, 133, 136,
    137

Kanter, Rosabeth Moss, 39, 70, 79,
    82, 108
Kappel, Frederick, 176
Katzenbach, Jon, 99
Kelley, Brian, 142, 143
Kewill.Net, 128
Kinney, Sam, 116, 127
knowledge
  converting personal to
    organizational, 26
  exchange of, 137–138
  filtering of, 46
  shared, 41
knowledge assets, 23
Knowledge Exchange, 32
knowledge management, ix
  future of, 45–46
  interpretation of, 24
  keys to effective, 26
  opportunities for, 13
  skills for, 28–29
Koehler, Rob, 87
Kwik Save, 77

Laaksonen, Juha, 160
Latham, Mark, 200
leaders/leadership. *See also*
    management
  developing, xii–xiii
  future of, 190–191
  need for, 178–180
  skills, 16, 177, 182, 197
  styles of, xiii
learning about customers, 54–56
Learning Lab, 87
Lee, Hau, 137
legacy structure/systems, 19
Leifer, Larry, 26
Levi Strauss, 62
L.L. Bean, 64
long-term relationships, 156
Lowy, Alex, 90
loyalty
  corporate, 91–92
  customer, 61
  employee, 109–110, 111
  to teams/groups, 99–100
Lucent Technologies, 169–170
Lurie, Mark, 100

MacCormack, Alan, 42
management. *See also* leaders/
    leadership
  of alliances, 180–182
  of change, 178–180
  of collaboration, 182–185
  of communications, xi–xii,
    177–178
  future of, 190–191
  at head office, 185–188
  of inventory, 135–137
  of mobility, 100–102
  rules of good, ix–xiii
  skills, 16, 25, 191

supply chain, 15
  of talent, 69–70, 188–190
marketplaces, electronic, 124–126
Marks & Spencer, 158
Martin, Peter, 21
Martinez, Pete, 17
mass customization/content, 61–63,
  144
Matra, 163
McDonald's, 66
McKinsey & Company, 43, 146
Media Laboratory, 32, 164
mergers, 35–36, 77, 163, 180
Merrill Lynch, 86
Metro, 120
Microsoft, 60, 154
millennium bug, 11
mission of companies, 96–100
MIT Media Lab, 164
mobile learning, 87
mobility, 94, 100–102
Monster.com, 76, 89
Morris, Michael, 108
Motjitbai, Avid, 63
Motorola, 103, 183

Narayandas, Das, 127
Nasser, Jacques, 97, 179
National Semiconductor, 44–45
"Nature of the Firm, The" (Coase),
  155
negotiations, 108, 119
Netravali, Arun, 170
networks, value of, 154
Neumann, Thomas, 74
New Deal at Work, The (Cappelli),
  76
New Ventures Group, 169
Nike, 51, 54
Nordstrom, 64

Nortel Networks, 158–159
Nuti, William, 97

OASIS, 123
Office Depot, 65
Open Source software, 42, 166
Oracle, 16, 119, 172–173
outsourcing, 153, 194, 196
  corporate structure and,
    158–161
  free agents/freelancers, 2, 79, 89
  suppliers, 145–146
  talent, 82–84
Ozzie, Ray, 36–37

partnerships, 128, 181. See also
  alliances
patents, 24, 44–45
peer reviews, 32–33
peer-to-peer applications,
  194–195
Penzias, Arno, 12
Phantom Works, 167
Piller, Frank, 144
Pine, Joe, 52
Pink, Daniel, 15–16, 79
portals
  Internet, 128
  intranet, 103–105
Pratt & Whitney, 87
PricewaterhouseCoopers, 56–57,
  172
privacy, 55
Procter & Gamble, 60–61
product procurement, 121–123
profitable customers, 56–58, 67
proxy votes, 200, 201
Prozac, 61
Prudential Insurance, 80–81

purchasing/purchases
  company methods of, 115–117
  consequences of online, 130–131
  controlling indirect, 118–120
  electronic marketplaces, 124–126
  product procurement, 121–123
  restructuring, 126–130
  use of Internet by managers, 114

Ramakrishnan, Chittur, 98
Rasul, Firoz, 181
real-time companies, 197–198
recruiting, 195
  cooperating with other companies
    for, 83
  customers, 48, 59–61
  insiders, 73–74
  outsiders, 75–78
Reflect.com, 62
Reich, Robert, 72
Reichheld, Fred, 61, 73
research and development (R&D), 24
retention
  of customers, 48, 59–61
  of employees, 79–82
returns of merchandise, 62, 64
Reuters, 170
rewards, 167, 188–190. *See also*
  incentives
Robertson, Dennis, 156
rogue purchases, 117, 120, 121
Roizen, Heidi, 108–109
Rosen, Sherwin, 72
RosettaNet, 123
Rothschild, James de, 95
Ruane, John, 67
rules
  80/20 rule, 49–50
  of good management, ix–xiii
Ryanair, 49

salaries, 82, 190
Sanders, Wayne, 177
SAP, 87, 98, 117, 119, 120
Saturn, 138
Schmidt, Eric, 73, 102
Schrage, Michael, 107
search engines, 30, 33, 195. *See also*
  Internet
Securities Act of 1933, 9
Securities and Exchange Commis-
  sion (SEC), 200
Seegers, Harvey, 123
segmentation of customers, 57–58
Senge, Peter, 136
Shackleton, Ernest, 178–179
shareholders, 199–202
Siemens AG, 77, 98, 184
skills
  analytical, 38
  communication, 98, 179,
    190–191
  decision making, 38–39
  knowledge management, 28–29
  leadership, 16, 177, 182, 197
  testing employee, 77
slashdot.org, 42
sliver companies, 5
small companies, 5, 157, 170–171
Smart cars, 144–145
Smith, Douglas, 99
*Social Life of Information, The*
  (Brown and Duguid), 101
Somerfield, 77
source codes, 42
Spaarbeleg, 167
Stallman, Richard, 43
standards
  agreed-on, for online purchasing,
    126
  centralizing, xii
  importance of, 187–188

OASIS, 123
  setting, xii
Stanford University, 87
Star Alliance, 163
Starbucks, 164
State Street bank, 50
stock-market valuations, 25
stock option grants, 183
Streamline, 164
subsidiaries, 168–169
Sun Microsystems, 169
suppliers
  benefits of integration, 139–141
  dealing with, 159
  difficulties of integration,
    141–145
  exchanging information/trust,
    137–139
  impact of Internet technologies
    on, 196
  managing inventory, 135–137
  spreading network of, 148–149
  strategic supply management,
    145–148
supply chain management, 15,
    133–134, 145–148, 196
SurfControl, 110
Sveiby, Karl Erik, 24–25
Swinerton & Walberg Builders,
    35
Swire, Claire, 110
systematizers, 7


takeovers, 35–36, 180
talent. *See also* employees
  locating, 70
  managing, x–xi, 188–190
  outsourcing, 82–84
Tapscott, Don, 90
Taysom, John, 170

teams/teamwork
  for finding good people, 78
  rewarding, 189–190
  and use of Internet, 99
  virtual teams, 95
  *Wisdom of Teams, The* (Katzen-
    bach and Smith), 99
teleconferencing, 21
Tesco, 122
testing employee skills, 77
Texas Instruments, 44–45, 140
Thompson, Leigh, 108
Ticoll, David, 90
time-wasting by employees,
    109–110
Torvalds, Linus, 42
ToySmart, 55
tracking sales, 67
trade unions, 97
Trading Partner Network (TPN),
    128–129
training employees, 84–89
trust
  alliances and, 181–182
  brands and, 51–54
  creating, 101
  establishing, 55
  online exchanges, 125
  with suppliers, 137–139
T-shaped management, 184–185
Tulgan, Bruce, 70, 82
turnover rates of employees,
    81–82


unions, 97
United Companies Financial,
    199–200
United Parcel Service (UPS), 81
United Technologies Corporation
    (UTC), 117, 118–119, 147

universities, 203–204
unskilled workers, 72
UTC. *See* United Technologies Cor-
    poration (UTC)

Valley, Kathleen, 108
vendor managed inventory (VMI),
    138
venture capitalism, 40
video conferencing, 86
Vodafone, 40
VooDoo Cycles, 62–63

Wagoner, Rick, 21
Wallman, Steve, 201
Wal-Mart, 65, 164–165, 166
Warner-Lambert, 137
Warwick University Business School,
    185
Watson, Thomas, Sr., 93
Web design skills, 70
Welch, Jack, 16, 176, 179

Wellman, Richard, 87
Wells Fargo bank, 63
Windows, 154–155
winner-take-all effect, 72
*Wisdom of Teams, The* (Katzenbach
    and Smith), 99
Wohl, Ron, 128
World Wide Web Consortium,
    123
"wow" experiences, 52

Xerox, 33
XML. *See* Extensible Markup Lan-
    guage (XML)

Y2K, 11
Yahoo!, 53
Yates, JoAnne, 7

Zaplet, 36
Zinow, Rainer, 87

# About the Author

FRANCES CAIRNCROSS is a Management Editor on the staff of *The Economist*, where she has worked since 1984. She has had responsibility for the Britain section and for coverage of the environment and media. She now writes mainly on corporate management.

Cairncross is a graduate of Oxford University and Brown University. She chairs Britain's Economic and Social Research Council, and is an Honorary Fellow of St. Anne's College, Oxford; a Visiting Fellow of Nuffield College, Oxford, and a Nonexecutive Director of the Alliance & Leicester Group. She has an honorary degree from Glasgow University.

Her previous books include *Costing the Earth: The Challenge for Governments, the Opportunities for Business* and *The Death of Distance: How the Communications Revolution Is Changing Our Lives.* Both are also published by Harvard Business School Press. She is married to Hamish McRae. They have two daughters and live in London.